My Dear Daisy

MY DEAR *Daisy*

Letters to Fulham from the Front

*The letters and papers of
Private William Stocker RAMC
5th (London) Field Ambulance TF
1914 – 1918*

Edited by
KAREN STOCKER

Copyright © 2017 by Karen Stocker.

Library of Congress Control Number: 2017900626
ISBN: Hardcover   978-1-5245-9641-5
              Softcover   978-1-5245-9640-8
              eBook   978-1-5245-9639-2

All rights reserved. No part of this book may be reproduced or transmitted in any form or by any means, electronic or mechanical, including photocopying, recording, or by any information storage and retrieval system, without permission in writing from the copyright owner.

Any people depicted in stock imagery provided by Thinkstock are models, and such images are being used for illustrative purposes only.
Certain stock imagery © Thinkstock.

Print information available on the last page.

Rev. date: 02/15/2017

To order additional copies of this book, contact:
Xlibris
800-056-3182
www.Xlibrispublishing.co.uk
Orders@Xlibrispublishing.co.uk
753370

The Fifth the fliers
The Fifth the triers
The Fifth that never tires
And that never makes a fuss
Oh! we will tell you on the strict Q.T.
Just the sort o'kind o'chaps we be
We are the Fifth London Field Ambulance of the RAMC

Chorus of the Fifth
Reginald H. Wyatt
History of the 5th London Field Ambulance TF c.1935

*

In drippin' darkness, far and near,
All night I've sought them woeful ones.
Dawn shudders up and still I 'ear
The crimson chorus of the guns.
Look, like a ball of blood the sun
'Angs o'er the scene of wrath and wrong
"Quick! Stretcher-bearers on the run!"
O Prince of Peace! 'Ow long, 'ow long?

from **'The Stretcher-Bearer'**
Rhymes of a Red-Cross Man
Robert W. Service, 1916

To all peacemakers and healers.
And to my nephews Noah and Nahum Stocker.

I would like to thank the members of my family who shared their memories and photographs and everyone who encouraged me and gave so freely of their time, help and advice. Special thanks to:

Alex Bear; Annette Payne; Ashley Stocker; the Blair family of Calgary, Canada, especially John's sons Jim and Dave; Bruce Stocker; Christophe Vincent of *l'Avenir de l'Artois* newspaper; Connie Radford; Donald Munro of Brisbane, Australia; Eleanor McMurchy of the Lethbridge Genealogical Society, Alberta, Canada; Helen McCarthy; Jamie Nimmo for showing me where to find trench maps and how to locate the Cough Drop; Joanna Swanston for the map; Julian Stocker; Mike Gilbart-Smith of Twynholm Baptist Church, Fulham; Mark Grahame; MC in Arundel, Sussex, for keeping my thumbs functioning and my hands typing; MECJ, also in Arundel, for keeping my brain functioning and for tolerating my warped sense of humour; Cdr Paul Windsar; Philip Stocker; Tony Mickle; Tracey Jennings of Shorthand Transcription Service. Special thanks to Isobel Harvey, for so much good advice, for checking the entire manuscript twice and for encouraging me when I was close to giving up.

And my thanks to all members of staff in the Archives and Local History Centre at Hammersmith Library, the Imperial War Museum, the British Library, the Wellcome Library, the Commonwealth War Graves Commission, and the National Archives at Kew who so willingly helped this bewildered novice researcher to find her way around their collections.

Karen Stocker

Contents

Introduction xiii

1914 1

1915 20

1916 101

1917 135

1918 193

Afterword 243

Appendices
  1 Map of the area where Will served 251
  2 Going Home, Will's account of the day he was injured 252
  3 Transcript of a tape recording made in 1989 of Will talking about his war experiences 259
  4 'A Meditation from the Front' by Alexander Stocker (abridged) 266
  5 Songs mentioned by Will 268

Sources and Bibliography 271

Index 275

Introduction

William Stocker (Will) was born in Fulham on 14th September 1892, the middle child of the five surviving children of James Stocker and Ada Holgate. He had an older brother and sister (Henry or 'Harry' and Ada) and a younger brother and sister (Alexander and Irene). His father, James, the son of a silversmith, had been a grocer at 334 Lillie Road, Fulham, but around 1909 the business started to fail. The family moved to Waldemar Avenue, Fulham, where James became an insurance agent working from home. Ada Stocker's father, Joseph Holgate, was the founder of several temperance eating houses and pie shops. While James was a gentle fun-loving man called 'Dada' by his children, Ada was a morally strict disciplinarian.

Daisy Edith Palmer was born in Fulham on 21st April 1893, the eldest of four girls: Daisy, Ivy, Edie, and Elsie. However, while the other three girls lived with their parents, from at least the age of six, Daisy lived with her mother's sister Miss Ada Maisey, a dressmaker. After leaving school, Daisy went to Clark's College in New Cross, London, for secretarial training.

*L-R: Mother and 'Dada', older brother
Harry with younger sister Irene,
older sister Ada with her husband Ernest
Owens and son Basil. Late 1914.*

Will's younger brother, Alexander c. 1914

Will and his family were all members of the Church of Christ at Twynholm Hall, Fulham Cross in London. The church promoted simple living, plain worship, personal piety, service to others, and obedience to New Testament principles. Members often referred to each other as 'brother' and 'sister' rather than Mr, Mrs or Miss. The Twynholm building had originally been the Queen Anne Coffee House before being taken over by the Church of Christ in the late nineteenth century. Twynholm Church had many groups and societies, including bible study, an orphanage, a Band of Hope temperance group and a Total Abstinence Society. They also had their own district nurse and social worker. All of Will's family were involved in the church in some or other capacity. Daisy, her aunt and sisters were all members of Twynholm Church while her parents were not. Many of the people mentioned in the letters were members of the Twynholm community. RWB was Robert Wilson Black, whose family were founder members of the Twynholm church. WM was the minister, William Mander. Local folklore had it that when preaching he had a habit of suddenly booming loudly to wake anyone who had dozed off. During the War, many fund-raising events took place to send parcels of 'comforts' to the Twynholm members who were serving abroad. The sum of £6 was raised in 1916 through the sale of copies of Will's father's poem '*In Memory of Our Brave Boys*'. As yet, no surviving copies of this poem have been found. Twynholm is still active at Fulham Cross and is now a friendly and welcoming Baptist church.

Joyful Tidings was the monthly news-sheet of the Fulham Cross Christian Mission at Twynholm. Its header in the first issue was, 'God grant that Joyful Tidings may diffuse sunshine and cheerfulness into five thousand homes and tens of thousands of hearts each month in Fulham, Hammersmith, West Kensington, Chelsea and other contiguous districts of south-west London!' In his letters, Will often mentioned receiving the paper. *Joyful Tidings* was produced between 1893 and 1970 and Twynholm Church still possesses a complete set of bound archive copies. They were found in the corner of a damp basement by the present minister, Mike Gilbart-Smith. He brought them upstairs and carefully dried them out. They have proved to be a gold mine of information.

A view of Twynholm from Joyful Tidings 1900

Joyful Tidings front page December 1916

When war was declared, Will was working as a clerk with Western & Son, a firm of solicitors in The Strand, London. On 1st September 1914 he enlisted into the 5th (London) Field Ambulance, Royal Army

Medical Corps. It was a territorial (part-time volunteer) unit originally formed in Greenwich. The 'old boys', as Will calls them, were called up on the outbreak of war on 4th August 1914. After basic military and medical refresher training in Blackpool, the unit was sent to Hertfordshire to await reinforcements prior to being posted to the Front with the 2nd (later 47th) London Division. Will was posted to Hertfordshire on 9th November 1914, ten weeks after enlisting, having done his basic training in London. In March 1915, the 47th Division went to France, only the second territorial division to enter the war zone. It remained on the Western Front for the duration of the war.

Three field ambulances were attached to the 47th Division, the 4th, 5th, and 6th (London) Field Ambulances, all territorial volunteers. They worked closely together, helping each other and each is often mentioned in the War Diaries of the others. The War Diary of the 5th (London) Field Ambulance is complete from April 1915 to May 1919, except for the first eleven days of October 1916 which are missing. It has been used to help determine where Will likely was at any given time.

A field ambulance was not an actual vehicle although transport vehicles, both motor and horse-drawn, were part of it. It was a mobile unit responsible for a number of areas along the casualty evacuation chain: the Bearer Relay Posts which were close to the Regimental Aid Posts in the front line, taking casualties back to the Main Dressing Station via an Advanced Dressing Station (ADS). It might also establish rest areas, baths, and small local hospitals. The members of the Royal Army Medical Corps were strictly non-combatant and unarmed, although some officers did carry a weapon for self-protection.

> "... a Field Ambulance is therefore a maid of all work ... it must turn its hand to anything and adapt itself to any work ... in resting times one section may be running a hospital in some chateau, another may be working a bath and laundry and the third may be keeping a rest camp. There are not many things that a Field Ambulance does not know nor many sides of life that it has not seen."
> **A Physician in France – Major General Sir Wilmot Heringham, London 1919**

Will remained in the Royal Army Medical Corps throughout the war and was stationed on the Western Front from March 1915 until March 1918 when he was injured and sent home. He corresponded throughout with his fiancée, later wife, Daisy.

Despite telling her not to keep his letters, she did keep most of them. They were found some time after Will died when his bungalow was being cleared. They had been packed away in a box at the back of a cupboard by Daisy many years earlier. They were threaded on ribbons in batches of approximately six months; some of the ribbons had disintegrated, causing the letters to spill and be mixed. It took some time to put those which had escaped back into order. Where a letter had no date at all, decisions were made by comparing the content with the War Diary, type of writing paper, use of pen or pencil, and style of handwriting. The type of paper changed frequently as he rarely had the same make of notepad twice. His handwriting is changeable. He was interested in calligraphy and his writing varied between the several pens and pencils which he used. He also was liable to lapse into shorthand halfway through a sentence and there are some P.S.s and entire paragraphs scribbled up the sides of letters.

As well as various cards, there are about 330 letters, some of which were written over several days. Twenty-five of them were written between 1908 and 1914, mostly from 1910 and 1911. The first earliest letter is dated 7th October 1908, when Will was just sixteen and Daisy fifteen. There are none at all from 1912 and only one each from 1913 and 1914. Most of these early letters concern chess tournaments, football matches, and times and places where Daisy and Will were to meet. A letter of 16th September 1911 gives an early hint of Will's sense of humour: *'I presume you are aware that I am playing again today & I believe the opposing team are a rather rough lot emanating from Chiswick, so you won't be surprised if I am brought home on a stretcher!'*

Of the pre-war letters, only the letter from July 1914 has been included; it was written while Will was on a walking tour in Germany. A few letters seem to be missing entirely, with torn corner scraps still held in place by other letters, while some have parts of pages torn off. Will did not always put complete day and date on the letters, and then not always in the same format. Some of the letters have the day written in Will's handwriting and a date pencilled in Daisy's writing, probably the date of the letter's arrival. Only two envelopes had been kept, so there was no help to be found there. One letter was dated from the heavy impression made by the postmark through the envelope onto the letter. The dates have been edited to use a consistent date-month-year format. The actual day of the week has usually only been used where Will has written it.

The content of the letters has not been altered although most of the closing salutations have been omitted. The only ones included are those which depart from the standard 'yours sincerely' or 'yours truly' which are the most usual ways in which Will closed his letters. Punctuation and grammar were amended in a few places but only going so far as to improve the readability of the letters. The sense (or lack of) of the original letters has been retained; for example he confuses the verbs 'to lay' and 'to lie'. These have been left as he wrote them. Will uses ~~~ to indicate that what he is thinking should be imagined by Daisy. In the early months, they set each other questions on biblical subjects but this stopped as the war progressed. Most of these and the only surviving answer have not been included.

This envelope from March 1915 is one of only two which survive: note where Daisy has written the dates of a batch of letters. It still contains some pressed flowers: a daisy, some forget-me-nots, and a white clover flower (which means 'think of me' in the Victorian language of flowers)

Despite his often asking Daisy to check letters which were going to be read by other people, Will was not writing for publication. He wrote with a lot of underlining and use of 'hem!' and 'what, what!' Other letter writers from the period, including his comrade Frank Orchard, show similar styles of expressing themselves.

Fortunately, several of the photos and postcards to which Will refers have survived. Many have been inserted into the text. Unless otherwise stated, all illustrations used are from those kept by Will or Daisy and now in the editor's possession. Also included are a few newspaper reports, excerpts from various War Diaries, stories, and anecdotes told to family members, and comments kept in a small notebook made by Daisy in 1960. All the excerpts from War Diaries are from that of the 5th (London) Field Ambulance unless otherwise stated. Attempts have been made to identify each person to whom he refers, particularly his military colleagues.

None of Daisy's letters to Will have survived; military orders were to destroy personal letters once they had been read. And there was only so much that he could carry around with him. Although Daisy's letters do not survive, some of their content can be made out from Will's comments. Will also wrote to his parents and brother Alex; none of these have survived. When asked, Alex's son, Peter, remembered that his parents had had a big clear-out of papers when they moved house in 1961.

Will's letters capture the mood of the time as well as hinting at the ups and downs of his relationship with Daisy. They show some of the mentality of the time and highlight some of the contradictory attitudes and strains which the war engendered. It is clear that even Daisy herself did not really understand what the men at the Front were going through. Conversely, Will did not understand that Daisy had a life and a job as well and sometimes wrote as though all she had to do was to sit at home and await his instructions for items he needed sending to him, usually tooth powder, boot laces and notepads. They often seem to be bickering and sniping at each other by post, particularly where music lessons are concerned. Will was always fond of music and simply could not understand that while Daisy had a beautiful singing voice, she clearly disliked playing the piano.

Unfortunately, a lot of the war experiences were saved for separate letters which were to be circulated around the family and these have not survived. The letters which Daisy kept are the ones addressed solely to her. They speak volumes about the stresses and frustrations of separation, although there are moments of humour. Although Will was the one away at war and Daisy safe at home, it seems to be more Daisy who needed the reassurance as to Will's feelings. In a few places, reading between the lines of what Will has written, it seems that Daisy might have been suffering from mild depression, then a barely acknowledged illness. And Will himself, while pompous and arrogant at times, somehow remains vulnerable. His own morale clearly starts to deteriorate as the years pass and his war experiences become worse. He copes with his situation but does not revel in it. He was from a generation brought up to hide their emotions, so it is remarkable that he could express himself at all. And always he is looking to the future with his insistence on saving and frequent requests for his latest bank statement. Most of the discussion of house buying in 1918 and the constant exhortations for economy have been edited out.

William Stocker was a devout Christian and at the same time a peace-loving patriot. Enlisting in the Royal Army Medical Corps helped him to reconcile this personal conflict. His letters reflect on his attitudes to war and faith as well as giving anecdotal evidence of the daily life and routine of a soldier during the Great War. His expressions of his faith may seem a little cloying, but it was obviously a source of strength and comfort to him. Although both Germany and Great Britain invoked the deity and were sure that God was on their side, Will saw that the war, indeed any war, could not be God's will.

Karen Stocker
Editor
Granddaughter of Will and Daisy

1914

Thursday 23rd July 1914
Trier
Dearest,

    We are now in Germany, and I am writing this just after breakfast. Yesterday we walked 30 miles from Luxembourg to Trier and my poor trotters painfully realize the fact. Luxembourg is a splendidly situated town after Edinburgh's style. In the evening we went to the Place d'Armes, the centre of the town, where there is a bandstand in a large open space and the whole town, more or less, congregate there gaudily clad, somewhat like Hyde Park bandstand. We made use of some seats and a little table and ordered lemonade and beer respectively and sipped it while listening to the various selections. Jolly fine too. I can't write much about Trier, I have not had a chance to have a look at it yet. We are going to survey the place when I have written this epistle, after I have been to see if you have kindly sent me a letter Poste Restante at Trier PO. I have seen some <u>beautiful</u> scenery and some peculiar sights which I must tell you later on when I return home.

    We have decided to alter our course a little and so if you wish to write (and I sincerely hope you will) please address as follows:

<u>Write on</u>	<u>For</u>	
Saturday July 25th	Mayen	Eifel, Germany PL
Sunday	Adenau	" "
Monday	Blankenheim	" "
Tues	Montjoie	" "
Weds	Liège	Belgium PR

    It seems years since I saw you and I shall be glad to get back to see you again, although I don't want my holiday to go too quickly. Did I understand you to say that you had a dozen or thirteen open air addresses ready for me? I could not quite read your figures.[1] Well, now I'm off to the Post Office and if there's not a letter for me, look out.

WALDEMAR RESIDENTS EXPERIENCES IN THE WAR AREA

Mr Henry Norman of Waldemar Ave, Fulham, recently returned from a tour of the war area at present occupied by the troops. Mr Norman, who is secretary of the Fulham Congregational Literary Society, told this paper an interesting story of his experiences. 'In company with Mr William Stocker, who is a well known member at Twynholm Hall, I left Dover on July 17th for Ostend and Brussels. From there we went on to Namur by train and then walked to Dinant where we could not get accommodation and spent the night in a wood. Next day we went on to Arlon, on the frontier, and the following day we entered Luxemburg. From there we rode over the frontier to Trier in Germany. It is an aeroplane station of some importance and has a motor cyclist battalion of the Germany army quartered there. The motor cyclist soldiers were very much in evidence all the time, dashing all over the place. We followed the valley nearly up to Coblentz. Everybody we met was talking and wondering whether it would mean a war. On Friday night, July 31st, we reached Mountjoye, a small town in Germany. It seemed in a state of great excitement. The populace were gossiping in crowds in the streets and there were soldiers everywhere. As we sat in a café having dinner, a newsboy rushed in giving out these little news sheets. As you can see they contain a proclamation stating that martial law is now in force, and ordering all foreigners without passports to leave the country within 24 hours. We soon saw what martial law in Germany meant. The roads were closed to all private motor cars and troops were controlling the railways. We slept there that

---

[1] He is teasing her. They often wrote to each other in shorthand, so it is likely that Daisy had written something about 'open air kisses'.

night and on Saturday morning we got to Aix-la-Chapelle. The railway line was guarded by troops, and the stations were in the hands of the military. We wanted to get home via Belgium, but no through-trains were running and no through-tickets being issued. We picked up a train to Herbesthal, a frontier station. We had to get out there and walk three-quarters of a mile to Welkenraedt on the Belgian frontier. On the way we were shepherded by German troops. I tried to turn down a side street but soldiers were drawn across it and I had to go on the appointed way. All the German troops were in full kit and had the well known brown holland covers over their shining helmets. From the Belgian frontier we got a train to Liège. It was filling with soldiers then. It was the same in Namur. We went up to the old dismantled citadel and saw the hills round with rings of trees on the top but no obvious forts. Our train from the frontier into Liège was packed with refugees, mainly Belgians, who seemed heartily glad to get out of the country safely. From Brussels we got to Ostend and after a long delay got a boat across to Dover, reaching there at four o'clock on Sunday, August 2nd. Although England was not then at war we were met by torpedo boats before we reached the harbour, where search lights were playing on all the shipping. In Germany the general impression was that England would not go to war on behalf of France and Belgium, but would be content to look on and later share the spoils.'
The Fulham Chronicle 21st August 1914 (abridged)

In later years, Will described how an official in one town, realising that they were British, took him and his friend aside for a quiet word. They were advised to go home as quickly as possible because things were looking bad and he did not want them being stranded in Germany if war was declared. Several of the locals, with whom they had become friendly, came to the station to see them off, wishing them good luck and asking them to come back soon to finish their holiday. They never did go back and they never heard from any of their new friends again.

Throughout August 1914, the Fulham Chronicle newspaper reported on the recruiting going on in and around Fulham, giving places and times where the various corps and regiments were holding sessions. Will's younger sister, Irene, told how he had "thought about it for a week or two before deciding what to do". Many years later, Will told his son, Bruce, that he had been travelling on the top deck of a bus with a friend from Twynholm when they saw an RAMC poster. He decided in that moment that that was what he was going to do. He enlisted into the territorial RAMC two days later. Although Will's service records were among those destroyed during the Blitz in 1940, the War Medal rolls in the National Archives show that he enlisted on Tuesday 1st September 1914. We do not know exactly where he was between 1st September and 9th November but it is most likely that he was in training at the territorial RAMC headquarters at the Duke of York's Military School in Chelsea and going home each evening as his billet.[2]

c/o Mrs Barber, Batterdale House, Pond Hill, Hatfield, Herts
9th November 1914
Dearest,

Arrived safely.[3] Billeted with 4 others in one room of the above cottage. Mattresses on floor. Quite comfortable. The RAMC already here are very rough, not to be compared with ours, but anxious, very anxious to make friends. Just had tea. What! What! My billycan half-full of tea and a ¼ of a loaf with a bit of jam smacked on and then chucked out to walk along the high street to billet place with the stuff in our flippers.

PS. . . . Got a nice overcoat. Write fuller later.

---

[2] 'Recruit drills and preliminary training exercises were carried out during the first three weeks . . . in open spaces in and around London. All ranks, with few exceptions, living at their homes and mustering at their Headquarters daily, for training . . . all parades at first took place in ordinary civilian garb.' **History of the 60th London (2nd/2nd London) Division**

[3] 'A large draft was sent from Chelsea to Hatfield on November 9th to complete establishment. The personnel was now that which was to work together for the next four years.' **The History of the 5th London Field Ambulance TF**

11th November 1914
Dearest,

Before I tell you about anything else, please send me on my locket, not the chain. Mother will find it for you. <u>When</u> you write me (haven't received anything yet) address me as 'Mrs W Stocker' at above. If you put 'Private Stocker' it will go to the Town Hall and I shall have to wait for it. We're at present sitting round table writing love letters.

I'm getting on alright. We've got decent diggings: one room for 5 of us, mattresses on floor. Doesn't sound nice but it's great. Nice fellows. One is an out and out Christian, associated with the Brethren, and the others (except one who goes about half asleep) are very decent. We've stopped (Blair and I) all swearing indoors (strong adjectives etc) but the chaps don't want any checking now they're quite respectable.

Will in November 1914

The fellows already down here are absolutely awful. Our fellows (ones from Chelsea) are <u>much</u> superior to them. The way we get our grub is awful but nevertheless amusing. We have to go to the Town Hall for it, line up inside, one of the above mentioned hooligans dips a tin can in a cistern of tea and chucks it in our 'billycans', we pick up a chunk of bread (chopped up by another hooligan), the 3rd ruff smacks on a bit of bacon and we hop off down the street with tack in our flippers. That's our breakfast. I did a bit of spinning for tea. It was raining and so I told corporal hooligan I couldn't go along the street with jam on my bread, for it would be washed away. And looking very innocent I asked if I could take home a pot of jam for our household. "Not usual he said. But if you're not swanking me you can take home the pot and the <u>others can share</u>". He also gave me bread for 7. But the others had already got their rations and so now we have got a pot of jam and about 3 loaves to spare. So we shan't starve.

A fellow in my carriage coming down complained of a headache, now he has scarlet fever very badly. Some of us in the carriage they have isolated in case of trouble, but they have looked at me and let me free. We are not allowed out of Hatfield more than a mile any day and we are allowed home about every 8 weeks. Rotten isn't it. Nothing whatever on in the evenings. No pictures etc. I've bought a little cherry pipe (excuse me won't you darling) and we sit in talking, arguing temperance, Christianity, etc and reading. Last night the lady asked us into the sitting room. I played dozens of songs and we all sang. Just about to do the same now. Our diggings are fine. Some of our chaps are sleeping in empty haunted houses on hard boards. They reckon we are in Buckingham Palace here at Batterdale House.[4]

Excuse rotten writing in hurry.

PS. . . . Let Mother know how I am getting on. I shall shortly be making arrangements for you to come down one weekend.

Thursday 12th November 1914

Dearest,

Just got your letters at Town Hall. Don't put 'Private RAMC' anymore. I'm glad you like the photo. I'm not particularly struck with it. Criticism – one eye too much pronounced. If the partially closed eye is effectively altered a minute fraction (or the other eye) I think it will be a fine photo. Otherwise hair etc is very good. Ask all at home to severely criticize it and let me know precisely their remarks, and return photo again with criticisms. Although it will be awkward to sit again for some time to come I'd rather wait (if it means months) than mess things up. Any rate let me know what they <u>all</u> say at home. There may be a possibility of my coming up to London a few days hence with Blair to get an engagement ring for his girl, who is in Liverpool. <u>If</u> I should come up I'll arrange to

---

[4] Batterdale House was a six-roomed Georgian house.

meet you. But they're awfully strict here and I don't think it will come off.

Don't forget my locket. Also send my football togs. <u>See you send the proper things</u>. I don't think I have a decent pair of stockings. If I have not buy me a pair about 1/- to 2/- and send me them on quickly please, dear. Of course you will pay for socks etc out of my own money. Ivy's socks fit me finely. Another medical exam we have had today, hooligans and gents. Excuse my shocking writing.

PS. . . . I may be shortly writing to ask you to come down next Sunday week.

PPS. . . . Just received another letter here but put 'Mrs' in future to insure proper delivery. The postmen here have had orders to take all letters to 'privates' to the Town Hall, that is why I am asking you to address me as 'Mrs'.

Sunday 15th November 1914
Dearest,

Thanks awfully for parcel. Very nice. Sorry to hear about your business, but still, if you want my assistance, and you must, I shall consider it an honour to help you.[5] As for next week, you must come down. You don't reckon I'd allow you to pay your own fare, in any case. You have my book, so help yourself. My interests are yours: yours are mine. We will arrange later about time.

I don't remember whether I told you, or Mother, but I have now taken on cook's job with my friends. Start 5.30 in the morning and at it nearly all day. We have all bought blue engineering trousers and bib and with our little hats, we look hot stuff. Our own sergeant from Chelsea came to our billet and asked for volunteers and we agreed to all go. The present cooks except the sergeant cook, have today been discharged. Our fellows (Chelsea boys) are very pleased; they anticipate things a good deal cleaner, for the cooks looked awful. Our fellows complain greatly about the 5th already here. There's nothing else the fellows talk about now but the awful hooligans. They approached the officers and have asked to be put together in one section. And the reason we have been asked to cook

---

[5] Daisy had been laid off work temporarily.

is on account of complaints about the food, or rather the coalmen who cook it.

I don't know when we shall go away, it may be a day or two or after Christmas. By the way, what is the weight of my scarf? We have had an argument about it.

I expect you would like to know if I am really happy. Well, I don't know. It's not bad. My billet is fine and that's a lot. You asked me in one of your letters, whether the fellows in my billet are of Chelsea. Good Heavens! Yes. You will see them next week yourself. Very good of you to trouble so much about my football togs. Well I must now close, it is nearly 7 o'clock and we are all going into Mrs Barber's drawing room to sing etc. Mind you keep happy, I mean really hilarious, anticipating not our meeting next Sunday, nor my final return home, but, ah! What! What! 'There's many a nice little - - been planned in the twi twilight'.[6]

PS. . . . John (Blair) is still at his epistle. I have written home, and am about to write again. But I may miss putting in one letter to you what is in Mother's and vice versa so transfer information.

Monday 16th November 1914

Dearest,

Thanks for letters. Have received locket safely. With regard to my photo, I think it would be worth while to have it finished, and if they can properly just alter the eye a little, to do so, but if they really consider it will be alright when properly done, without any 'touching up', to leave it alone. I also see that by paying 4/- extra, I can get a dozen photos and an enlargement. If you think it wise, have the dozen, pay for them out of our common fund, and you can have the enlargement. Just please yourself.

The fellows, 'our boys', are awfully pleased that we are taking over the cooking and some more of 'our boys' are coming down tomorrow and some of the 'old stock' are leaving and so things look much better. We have already turned a 'Black Hole of Calcutta' (cooking house) into a 'White City', but us cooks have jolly long hours and very hard work. I started today at 6 a.m. (I got up 5.30)

---

[6]   *In the Twi Twi Twilight*, a song by Charles Wilmot and Herman E. Darewski.

and finished at 6.45 pm. The ordinary trooper commences at 8.45 and is done at 4 pm. So you see we have sacrificed a good deal in becoming cooks. I must now get to bed for it is 10 o'clock and I am tired.

Thursday 19th November 1914

I expect you are eagerly anticipating this letter re time of train. I hope to finish on Sunday about 2.30 and I see there is a train which leaves Kings Cross at 1.32, B Platform and arrives at Hatfield at 2.23. I believe the fare is 2s/11d from Kings Cross. I shall be outside the station. I'm not allowed inside. I enclose 10/s to pay fare and sweets etc and the rest please bank.

If you can conveniently manage it, bring down my swagger cane. Needless to say I've already broken one down here and I've only used it twice. By the way I hope you have got my paper from Charlie. If you have you might send me a sample. I would like you to bring a finished photo with you Sunday if they are done. I'm awfully anxious to see you. We'll go for a 'walk, walk, walk, a quiet old – and a talk, talk, talk'. My word! Won't we enjoy ourselves. A pity it's not Wimbledon. I told Mrs Barber my girl is coming down and we are going to have tea with her.

PS. . . . I don't think we are moving till Spring. Bring me up a waistcoat of some description if you will. I should be awfully obliged if you would buy & bring me on Sunday one good military brush. Don't pay too much for it, but get one that is nice and stiff, really stiff.

Tuesday 24th November 1914

Dearest,

Sorry I did not have time to write to you last night. Mr Horrocks[7] has just been telling me (and the others agreed) that I ofttimes remind him of early photographs of Asquith. What a compliment! I'm anxiously waiting for my finished photograph. If

---

[7] George Gibson Horrocks – originally with the 5th London Field Ambulance, he transferred to the 85th (3rd) Field Ambulance in May 1915 with several other men from the 5th LFA.

the enlargement is done with the others, I should be awfully obliged if you would send me it also. Needless to say you will pack it well.

I am glad you so enjoyed yourself on Sunday. I was really very depressed until you came, over Blair, but now I'm perfectly happy. Ripping walk on Sunday, wasn't it? Wait till I come home again for good and I guess we'll make up for lost time. I'm looking forward to the time when you will sit down at the piano and play and sing to me *The Rosary*, *I Hear You Calling Me* and so forth.

I want you to let me know what you would like for Xmas. Send me a list, a nice long one, to choose from. If you can't think of anything, get suggestions from your Aunt. I'm glad you wrote to Mrs Barber, I know she much appreciated it. Of course you will tell Mother how I am getting on. Don't forget to tell them about the tapping at the window. I enclose Postal Order for 10/- for you to bank.

Friday 27th November 1914
Dearest,

Puzzle find me! What do you think of it? It has just come. Don't I look gloomy. Thanks for letters. The military brush is very good indeed. Nice and stiff. The socks are alright, but they are not quite such a good fit as Ivy's. As far as a Christmas present is concerned, I really can't say. Perhaps you would like to send me a few suggestions of things you would like to buy me. I'm anxiously waiting for a finished photograph from you, especially the enlargement. You also ask me about Blair. There is no change in my attitude towards him.[8]

Tomorrow's match against Hatfield Town I'm longing for. I heard tonight that the Sergeant Major said referring to me 'he's a magnificent player and I would not mind betting he gets through 3 times tomorrow'. My word, What! What! And when I enquired as to whether I was playing tomorrow for certain, they said *your* name was put down first. So they are expecting great things. Let's hope they're not disappointed.

---

[8] They had argued over religious differences.

I am glad to say my cold is much better, and I hope yours is well also, including the ~ ~ . I enclose Postal Order for 10/- for bank.

Sunday 29th November 1914
Dearest

Sorry I have not written to you oftener, but I don't get much time, and I have written home 3 times this week. I am writing this in the cookhouse 3.45pm while waiting for water to boil for tea.

Your aunt and mother may have a photo willingly, and I suggest the following people for the others:- viz ten. 1 Mrs Barber (has the one you sent me, and is very pleased with it) 2 Mother 3 Harry 4 Ada 5 Alec 6 RWB 7 Mr Andrews (school teacher) 8 Mr Brotherton (school teacher) 9 Uncle Bob (Robert Stocker, the silversmith) 10 Myself. This is open to alterations. From what I can see of it I shall want ½ dozen more, and I could easily get rid of another dozen. For instance, I should like to give one to:- 1 Uncle Harry 2 Uncle Will 3 Uncle Will (Hackney) 4 Uncle Arthur 5 Uncle Henry 6 Mr Mander 7 Mrs Perkins 8 Mr Melville. What do you think? Ought I to get any more? Of course they should be cheaper, about 6/- dozen. I don't want to offend anybody by giving to one and not to another such as Uncle Bob and not Uncle Will and Harry. I'm open to suggestions from you. You might show list at home (my place) and get suggestions. I don't want to waste any more money, if possible, on further copies. When we have settled what we are going to do, I think you had better send me a supply of note paper and envelopes to send them off.

Re Christmas present. A music case and music I naturally consider a good suggestion, but if you would like a fur (and apparently you would) I should get one. And if you consider you can get better value at a sale, by all means get it now if you like. Well, I have made tea and I think I deserve to go to my billet.

Monday 30th November 1914

Dearest, please do not write any more trying to make out I'm getting sick of your letters. Because you know very well I'm not. I think your suggestion for a Christmas present is a very good one. I think I would prefer a signet ring, if it had my initials on it, for my little finger. As a matter of fact I had it in my mind.

I was sorry to read about the enlargement, but nevertheless, I think it wise. As for coming home, that seems almost impossible. And I should not be surprised if I am abroad at Christmas. There is a some official report that we are shifting Thursday either to Braintree or Harwich. Whether it is true or not I should not like to say, but there is something in the wind. And also that we go abroad on December 20th. If we do not go away, <u>perhaps</u> we can make arrangements for your coming down, but don't reckon on it. I suppose you are still transferring news at home.

I've been wondering today whether you are still continuing your exercises, music practice etc. Let's hope you are, dear. If you should come down on Sunday, wear your black v-shaped blouse if you still have it in use. Can't write any more at present.

Daisy in her black V-necked blouse, her RAMC sweetheart brooch is just visible

2nd December 1914
Dearest Daisy,

I feel I would like to write a lot tonight, I'm joyfully upset. Blair and I have just been quietly talking together about our misunderstanding. And I can really write no more about the subject, but say, that in the future we shall be bosom companions. It's a misunderstanding, I'm sure. He is a fine fellow. Can't write anymore tonight dear. Please come Sunday same train unless I hear anything. I'll write you tomorrow properly.

PS. . . . I started a second letter but really can't finish it.

Started Thursday 3rd December 1914, continued Friday
Dearest,

Glad to hear you are still practising. Don't be discouraged. 'Rome was not built in a day!' Re photos. Extra ones are jolly dear and not worth it. Re Christmas present. I don't quite understand you. I meant to imply that being so fond of music I should naturally prefer music, but I would like very much to buy you a fur. If you intend to buy a fur, buy it now (a good one) you know what I mean and appear with it on Sunday. I don't suppose I shall be home Xmas. I've had a hard day today. Started at 5am finished at 7.30pm.

I'm a jolly long time hearing from you. Have you forgotten my address? Every post brings disappointment. Catch the same train, and should I not be at the station, please go straight to Mrs Barber's on Sunday.

PS. . . . I think you had better buy a fur at once and appear with it on Sunday.

John Blair *Will Stocker*

5th LFA RAMC cooks, 3rd December 1914
L-R: Sgt Arthur Archer, Arthur Hearn and John Blair at the chopping bench, Will Stocker centre, sharpening his knives; the three men on the right include Lionel Calcutt and Cecil Carrington with one unknown, but the photo is not labelled which is which

Wednesday 9th December 1914
My Dearest,

Sorry I have not written before, I am very busy and have a sore throat and don't feel very grand. In fact I was not going to write this letter. And after I have written it I'm going to bed, the time will then be about 6 o'clock. I shall keep the photograph you sent me for sending to RWB. You have not yet sent me the other photos to send off. You need send no paper, but you might get a packet of envelopes large enough to send them off in. I can't get any down here. I have written to Mother asking her not to telegraph about Irene because they enquire into them, but to write a letter only to the same effect about Thursday morning.

One of the officers, I understand, told some of the fellows that there will be no Christmas leave. Well I can't write anymore dearest, tonight.

Thursday evening 10th December 1914
Dearest,

I expect you will be glad to hear that my throat is much better. Yesterday I had a rotten headache, and I kept gargling my throat with permanganate of potash all day and I went to bed last night at 6 but I really feel practically all right now except for a slight soreness of the throat. I have not heard from Mother re Irene so I suppose she doesn't think I ought to come home on a near approach to a fib. You have not told me the result of your conversation with her. You simply say in your letter that you told Mother how I was getting on, nothing about the Irene ruse. It's too late now.

When you next write me, send me on the words of that song we heard sung by Ivor Walters about sweet harmony. I want it for an autograph book (Miss Windybanks). If you could get it either from Coleridge's works or from the commencement of one of the chapters of 'Duty', Smiles, which is in the library, I would sooner put in that verse which runs something like this.

> 'He liveth best who loveth best,
> All things both great and small
> For the dear Lord who loveth us,
> He made and loveth all'

I am not sure whether this is correct.[9]

By the way, I should be ~~awfully obliged~~ very glad if you find out whether I have any outstanding books from the library. I don't want to have to pay £100[10] fine when I return. I don't know whether I mentioned it in the last letter, but I should be very glad if you would thank your mother for the tomato pickle. I don't know yet whether it is my turn to come home Sunday. If I don't get Xmas off I'm going to bunk.

PS. . . . I hope you are not keeping all this scribble, you will have a lively collection if you do. I think I should give Mrs Perkins her photo, the same with Ada, Harry, Mother, Alex etc. I'll write the others <u>when</u> I get photos. Hope you are in A1 condition and practising well.

Tuesday Eve 15th December 1914
My very dearest,

Better late than never. I believe we are going to St Albans on Sunday, but I'll write you later about that. Another rumour reports 'No Christmas leave'.

Dearest, if you can write me in your next letter giving good reasons why I should not smoke, I'll smoke no more. No photos have arrived yet. Hope you got home all right on Sunday. Just been playing on piano *'Somewhere a Voice is Calling', 'Flight of Ages'* etc. Two minutes to catch post and buy stamp. Goodbye

Thursday 17th December 1914
Dearest,

No Christmas leave for me. This morning we had to draw for it. 15% only are going. About one in every six, you see. I drew a blank. It's bally rotten. And I believe I'm in for a lively time cooking Christmas. I'm not sure what I shall do exactly but I may not be

---

[9] This is from 'The Rime of the Ancient Mariner' by Coleridge. Smiles used it at the start of chapter xiv of *Duty*. 'He prayeth best who loveth best, All things both great and small; For the dear God who loveth us, He made and loveth all.'

[10] British currency at this time was the pre-decimal pound (£), shillings (/-), and pence (d), 12 pennies to a shilling and 20 shillings to a pound.

busy and we must see what we can arrange about your coming down here. I must see you if possible.

We played a big match today in the Territorial Cup against the 20th Division and after a rough and most unsatisfactory game we lost 2-0. So you see I'm not very happy.

Friday 18th December
Dearest,

I suppose you have received my letter asking you to come up Sunday. Before I go any farther, please bring me a 1/- box of Eucryl tooth paste with you. Of course you will come the usual time, and a black blouse.

We have been told today that all leave is stopped. Fellows were selling passes for £2 and over yesterday. Now they are worth anything from 5/- to 7/-. Just an outside chance that the last order will be rescinded. This is official from the Colonel. I received my first Christmas box today, a dose of vaccination. I have some Christmas presents for you to take home with you. I want you to get me a razor about 1s/6d in London for Dad. I have something for the others. You won't get a brilliant razor for 1s/6d but you will get a fair one. Bring it up when you come on Sunday. I have not written to the others at home, so you will let them know the news if you can. I don't get much chance to write. I would like my ring Sunday.

What do you think of my card?[11] Please don't send me one. When you come on Sunday we must chat about what we are going to do Christmas. I hope you are keeping fit, although overworked (hem!). Of course you must tell Mother, it would not be much use her coming up on Christmas, but I wouldn't mind a Christmas pudding sent down by you on Sunday for Christmas. As for Christmas Day I expect (I don't really know) I shall be at work all day except evening. I don't know whether you could stay here Christmas night. I don't see why you can't. We must discuss that later. Goodbye till Sunday.

---

[11] It is made of green celluloid with a pink foam rose on the front.

21st December 1914
Dearest,

I have enquired re your coming down Christmas Eve and the lady I mentioned cannot put you up. I have asked Mrs Barber if she knew of anybody and she suggested that the chap who came in while we were singing yesterday, if he had no friends up. Mrs Barber also suggested your sleeping in with Miss Windybanks[12] and we left it that she would enquire and let me know what she could do. The fellows in my billet suggested buying a present for Mrs Barber and they want you to get in London a bread knife and board about 7/- not more. Don't get a 6½d mucky arrangement. Pay about 7/- not much less. Bring it Christmas Eve.

> *"The people of Hatfield gave a Christmas banquet for the members of the London Regiment and the RAMC billeted on the town: 'To round off the day there was a concert in the Public Hall led by the choir of the RAMC featuring contributions from all ranks with songs, both serious and humorous, recitations and monologues, and closing with the National Anthem'."*
> **Wardleworth:** *William Reid Dick, Sculptor*

30th December 1914
Dearest,

Thanks for letter. Sorry, ~~awfully~~, very, I have not written before. Re St Albans. I understand from a most reliable source that we are not going to leave Hatfield now, St Albans cannot find enough billets for us. Needless to say, I'm very pleased. No remarks whatever were passed re yourself except what I told you. When you come up next time you can take my photo back with you. As a matter of fact, I don't know why you sent it dear.

I asked Mrs Barber what her bill was yesterday and she said 2/6. I then said 'That's too little, I expected to pay 10/-' and she said she would not think of taking that. Mr and Mrs Barber said that they thought you were a very nice young woman and that they were only

---

12   Ada Windebanks lived with her aunt, Will's landlady, Mrs Barber.

too pleased to have your company. And I paid them 5/-. They spoke very nicely about you and hoped we would come and see them after the War. I hope you don't feel too lonely now, I thought it was rather suggestive when you said you would like to come and work in the cookhouse among us <u>all</u>. A case of 'Put me amongst the Boys'.[13] Naughty girl!

Last night Blair and I went for a ripping walk for about 2 hours. It was a grand moonlight night and we both thoroughly enjoyed our walk. But I wish it had been you instead of Blair. We spoke about various topics. And he asked me when was I going to get married and I said 'When I'm 30'. 'A fact' he said, and then I told him that if and when the war were over I could see my way clear (that's if the war lasted about 3 years) I should not be at all surprised if I ~~. He is jolly keen on ~~getting married~~ making a fool of himself. Well I must now conclude wishing you A Happy New Year

~~Your loving husband~~ Yours sincerely

---

[13] *Put Me Amongst the Girls* was a song by C. W. Murphy and G. Arthurs.

1915

Saturday 2nd January
Dearest,

Have just returned home from a football match, which we won 7-0. I understand that it is official that we leave for St Albans on Thursday next. You seem to be under the impression that it is not very nice there as far as comfort is concerned. I've heard very different, the fellows are keen on going.

I enclose POs for 27/- which please bank. I expect you will be receiving some money from Western's next week. Let me know when you get it. I have given up smoking as I promised in the new year. Have you any more resolutions you consider I ought to make? I wish I could have been with you at the Watch Night Service[14] but never mind. The War may be over by this time next year. I'm thinking of turning up cooking. Getting 'fed up', so don't be surprised to hear I have gone on duty again. It is practically official that we are going to get 3 or 5 days leave soon. We expect to start in batches the week after next. It will be jolly fine if we do, won't it. We'll have a ripping time together.

Thursday 7th January 1915
My dear Daisy,

We are not going to St Albans today, it is again postponed. All leave has been stopped, those who started on Monday on their 6 days leave have been recalled. What for, I can't say. My 6 days leave would have been due in about 7 weeks time. The rumour is that the leave will start again on Monday and only old men will go, not the 'Chelsea Boys'. About 10 per cent a week.

You say in your letter that I fail to answer your questions. May I say I fail to understand what you mean. Will this do:-

Do bandsmen fight? No, not as a rule. They are stretcher bearers, known as Regimentals.

---

[14] The New Year's Eve Service at Twynholm Church, Fulham.

'Do you think him lucky' referring to Alex billeting with Dixon?[15] Have not the remotest idea.

Is it my turn to come home? Probably in a fortnight. Wait and see.

Thanks for Joyful Tidings. Glad to hear about your studying theory. Let's hope you will study. You don't seem to have done much yet. I'm not leaving cookhouse after all. I applied to, but officer and sergeant cook said they were 'very pleased indeed' with me and would I reconsider. So I shall not go now. Don't come on Sunday. It's my day on. I expect it will be wet and save the fare too. I <u>may</u> be home the Sunday following. Brewer's book I'm making good use of.

Written in spare time between chopping meat and cutting bacon.

PS. . . . I should be glad if you would tear up my letters after you have read them. They are not ornate. Did you do any exercises last night? Stop Press. Just heard, we are going to St Albans tomorrow and the Front in a few days.

7th January 1915
Dearest,

On second thoughts, I shall be glad if you will come on Sunday at usual time. I really must see you. It's my late day and I shall not be off till 5 o'clock, but after dinner I can light the copper for tea and then leave it for an hour or so and then I can see you for a while in the afternoon. Let's hope it's fine in the evening. I wish I could go home Sunday, but I can't. To be perfectly frank I feel awfully spoony. When I do come home we must make up for lost time. Shall we?

I'm sitting on my mattress writing this. I wish you were by my side and all the others were out of the room. I do feel like squeezing you tonight, especially if armour plates were not there. Hem! Well goodbye dear. I feel lonely tonight somehow. Don't forget to come Sunday.

---

[15] Percy Dixon of Fulham enlisted 20th November 1914 and served in the 2nd/6th London Field Ambulance with Will's brother Alex.

9th January 1915
Dearest

Thanks for letters especially number 1. You seem to be under the impression that I was 'ratty' when I sent my 'first' letter. As a matter of fact I was rather hilarious and sent it 'to be funny'. When I got your reply to it I thought I'd gone and done it absolutely, and when I read the PS ~~ well, say no more. Never mind, we'll make up for it on Sunday. I hope to have such a ripping walk in the evening with you. Might I be forward enough to ask you to leave off your armour plates. If I should not be at station you may see me come out of the Town Hall. I have some more money for you to take back. You might let me know how I stand when you come down. Don't trouble to get out an elaborate Balance Sheet.

By the way, Mrs Barber asked me to thank you for your cough drops, or was it corn cure, I forget now. Remind me I've got something to ask you when you come.

P.S. Don't forget your exercises tonight, there's a good girl.

12th January 1915
Dearest,

Thanks for letter received yesterday. Before I write any further, might I remind you to look for my Address Books.[16] I have written to Mother sending her some dripping and she will pay you the postage which please bank.

Yesterday a list was posted of our various duties and both Blair and I have been put as stretcher bearers and old men have been allotted cooks. Our sergeant is very disappointed and is going to see the officers and try and get us as army cooks. The newly appointed cooks are going under a special course of training starting today at Hatfield House and I believe when proficient will get 6d a day extra.

Wasn't it a rotten day Sunday? I wish the rain would keep off when you come down. There was one thing you said on Sunday, which I hope you won't mind me mentioning again, but it was most unkind of you to have said, namely, re my

---

[16] He means a collection of religious texts available from Twynholm Church.

affection toward you. One or two sentences, no doubt you will remember them, & I thought at the time it was, to say the least, quite out of harmony with our present friendship to mention and although I assured you, that you were wrong, you wouldn't believe me. Dearest, you will really very much oblige me if you don't talk in that way again. As a matter of fact I've taken it to heart this time and I'm afraid you will have your work cut out to dissuade me now of your opinion. Actions speak louder than words. <u>Perhaps</u> some day you will believe me. Will you please tell me in your next letter if you are keeping my letters. If you will promise to tear up the pencilled letters I've sent you I'll write decently in future which you may keep. I am yours <u>sincerely</u> (although you doubt it)

PS. . . . Tear up this please. Will you buy me in London a cheap but good reliable stylo. Send it with next letter.

14th January 1915

Dearest, although you doubt it,

Have just finished reading your letter. I'll do my utmost to get up next Sunday but I've got a hard job. How would you like to be in Miss Tweed's shoes?[17] It won't be long dear, I hope, before you are Madame Stocker. Can you imagine anybody calling you Mrs Wm Stocker? My Word. As far as we are concerned you are that now. 'What's in a name' Jolly lot. Eh.

Can you think of a good reason for wangling a weekend, that is Saturday and Sunday, pass. I believe I could get a pass on teeth, having some false put in at back. The question is, is it worth while to pay say 30/- for new ones in order to get a weekend pass. You will remember the dentist has 21/- of mine. I've written to ask Harry to come up on Sunday if I can't get off and bring Annie.[18] If you want me to come home Saturday and Sunday, think of a good excuse.

Yours sincerely, although you doubt it

---

[17] Daisy Tweed of Fulham was married a few months later.
[18] Annie Black, the fiancée of Will's brother, Harry.

15th January 1915
Dearest,

Have just finished reading your letter and in compliance with your request I'm writing per return. Although you write in such an assuring manner, to be perfectly frank, I still hold the same view. So many times have you told me that I'm not keen on you, and that the true engagement was as good as 'a case of have to' that I can't alter my mind yet. That you have confidence in me as far as being genuine and steady and so on, I'm certain, and as far as your affection towards me is concerned, that's obvious, but you must admit that times out of number you have (not in fun) broadly insinuated what you said so deliberately on Sunday. While you were writing the letter I've just received, I have no doubt your mind altered. Sentimentality, feeling & emotion for the time being, upsets ones usual thoughts so very often. I'm very glad you have written as you have, because although you have not altered my mind so far, if you are always as sincere as you were when writing that letter in your expression and words, my present view may change. I shall try and not ponder over the sentences which grieved me last Sunday and when I next see you I shall be only too pleased to be convinced I've made a mistake.

All leave has been stopped for Sunday and so I expect I shall be delayed yet another week making me due home a fortnight Sunday. I heard nothing about St Albans and don't want to. I'm trying to stop on as cook. Candidly speaking I believe it's a safer job and I think it's my duty to look after myself not for my own sake, for if I'm killed it won't affect me, but I'm anxious to return to you, my people, and to do a little good in the world.

Thanks for the pen. It's good of you to send me on everything I ask for so promptly. I shall expect it tomorrow. In conclusion may I say that one sentence in your letter seems to corroborate my present view. 'I realize you are capable of strong affection, and honestly, I think I have a fair share of it'. It seems to imply a divided affection, whereas my affection (not part of it), is centred on you.

PS. . . . I sent my Mother some dripping a day or so ago, I heard nothing further. Do you know if she has received it.

19th January 1915 <u>Extremely Busy</u>
My dear Daisy,

Thanks for your letter. I'm sorry to hear you are not well. I believe I know how you caught a chill. Look after yourself won't you. Colds don't aid development. I agree with you about our walk. It was ideal. When the war is over we must go to Hatfield in the summer. A motor-bus ride and on top all the way. Half our billet have gone to St Albans. I go tomorrow. I expect we shall get split up a bit. I hope I get Chelsea Recruits in my billet. I believe I shall have my leave 3 weeks hence and I shouldn't be surprised if that will be the last time you'll see me before I go to the Front.

You might tell Ivy I think it very kind of her and tell her 'Will says he is going to write you'.

The Wesleyan Church in Marlborough Road, St Albans. It is now a Methodist church.

5th LFA RAMC, St Albans
21st January 1915
Dear Daisy

I've got here. I'm billeted in a Wesleyan School Room[19] with about seventeen others including Blair and Hearn. I slept on a couple of forms last night and slept well: no mattress. Tonight I've got a straw mattress. Mostly Chelsea fellows in our billet. I should have been about 1¼ miles off but being a cook I asked to get near the cookhouse and was successful. I say cookhouse, but it's a dirty old yard, no arrangements whatever. Today we've had a shocking time cooking in the rain. Pouring in torrents. We are erecting sheds etc and I believe we'll soon be alright. Sooner be at Hatfield though. I've just had a wash: first since last night and I'm feeling fit and fairly happy. As you will see this is written in the YMCA where we have our meals. Everything seems peculiar, but I have no doubts I shall jog along alright.

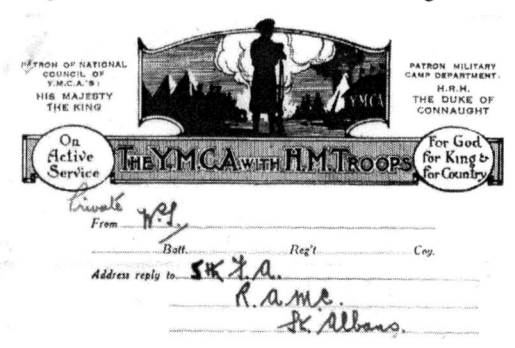

I hope you got my big box and also my letter, I couldn't possibly write sooner. I've been <u>absolutely</u> rushed off my legs the last 2 days. Not a minute to spare. I'll write again soon. I haven't written home yet so if you get a chance you might convey news home.

PS. . . . I very much like my pen.

22nd January 1915
Dearest,

I have just finished my days toil and have a slight headache. We've had a shocking day today. Worst in all senses since I enlisted. Our cooking yard was awful. I've been dodging about in the pouring

---

[19] The school room at Marlborough Road non-conformist chapel. Other accommodation was provided at the Salvation Army barracks and the hat factory.

rain all day. I believe things will be better tomorrow. One thing I'm certain of, they can't be worse. It really seems a month quite since I saw you so many things have happened. Don't worry about me I haven't caught a chill yet and my billet is quite alright and those two items being A1 is all that's necessary. Well, not exactly all, but a long way towards it.

I'm enclosing some razor blades which please get sharpened quickly: just off Waldemar Ave there's a shop and I want you please to get and forward a one-penny looking glass from the Penny Bazaar and a 1d boot brush (two), Star Boot Co Ltd. I hope you will put your dignity in your pocket and go to the Penny Bazaar.

I'm anxiously awaiting a letter from you and I expect I shall have one in the morning. Tell them at home how I'm getting on. I don't know whether it's the magic in writing to you but my headache has passed away really while writing this letter and I've had it all day. I enclose a postal order for our future home.

Saturday 23rd January 1915
Dearest,

I'm waiting waiting waiting for a letter from you. I've got on a little better today except for the fact that in pushing along a coster's barrow down a little yard in order to get some meat, I ran in a wall and hurt my finger. I've been to the hospital and it's alright now. Let's hope it gets poisoned badly so as I can get some leave. Before I go on any further I should be ~~awfully~~ obliged if you would send me along as soon as possible my grey trousers. I'm really sorry to have to trouble you so much dear, but I'm sure you don't mind. I shall be glad when I get the other things I asked for.

I heard the other day that Ernest is not doing at all well. Rather hard luck isn't it. I expect I shall have to wait some time for my money. We want to save all we can now.[20] I enclose a letter I had from Andrews[21] today. Please write often won't you.

---

[20] Will had loaned money to his brother-in-law Ernest to help him start his own butcher's business.
[21] Will's old schoolteacher, Harry W. Andrews.

25th January 1915
Dearest,

I have finished for the day. John and I have arranged to get up at 5 o'clock & get breakfast and the others arrive about 8. It was John and I who suggested it and the others jumped at it. But we finish at dinner time. Another cook has just had an accident, a skewer has run in his hand and Calcutt[22] is also on sick leave. I have arranged with my Captain to be a cook at the front, a hospital cook. I went with JB to Hatfield on Sunday. We walked both ways.[23] They were very pleased to see us and Miss Windybanks asked to be remembered to you and hopes your cold will soon be better. I do too. John and I are going to bunk to London on bicycles next Thursday all being well. So I may see you soon. The question you ask about leave I can't answer now. I'm not sure when I'm coming. But there's no doubt we are off in a few weeks to the Front. We are being measured for special boots for cold weather and we are to have two pairs of socks in them. So we are going soon.

I'm going now to see if you have sent the things I asked for. In future write to the YMCA. Please send me my Address Book, I'd like to show it to Blair. Ain't I a nuisance asking you to send so much? May I say in conclusion I liked the extracts you marked out in JT and also the verse in your letter. I must now bid you adieu.

PS. . . . You can guess I didn't write this with a stylo. JB's writing an Epistle, I mean <u>volumes</u> to his girl. You sometimes put x in your letter, what does it mean?

Tuesday 26th January 1915
Dearest,

I'm sorry to hear you are still in bed with your cold. I wish I could come home and see you. I tried to wangle home this afternoon but it wouldn't come off.

Blair suggests asking down his girl in the event of his not getting leave. I expect if she comes down she will stay for a week. He also suggests my asking you to do the same. I expect we shall be going

---

[22] Lionel Hamilton Calcutt.
[23] A round trip of about ten miles.

away soon and I should like to see you and spend some time with you before I go. So if I don't come home I shall make arrangements for you to come down here: Blair's girl and you could share the same rooms. I understand you will be asked to have some time off shortly. What do you think? I've been trying to work out my Sunday leave and it will be, I think, next Sunday fortnight. A long time yet, but time soon passes (sometimes). If in my travels I see any little things that you could 'bottom drawer' shall I buy them? Or do you think the possibility of my being a FM greater than my being a WM?[24]

I'm coming home Thursday I hope.

Friday 29th January 1915
Dearest,

Expect you got my postcard saying I arrived home alright. On leaving you I rode for all I was worth. It's up hill nearly all the way to Finchley and when I met Blair at 4.05am the perspiration was rolling off my face and I felt as if I had ridden 100 miles.[25] I hadn't gone but a mile when Blair kindly offered to help me along. I felt very rotten when I left you, but I didn't like telling you exactly how I felt and so you can quite understand how done up I was when I met Blair. But still I pushed on, Blair suggesting that we should take our time and get to St Albans about 6.45 when it would be light and the barricade shifted. Finally I had to get off at every hill, which seemed to buck me up for a minute or two. Whenever we saw a light on the road we approached it very steadily. At last, at last, we reached the barricade. Blair by this time was about 20 yards ahead of me and he rode straight up to it and I slacked behind and jumped off fully imagining he would be caught, it seemed as if he did not notice it. There were several soldiers with fixed bayonets. Then Blair said to these fellows 'I suppose I can go through' in a somewhat confident manner and the reply was 'Yes'. As soon as he got through I jumped on and rode through and said nothing. Blair had a mackintosh on and looked like an officer, so perhaps they took him for one. No sooner had he got through than he sprinted for all he was worth, but

---

[24] Foolish man, wise man? Possibly a reference to a biblical parable.
[25] Fulham to Finchley is about eleven miles, then another twelve to St Albans.

I could only dawdle and I met him waiting and hiding in a hedge to see if I was alright. We got to the cookhouse at 6 and the other fellows (3 of them) had got up at 4.30 and everything was in order. I was starving and went down to the quartermasters stores and got a few biscuits. I then sat down near the Army Service Corps in the dark and went to sleep in a second. The ASC man woke me up at the approach of an officer. I then had a big breakfast and went home about 8 o'clock and went to sleep, there being no parade for cooks.

I've just got up and had my dinner and don't feel too grand. Blair asked me not to come down to the cookhouse as the other sick cooks had returned and the 2 pro-tems are helping too, so I gradually sauntered along the street to the YMCA to write you a letter. I may go back to the cookhouse and render a little help and I may not. And if I don't feel fit tomorrow I shall have a day off. It will be my first day off. And all the other cooks have had days and some weeks off and so you see they'll have nothing to complain of, not to say they would, they know jolly well that I'd slip into it if I was anything like fit. Perhaps after a good night's rest I shall be all right. I expect I shall turn in at 7 or thereabouts.

I was disappointed I couldn't take advantage of your cooking, but really dear, I felt so rotten that I couldn't possibly eat it. You'll let me off won't you. Nevertheless I'm glad I came home.

30th January 1915

Dearest,

Have been to see pictures with a friend. A fellow of course. I feel much better today and I played in another big match for RAMC against the London Irish Rifles and after a strenuous game we won 4-2. This we consider very good as the Irish Rifles beat the 20th who beat us 2-0. We are the first to beat the Irish Rifles. Hall and Bell[26] were spectators.

Do you remember I asked you about the bottom drawer which you never replied to. I should like to know. I enclose a note for 10/- which please bank. When you next get an allowance from business let me know how I stand.

---

[26] Walter Hall and Victor Bell of the Twynholm church congregation..

Mr Curtis wrote, in reply to a letter I sent him, today. He says he showed my letter round the office and also to Alfred & John. He also says Alfred got married a few days ago and now spending his ~~holiday~~ honeymoon in Cornwall. Silly chap. I expect he'll live to regret it. Some people have no foresight at all, have they? Nevertheless, I wouldn't mind being silly and short-sighted, would you?

I believe I have a pass for next Sunday. Let Mother know all the news won't you. Hoping your cold is getting better.

PS. . . . Why don't you believe in sprinkling and why not in confirmation?

1st February 1915
Dearest,

Thanks for blades received today. I have also to thank you for sending on that bicycle which arrived at shop today. In my last letter I spoke about enclosing 10/-, I'm sorry I forgot to enclose it. It's here alright this time. May I say before I go any farther that I'm anxious to see you in your new glasses. I expect you look er ~ ~ hem! hem! hem! I hope to see you next Sunday. I'll let you know definitely as soon as possible. I've just been looking in a jeweller shop window with Blair and he pointed out the type of ring he bought his girl and I did ditto. Do you realize that we have been engaged nearly a year. We were 5½ years getting engaged, I wonder how long we shall be getting married?

I went to the Wesleyan Church yesterday evening and the speaker spoke splendidly. I thoroughly enjoyed it and when I arrived home the organ in the Baptist Chapel where we are, started to play *'The day thou gavest Lord is ended'*. It was grand. It sent me into another world. I hope you are practising <u>hard</u>. You won't disappoint me will you.

Wednesday 3rd February 1915
Dearest,

Have you any idea what you would like for your Birthday? About ½ hour ago, at 6.30pm, I was sitting round a nice trench fire in the dark with Blair and another cook and the ASC cook talking about girls. I happened to cling Carrington around the waist and I said I'd like to be doing this in reality with you. The subject wandered on till I mentioned spooning[27] on the sofa, and Blair said he had only laid down once with a girl on the sofa and he considered it demoralising and would never do it again. I disagreed, and henceforth an argument, or speaking more correctly, a chat on the subject began. I said that if a fellow had been with a girl for nearly 7 years and was engaged he certainly was allowed a few liberties and I saw no harm in it. We wandered on and on till we were miles away from the subject. But I may say here that I believe that when a fellow is engaged he has taken on a great obligation and was morally, although not lawfully, married, and to break an engagement is parallel, although no equal, to a divorce. I told Blair that if he had no liberties given him when he really 'had a girl' and more especially engaged, he must never kiss his girl or hold her arm more than any other girl's. 'Spooning' with any girl I see harm in but if confined to a particular girl to whom one is greatly attached I can't really see any harm whatever. Any rate when Sunday comes we'll soon see, won't we. Marriage is demoralising in Blair's argument logically, and when it includes polygamy I agree it is gross immorality, but being confined to <u>one</u> it is pure and I think in a proper sense divine. Being confined to one makes all the difference.

    I haven't found out definitely about Sunday but my chances are very great. I went to the Wesleyan Church on Sunday by myself and it was fine. Last night I went with a Wesleyan in my billet to a recreation room in a private house open to Wesleyans. It was topping. Phonograph, a nice fire, bagatelle (is this the right spelling?). I want to get back early tonight to hear the organ in the church attached to my billet. I hope they play again '*The Day Thou gavest, Lord, is ended*'. When I heard it last it sent me in a whirl. I shall never forget it.

    I'm in much better form today, nearly perfect. Let's hope you are getting on nicely. Please Dear, do look after yourself. I expect you will soon be receiving my money from Westerns. Don't forget to

---

[27]   Cuddling.

send me on a Balance Sheet. You haven't told me whether you have let my people know the news re myself?

Goodbye for now (Excuse scribble)

PS. . . . I don't think you gave much of an answer re sprinkling and confirmation. Where do we differ (and give reasons for differences) from The Brethren?[28]

Thursday 4th February 1915
Dearest,

I hope you liked your brooch. I thought it very neat and pretty and I guessed you'd like it as a memento of my life in the RAMC. I want you to practise the piece of music I am sending under separate cover. I haven't found out yet whether I have a pass for Sunday, but today I asked C section corporal to enquire. I don't think there's much doubt about it.

We had a game of cricket yesterday in our cookhouse yard with a shovel and a milk can. I bowled. Only two cooks went in. One came out with a bruise on his arm as big as an egg and the other had a chunk knocked out of his finger, so the game was abandoned. They wanted me to go in and 'bat' but I wasn't having any of it. I've got two nasty cuts, I don't want any more.

I've been doing a little riding lately. The other day I mounted a large transport horse and I went up and down the yard quite gently, a Cossack couldn't have done it better. Yesterday, I got on a little Shetland pony belonging to the owner of the cookhouse yard. I won't go into details, but the next time he comes our way somebody else gets on and *I* throw the missiles.

Tuesday 9th February 1915
Dearest,

I hope you got home safely and kept dry. I got back all right and in good time. I expect the next time I get leave it will be the last before going abroad. It will be rather rotten for you not having 'your

---

[28] Will and Daisy were members of the Church of Christ. According to his marriage certificate, John Blair was a member of The Brethren.

boy' to take you for walks in the summer, won't it? That will be the time I shall be missed most. But other girls will be in the same boat.

Before I go any further may I ask you if you are still practising the piano. I've left home 3 months. You ought to be noticing a difference in your playing. I don't mean imagination, but reality. (Somebody's at the moment playing at the piano here '*Those Two Grey Eyes*' it sounds fine). You must pardon me making such an assertion, but you seem to me (I hope I'm mistaken) to be treating this matter very indifferently. To be perfectly frank you're disappointing me, as I expect you must know, with the interest you're taking. I noticed on Sunday when I came up that your piano is out of tune more than ever. I should be very sorry to even try to play anything on it. And I personally doubt whether you have done much practice. You know what you promised me dearest.

Now this is what I propose:- First of all that you get your piano tuned without a moment's delay. At my expense. And if you want any music or any aids to get on with to get them at my expense; & when your birthday comes I propose to pay for a tutor and additional music etc for a present. If you have any further or better suggestion I shall be glad to hear it. But I can propose till Doomsday and if you're not willing to take advantage of my assistance, nothing can be done. Dearest. This is the last time I suggest anything or offer to help you with playing. If this fails I shall give it up (not happily you can guess) as a bad job.

Saturday 13th February 1915
Dearest,

Thanks for returning my letter. I've torn it up now. Good riddance to bad rubbish. Let's have no more discord, but sweet harmony. Dearest, accept my apologies won't you. There's always beauty in a tiff, and that's the end of it: the joy of making it up.

It is raining very hard here and I've just been out purchasing. I intended to telegraph you to come up tomorrow, Sunday, but I think it will be too wet and I haven't made any arrangements and I don't fancy walking round and round the town in the pouring rain. Next Sunday it is my turn to stay late, but Sunday week I'll make arrangements for you to come up here. There is a remote possibility of my coming home

Sunday week. I'm going to try and get a special pass and in that case I shall have Saturday evening off as well. All I want is a good excuse. I said in one of my letters that I expect I shall only come home once before going away. Now I understand different, and from what I can see of it we shall stay here for many weeks to come yet.

We played another football match (or rather had a mud lark), we beat the Royal Engineers 7-1. I scored two goals. Next week we play the London Irish again.

I bought, a few days ago, a silver chain for my locket and identification disc to hang round my neck, not showing of course. Doesn't half look 'swanky' though.

Dearest, you won't write any more about my indifference or coolness towards you will you. Really last Sunday I didn't mean to be 'cool'. The subject of music didn't strike me till I got here, when I suddenly remembered it and your piano. I only want one request from you. Please accept my offer re music. Please don't refuse. I know you'll write and tell me you will, won't you dearest.

PS. . . . Please excuse mistakes, I'm in love.

Tuesday 16th February 1915

I hope you received my last letter safely I think it was in accordance with your request, which I got after I had posted my letter, the request that it should be 'a nice one'. And I'm anxiously awaiting your next letter. I intended to write you last night, but instead of writing I found myself sitting in front of one of our 'cookhouse' fires chatting with one of the cooks on the subject of dancing.

You will surprised to hear our leave has already commenced. Some went home yesterday for 6 days including day of departure and day for return. Those who went for a day last time and had to return have gone first this time. After these return some of the sections are going alphabetically and some according to seniority. About 10 per cent at a time. But the Captain of my section, Capt. Sandilands,[29] told our staff sergeant that his section would not take into consideration seniority or juniority or anything of that sort but that after the first lot return they would work from Z backwards

---

[29] John Edward Sandilands.

as he himself had been so unfortunate in leave and other things because his name commenced with 'S'. As to whether he will act upon this I shouldn't like to say, but if he does there being no Zs or Xs, Us or Ys in my section, I shall be home next week. Don't reckon on it though because it is quite probable it may not come off. It certainly sounds well. Then again, the cooks are trying to get their leave apart from the rest. If this comes off I may come home next week and I may not be home for a month or even 6 weeks. Lieut. Ware[30] told us cooks last Sunday that we would all be in France within a month. If this is so, some will go without leave or they will have to allow a much bigger percentage than 10 per cent. I took that information to be official till Lieut. Ware contradicted himself today and distinctly said that 'we shall not go abroad for some considerable time'. So I don't know what to think but I hope I get home soon. Please let Mother know this news.

I'm awfully keen on seeing you again but unless I come home beforehand on leave I can't, as far as I can see, see you till Sunday week when I hope to make arrangements for you to come down here. Well I must say farewell, Yours sincerely

PS. . . . I'm anticipating great things from you on the piano when I do get home next time. I've got another bit of a cold and for the last day or two I've been speaking in my boots. Something like a coalman. Anyhow it coincides with my cookhouse grub.

Wednesday 17th February 1915
Dearest,

Just been to Sergeants Mess to enquire about my leave. And the news I've got sounds all right. Our sergeant says that C section are working backwards as I stated in my previous letter and most probably my turn will start next Thursday. If I should come home you'll have to have the time off from business during my leave. Won't we have a ripping time. My Word! What!! What!!!

My cold has been much worse today and I intended to go to Hospital tomorrow and should they keep me in for 4 days I shall get 4 days leave as well as my ordinary leave, but unfortunately I feel

---

[30] Herbert Ernest Balfern Ware.

much better tonight and so I doubt whether I shall go on sick parade tomorrow.

You say you look forward to letters from me. I'm certain you are no more anxious and keen on getting letters than I am from you. When I go to the YMCA just round the corner from cookhouse every morning and get nothing I come away as if I'd lost a thousand pounds. I'll write longer later.

Thursday 18th February 1915
Dearest

Have reported sick today and am excused all duty. I've been given some funny tack which I have to take 3 times a day.

I was wondering whether it would be possible for you to spend a ½ day or weekend this week here. There is a Y.W.C.A. where I suppose you could put up. You had better get a train on Saturday afternoon which will enable you to be at the Y.W.C.A. Victoria Street at about 5 o'clock as I shall, if I'm fit, be playing football earlier in the afternoon. I'd ask you to come to the match but I don't know where we are playing. On Sunday I shall not be free till about 5 as it is my late day. But, however, you could come round and have a peep at our Chamber of Horrors in the morning.

Do you know I dreamt last night we were married. I wish it was true. I felt 'ratty' when I woke up and found it a farce. Still, it will be reality one of these days won't it. Just had a letter brought me from you. The omitted portion of the letter you refer to was accidentally left out and Ivy's brooch I can't get yet.

I know Albert Baswitz quite well and should be pleased to see him. When I get my leave it may be the last time you'll see me before I go away. Goodbye for now, I'm simply dying to see you.
PS. . . . The missing words in my last letter I now reveal 'My Treasure'.

Friday 19th February 1915
Dearest,

I think you had better go straight to the YWCA Victoria Street. At the moment I can't give you the exact direction from station but you can ask at station. If I'm not fit to play on Saturday, or the match is postponed, and you let me know when you will arrive at St

Albans station I'll meet you there. By the way please bring some of my money with you in case I haven't enough.

Do you know that Blair is going to get married. I suggested how he could quite easily manage it when he goes home on leave he says he's going to act on my idea. It's this. I asked him if married men were paid at his business and he said they receive 2/3rds of their money. So I said how much do single men get and he said nothing. So I said if you get married in a quiet sort of way, your wife can go to business in the ordinary way and you will get 2/3rds your money from business besides separation allowance which with your deduction of 3/6 from your 10/6 per week would amount to 16/- a week. So as a result you could save 2/3rds of your business money and 16/- making I suppose a clean save of something like 35/- a week. So if the war lasted a year (and I reckon it will last that) you will be able to buy a new home 52 × 35/- is roughly £93. Don't you think it's a brilliant idea of mine? I'd like to try it myself. I could save £1 and 16/- clean. Well I must now say goodbye.
PS. . . . I should think the YWCA could put you up alright. Excuse scribble.

Postcard of the 5th London Field Ambulance football team. Will is kneeling on the left of the middle row.

24th February 1915 (the postcard above was sent to Will's sister, Irene)
Home tomorrow. Find me in our famous team. Make me a trifle for tea.

Tuesday March 2nd 1915
Dearest,

I enclose brooch. You will see that it is of a slightly different pattern and I like it better. So I think you ought to have it and give Ivy the other one. It's the same price, 1/-. I'd like yours to be unique.

I thoroughly enjoyed my leave and I hope you did as well. I don't know as I'm much better for it. I've had a splitting headache all day today and feel right out of form. But I intend to take great care of myself and see if I can get fit soon. On reaching St Albans I was informed that we are going away on the 17th of this month. It's from a reliable source and I believe it to be true and I also heard that I shall not have any more leave before going away, I mean the usual 48 hours. But I'm under the impression I have a pass for next Sunday. You won't forget to write to the Building Society will you. And also remember to practise well on the piano, eat well, exercise well and get to bed early.
PS. . . . Keep smiling

Thursday 4th March 1915
Dearest,

Thanks very much for letter and enclosures. Your reply to the Building Society was quite alright, but I rather query whether my last sub was paid in January 1914, as far as I remember it was paid in June 1914. Don't you remember we've been reckoning as being 8 months in arrears making £16. What makes you think January now? Didn't they return my book?

The Building Society, as your PS clearly points out, are making a horrible blunder somewhere. If you could conveniently manage it you might 'phone through and get explanations that way, if they should delay answering your letter. You don't want to keep writing and waiting for replies otherwise you won't settle the matter before

March 11th when they promised to send a cheque. You know what I mean. Hurry them up. Make things hum.

I very much doubt now whether I shall be home Sunday. All leave is cancelled again. And the officer told me (Lt Ware) that we are going in a fortnight. The week after next. It's quite official now. We had another very strict medical examination yesterday and several of the corps have been rejected. They're turning out fellows every day now. Guerney has been rejected for one. I got through alright.

Should I not be able to get home before going away, I'll have you come down (if you will). Re the brooch. You'd better bank the money. Let them know the news at home won't you. Well goodbye, dear, for now.

PS. . . . Our motor ambulance men have just this minute had orders to push off with full war kit somewhere. Just saying goodbye.

PPS. . . . Blair and I weighed ourselves yesterday. He has got very fat in the face and looks much fatter than he did at Hatfield when without overcoats he weighed 10st.2lbs and I 10st.5lbs. I said the heavier pays and he said "You're not artful". He thought he was tremendously heavier now and I had not gained a fraction. He got on and to my astonishment weighed 10st.10lbs; then I got on and to his greater astonishment I weighed 10st.12lbs. So you see I shall soon be an elephant.

Friday 5th March 1915

My Treasure,

All men who have not already had leave have been sent on 48 hours leave today and it is certain now that we are moving in a fortnight. I believe we shall go to Winchester first for a day or two. As to where we are going, I'm not able to say, I expect it will be France, but wild rumours say Dardanelles and British East Africa. I don't take any notice of these.

I don't know yet whether Sunday passes have been resumed. I doubt it and even if they are, whether I have one and supposing I have, I can't see quite how the cookhouse is going on. Four cooks went home today. And another one besides myself anticipates a Sunday pass. I think you ought to come up on Sunday. I may be staying for tea, but that doesn't matter. You could catch a morning train which arrives at St Albans about 11 or 12 and come straight to the cookhouse and see me in my dress uniform. You could have a look round and go and have dinner somewhere and in the afternoon you could have a walk and we could go out to tea together. If I should not come home will you do that dear. So I'll take it for granted that if I write nothing to the contrary you'll be up Sunday. Will you please go to Mother at once and ask her to telegraph Alex as follows:- 'Will's up to say goodbye before going abroad. Please come home. Mother.'

If I should come up on Sunday he'll be able to see me before I go abroad. Should I not come up it will be a good excuse for him to get a Sunday pass. That's the only way I can think of that he can see me before I go. The others may be able to come to St Albans later on.

By the way if I shouldn't come home you could call at my house on Sunday and wait for Alex and bring him up here if his pass allows it. I expect he can wangle it. Personally I think this is a good suggestion. I'd very much like to see him before I go away and that's the only way I can think of. Take this letter to Mother's and if they have a better suggestion act upon it. I can't think of one. You know the position.

Monday 8th March 1915
My Treasure,
Thank you for your nice letter. I enclose as promised my Will. There need be no ceremony about it and no need to keep it sealed. You might let Mother look at it if you like. I have not sent off your bike yet, but will do so tonight if I get time. We have not shifted yet. The fellows think we are moving tomorrow, personally I think it will be a few days yet. I have not asked Mother to come down yet I'm simply waiting events. Keep smiling. Your greatest friend
PS.... Let Mother know the news.

Wednesday 10th March 1915
My Treasure,
Thanks for letter. I thank you for taking so much trouble about the Building Society. But do you understand it? Please don't agree yet although they have come down a bit. I can't see what they're driving at at all. It's Chinese to me absolutely. In fact it seems nonsense. If you know what they mean and can understand the

statement and agree with them, I should be awfully obliged if you would explain. It's getting on my nerves. It's bosh to me. I presume it's sense to you otherwise you would have told me you could not understand it. Didn't they send a letter? In future letters re this matter kindly send me your opinion. If you don't understand it please say so, if you do, say so. Let me know per return what's your opinion about this mad business. I have not the remotest what it all means. If you don't understand it write or phone or telegraph or go up or send somebody else up or employ a solicitor. Please do something to get at a sensible conclusion.

Thursday 11th March 1915
My Treasure,

We have not shifted yet. Most of our brigade have gone. I've sent home all my spare kit and cleaning materials according to orders. I expect you will be interested to know that all my curly locks have been cut off. We are all going to the barbers, on our own accord, and having our hair mown completely off. I look frightful; a few yards off and I appear to have no hair at all. I look a criminal now.

I'm anxiously waiting for a letter in reply to my letter of last night. I hope to get it tomorrow morning. Dearest, I hope my curtness did not offend you.

I wonder what this time next year will bring forth. Let's hope Peace and comfort. It would be peculiar to have me back again in civil life wouldn't it. I hope you are practising well and exercising too. I expect wonderful things when I return home again. I must say goodbye for now. Fondest love.

Private W Stocker 1857, 5th L.F.A.TF RAMC
British Expeditionary Force, France
Sunday 14th March 4.30 pm
My Treasure,

I arrived at Southampton this morning at 6.30 am and we are now lounging about the docks. I've just woken up from a good sleep on a hay stack arrangement. I'm fit and contented but I've been thinking of you all day. The moment I said goodbye I noticed you broke down and as a matter of fact I was unmanly too. Still, cheer up, I'm coming home again to you and I reckon the meeting will trebly compensate our parting. I'm looking forward to it now.

It's ripping weather here and I'm looking forward to a nice voyage. I've only a few wishes at the moment and I told you them last night. 1) Pray often. 2) Keep smiling. 3) Write me often. Goodbye, dearest, for now. Your future partner.

Thursday 18th March 1915[31]

Dearest,

Arrived safely in France. Channel crossing rough. Met Baswitz on board. Slept in the hold of the boat, extremely stuffy. Next day in a tent, then in a cattle truck 40 of us in which we travelled 2 or 3 hundred miles. Not enough room to lie down. Slept like this ⌐. Last night slept in a barn. I got right up on top of hay. Very comfortable.

It's novel marching along a street, kids hang round us in mobs. My French comes in very handy, I'm the interpreter of our billet. Aeroplanes fly over here every minute of day. Occasionally we hear distant booming of guns. No business yet, all travelling. I hope you're well. Personally I'm fit and happy. Simply waiting events. If you could forward me a pocket dictionary, small, I should be awfully obliged. Of course I mustn't put where I am, officers sanction our letters. Goodbye and keep smiling.

PS. . . . Send me a packet of postcards.

---

[31] **The History of the Fifth London Field Ambulance** has a brief timeline of the journey to France:
March 13th Entrained for Southampton
March 14th Embarked SS *Mount Temple*, *Viper* and *Copenhagen*.
March 15th Landed at Le Havre. March to No 8 Rest Camp. Havre.
March 16th Entrained at Le Havre. Detrained at Arques. March from Arques to Compagne-lès-Wardrecques
The War Diary of the 5th London Field Ambulance from before the 1st April 1915 does not survive. However, the War Diary of their sister unit, the 6th LFA, who departed the following day, states that they left Southampton docks at 8.30 p.m. and arrived Le Havre at 03.30 a.m., having been escorted across the channel by two torpedo destroyers. The crossing was made at night to minimise the risk of attack by enemy submarines. They spent the morning unloading horses, wagons, and equipment and then marched to the rest camp.

Friday
Dearest,

Pushed forward today a few miles. Have seen Indian Cavalry. Fine men they are too. Of course I have not received any letters from you yet, I suppose that's owing to our shifting about. Last night it was cold in our barn. Tonight we are sleeping in barracks, rough show. What one must expect war time. I met Victor Bell[32] on the road today. I'm in good trim still and that's a lot. But what I long for is that day when I shall return home to you again. My birthday, eh? My word What! I'm getting on with my French all right. I shall be quite hot stuff soon. Remember me to 'Prof' Curtis by 'phone. Goodbye for now. Warmest Christian love.

C Section 5th L.F.A.TF RAMC
5th Brigade, 2nd London Division
Sunday 21st March 4.30 pm – Tuesday 23rd March 1915
My dear Daisy,

Thanks for the two letters you sent me. I have sent you several postcards, which I hope you'll eventually receive. The weather out here is very congenial and up to the time of writing we have not seen the firing line and so I have nothing to report. Of course it's very rough and ready here. I'm at present sleeping on straw in a room accommodating about 13. There are about a dozen windows each end of the room and every one without exception is broken: open air treatment. Needless to say it is not what you might term 'tropical' and when I return I should make quite an efficient Nansen.[33]

---

[32] Now serving in the Royal Cyclist Corps.
[33] One of Will's colleagues, Percy Gardner, wrote to a cousin in Broken Hill, Australia a few weeks after this. The letter was printed in the local newspaper, *The Barrier Miner*, on Sunday 19th September 1915. In it he describes the discomfort of the crowded cattle trucks, the cold of the bell tents, the worse cold of sleeping in the barns with snow coming through the roof and the discomfort of marching on slippery cobbled streets.

I was surprised yesterday to meet Bert Coward and on board coming from England I met ~~Baswitz~~ who is a lieutenant in The ~~Lond~~[34] and I understand Hall has been enquiring after me.[35]

As to your question whether letters are censored both ways, I believe they only censor letters coming from the front. My letters are read by my officers first. In reply to your generous offer, I should be awfully obliged if you send me a good supply of chocolate occasionally. Tobacco does not interest me. And you might forward *Lloyds*[36] every week and *Joyful Tidings* monthly. Let me know how Beethoven's getting on.

The École de Jeunes Filles in Béthune

---

[34] The words 'Baswitz' and 'London' are heavily crossed through in the same ink as the rest of the letter: Will obviously realised that he would fall foul of the censor. Captain Albert Baswitz, 22nd London Regiment, lived a few streets from Will in Fulham. He would be awarded the Military Cross in January 1916. He was killed in action on 16th September 1916.

[35] Albert Coward and Walter Hall, both of Twynholm church.

[36] *Lloyds Sunday News*.

27th March 1915
My dear Daisy,

Thanks for letter received today. I have sent you several postcards and I shall be glad to know if you have received same. I am at present billeted in a school not many miles from the firing line.[37] I sleep on straw in a well ventilated room. Plenty of window frames but no windows. Nevertheless I'm in good condition and quite contented. I've met Bert here and also Fred Williams.[38] They are both billeted a few yards off. We have not been in action yet and so I've nothing much to report.

Monday afternoon 29th March 1915
Dear Daisy

Have just received parcel. Kindly thank the various subscribers for me. When I have finished writing I shall venture to try the contents. We have made another move since I last wrote to you. We are billeted in a school[39] and we are still within sound of the guns. It's very cold here at night, very. We have to be in by night, lights out 8.15. It's more comfortable here than at the last place.

I shall be obliged if you will send me in your next parcel: Eucryl toothpaste, safety blades ½ a dozen (occasionally a daily paper) and *Joyful Tidings*. I've sent a postcard to Irene, which might interest you.

---

[37] Collège de Jeune Filles, Béthune.
[38] Another member of Twynholm Church serving in the RAMC.
[39] 'In a school in Allouagne, near a church with a sad bell. They came back here several times in the first two years. It was like coming home' – from Daisy's notebook.

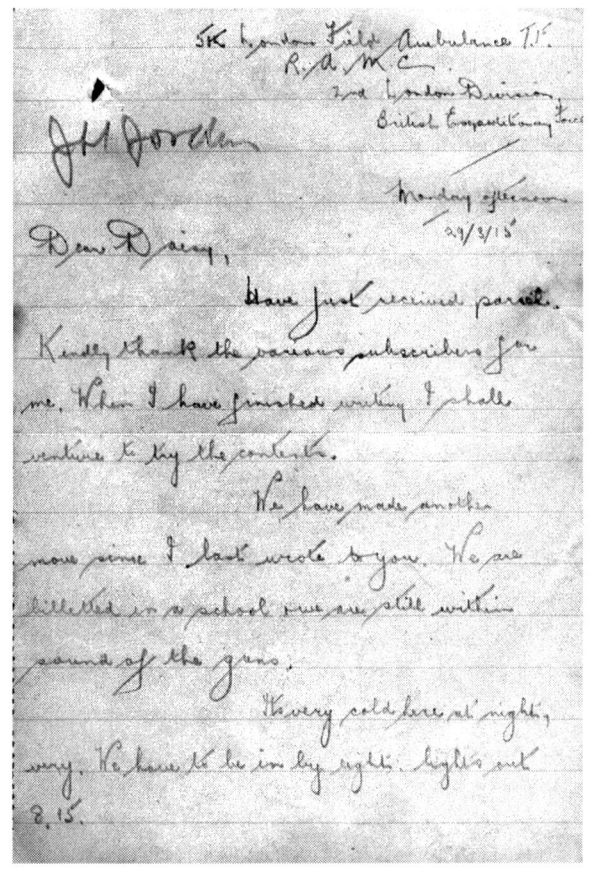

Will's letter of 29th March 1915
It has been censored and countersigned by Lt J. H. Jordan.

Saturday 3rd April 1915
My dearest Daisy,
   You will see by this envelope that it is a little more private than my other letters. I've had to be very curt in my letters, one can't express one's feelings properly when the letter is read by one's own Captain. Now for a nice letter, Eh! I am writing this in a café. In fact I've written all my letters in a café. Every night without fail I make for here, it's warm and comfortable. Our billet has no light and no fire. Now I can inform you that my Captain has told me I'm hospital cook with two old fellows, I'm to act as senior corporal and if I get on all right I shall be given stripes later. Sounds well doesn't it? So I hope to be a corporal in the near future.

I received your papers. Thanks <u>awfully</u>. Did you read 'Tips for Tommy' and the sermon by Enoch? Very fine articles. Where are you spending Easter, you simply say 'away from home'. I agree with you that when I return we must make for the Bridle Path because of its happy relations. You very much amused me when you said you'll soon forget the art of spooning. It looks like 'sprucing'; spooning should be written ͜ not ͝. You'll never forget the art of spooning, it's natural with your sex.

Re your admirer. You don't say who he is or where he comes from. I'd like to know. Don't write too much about him, I shall want to come home at once and square matters up. I've realized since I've been here the truth of the saying 'absence makes the heart grow fonder'. You can't imagine how I crave sometimes to come home and see you, although I'm quite happy and contented here. I eagerly anticipate letters from you. I'm glad I've got the locket. But by the way a few of us in the corps have been given a sort of letter case with writing paper and I have a little pocket arrangement admirably suited for a photo. Would you have your photo taken for me. About as big as a small postcard. Let the photo itself be as large as possible. Get it done quickly won't you dear.

I'm sorry to say I've lost my fountain pen. Perhaps you guessed that.[40] Well, I must say goodbye. Write often.
PS. . . . I've had a <u>nice</u> lot of letters from Mother.

(Contd) Sunday

I've just a few minutes to spare while waiting for stews to boil so I thought I'd try and continue. In your next letters it wouldn't be a bad idea if you send each time a little instruction about French, a sort of a very short lesson (copied from a book if you like) grammar

---

[40] This letter is written in pencil.

etc, useful hints and so on. Don't send me a book, I've enough to carry now.

You won't forget to do what I said re your birthday present. About the first thing I shall ask you to do when I return will be to play me something on the piano. By the way how are the dumbbells going on? You say in one part of your letter that some of the girls at your firm are playing about with other fellows while their own boys are at the front. I don't doubt it. It's a good instance of the 'fickleness of women'. They want a quiet hour with my Mother. You can't wonder at unhappy marriages and divorces when that sort of infidelity goes on. What a different world it would be if in all senses we all 'played the game'. It's 'man's inhumanity to man that makes countless thousands mourn'.[41]

My dear Daisy,
Thanks for your letter received yesterday. I'm still billeted in a school. Some of our fellows yesterday went to the trenches and I believe are returning in a few days.

Don't forget to send me in your next parcel another fountain pen in place of the one I've lost, ½ dozen razor blades and some bulldog buttons[42] and some leather boot laces. I'm told that by making arrangements with Lloyds they will send each week their paper to me. I shall get it earlier than if you send it. I hope you had an enjoyable Easter. The weather here wasn't very favourable, perhaps you had it better in London.
PS. . . . Keep smiling

Friday 9th April 1915
My dear Daisy,
I've just come across a letter which I intended to post a week ago. You won't forget to thank the various subscribers of my parcel. The dictionary I find very useful. I think it a very good choice.

---

[41] From *Man Was Made to Mourn* by Robert Burns, 1784.
[42] Bulldog was a brand of bachelor's button. They were made of metal and attached by being pushed through the fabric and anchored by a small split ring or clip. The idea was to save the bother of sewing on buttons which had to be removed each time the article of clothing was laundered.

Today I got a letter from Ivy and another from Ada and I'm anxiously awaiting the arrival of your letter. Ada says you're rather 'down'. If that is so, you have no reason for it. I'm in excellent condition and perfectly happy. Have you seen the PC I sent Irene? Perhaps you'll recognize some of the faces.

I believe in your last letter you said that you had waited over a week for a letter from me. May I say I write practically every other day. Possibly some of my letters go astray.

PS. . . . Keep smiling

My dear Daisy,

I have just received your letter of last Thursday. It sounds a little more cheerful than your previous letters. I think before you settle upon the photo, you had better forward me the proof and get it done in sepia if possible. You won't forget to forward me the razor blades I asked for and pen. I should also be obliged if you would let me have Alex's address. We are still billeted in the same little village.[43] Goodbye for now. The guns have been energetic today.

Tuesday April 13th 1915
Dearest

Another nice letter. What! What! I'm anxiously waiting to get your photo or proof and by the way your next letter also. It may be my imagination, but your letters are not over frequent are they. Perhaps I expect too much, but dear, I do appreciate your letters, especially now.

I am still billeted in a school 10 miles from firing line. Our fellows are taking it in turns to go, in parties of about 12, to the trenches for a few days simply for experience. They go up by ambulance motor. All the fellows are anxious to go. Although we are at present about 10 miles from the firing line, we can by motor, get to the trenches in about 20 minutes. Often hostile aircraft come our way, but they don't do much damage, occasionally they drop a bomb, but as a rule they get such a warm welcome that they soon hop it. We've seen two air duels here. I've seen several types

---

[43] Allouagne.

of soldiers here. English soldiers, Bengal Lancers, French cavalry, Algerian troops, Gurkhas etc. No Germans yet.

I'm in fine form here, I've never felt better in my life, although I'm sick (lovesick). Plenty of food, fresh air, sleep and work. Before I go any farther, please allow me to remind you to forward the following:- <u>1</u> Paper similar to which I'm now writing on for my case; get it perforated and same size etc if possible <u>2</u> Eucryl tooth powder 1/- box (which I asked for days ago and it hasn't arrived yet) <u>3</u> some socks, some of your hand knitted, a day or so will do for these <u>4</u> Gillette blades (asked for ½ dozen once) <u>5</u> pen, as before <u>6</u> Alex's address. Excuse my asking, won't you. By the way may I ask if you are carrying out my request re prayer.

Wednesday (contd)

How do you feel without me: ever lonely? When I return, we'll make up for lost time, won't we. It will be fine when we can spend our Saturdays etc together. I expect your birthday will see me away, but I reckon I shall be with you on my birthday. Do you know, personally, I shouldn't be over surprised (although it may seem ridiculous) if the war was over in two months. Hope so, eh? I reckon I shall see a little difference in you, re music etc, I'm getting on fine here and I feel as strong as a lion and as frisky as a monkey. Only those who are out here know how well the troopers are looked after. I'm growing a little tooth brush now, I shall soon be able to wax the ends.

I got your papers today. Thanks awfully. I believe I asked you to send in every letter of yours a lesson of some description in French. Haven't got it yet.

In the little village where I'm billeted I understand 30 have been killed in the French army. Awful, isn't it?

PS. . . . Keep smiling. 'Clouds will be sunshine tomorrow.'[44]

Dearest,

Thanks awfully for parcel. It was ripping. Pile heaps of thanks upon all subscribers. You asked me what I thought of the last parcel. I'm sure I said at least twice I liked it immensely. Before I go any farther

---

[44] *Oh Dry Those Tears* by Arthur Pryor and Teresa del Riego c. 1901.

might I suggest some things I should like in my next parcel:- a small nail brush, a hard one. Some Lifebuoy soap. I get tons of it here, but it's not over grand. Some cocoa in preference to sweets, I'm not a lover of sweets except chocolate, a tiny writing pad or more pcs. <u>Special</u> a few locks of your hair. Some cake made by you at my expense.

Now for your photo. Really I think it's very good. I have it in front of me now as I'm writing. It's very true. I have no complaints whatever. When you have it printed don't let the photographer muck it up by touchings. The more I look at it the more I like it. I wish it was you in reality. My word. What! What!! Dearest, you don't know how I crave to see you again. But it won't be very long now. Every day is a day nearer the Great Return. It must come soon. This time next year we shall be talking of my past in the R.A.M.C.

Myra[45] wants to know how I'm getting on with les petites filles. I haven't seen one, not one, worth looking at and if there were any here in this tiny village I couldn't have anything whatever to do with them. <u>My heart's at home in England</u>, my thoughts, in fact my all.

Thank Ivy for my socks but we can now send old socks to our laundry and have clean repaired ones instead or a new pair. Don't forget to thank your father will you.

Re my accounts. What on earth made you write saying you hadn't misappropriated any money. Good gracious! You do think I have a funny opinion of you. Did you mean it for fun? Re Corporal. Write me as Private Stocker till further orders not 'Acting Corporal'.

Will you please cut out each week the sermons in Lloyds they're fine. If you can, get the back numbers you have sent me for this purpose.

PS. . . . Some silly crow knocked over the candle on this card.[46]

Saturday

---

[45] Myra Perkins, a member of Twynholm Church.
[46] There are wax stains on the card. When they were behind the lines, they often slept in barns amid the dry hay and straw, having cigarettes before sleeping and using candles for light. In one place, one of the men sleeping downstairs had a bald head and they made a game of dropping candle wax onto his head. Smoking in barns was later banned by the army after several fires.

In a day or so we are moving, I believe up near the firing line. So we shall soon be in action. The fellows who have been up already are awfully eager to go. The big guns have been booming all day long and so I suppose we'll soon be busy. Don't like this pen at present. It flows like a mountain torrent.
PS. . . . Ask Mother to send me out the towels I sent home. Keep Smiling. Perhaps you'd be interested to know my hair after being shorn is like a curly headed negro's. I only use a brush.

Friday 30th April 1915
My dear Daisy,

Here we are again. I haven't written you oftener simply because I've had nothing fresh to tell you. I'm still at the same school, although today a party of our Ambulance including Bull and Calcutt left us today for near the trenches and so I expect we will soon follow. Terrific cannonading has been going on near here the last day or so. In the evening we play football and just lately we've been arranging matches with regiments having a rest. Of course you know the soldiers have so long in the trenches and a week or so rest. We've done rippingly and one most famous infantry regiment wearing kilts we beat 7-1 and another more famous perhaps territorial battalion we drew 3-3 and are playing again tonight. When we haven't got a match on we arrange concerts and we've some remarkable talents. We've had no casualties yet except 8 or 9 cases of German Measles. I think the fellows get it unloading cases from trains. Horrocks is away with it.

I believe I told you that at present we have a Field Laundry (in a school). So we get plenty of changes of underclothing and the troops also get a hot shower bath near here about once a week. But I find it inconvenient to go, so I borrow a tub and soon manage the business all right. Perhaps you are not aware that when a soldier has been in the trenches he has a bath and a complete change of clothing and so there are heaps of so-called 'Field Laundries' here.

You won't forget my locket. I get tons of letters now especially from you. Every day I get something, today I had 3. I'm glad you are going ahead with your music. I reckon you'll be quite 'hot stuff' when I return. It will be worth all the time and energy you put into it. You'll put me in the shade absolutely. You won't forget to go to Harry if in any way you consider he can render assistance. Re your photo. May I say again I consider it ripping. It's fine. I'd like to see it framed alongside of mine. They say anticipation is greater than realization. I'm ever anticipating the day of my return, but I wish it was realization. 7 weeks today since I left St Albans. It seems 7 months in one way.

Did you tell Mother I get few letters from her? I told you she wrote me very frequently. I suppose you misunderstood me. With your next parcel you might forward me some reading material. If you can get something after the type of Hall Caine *Eternal City* in paper cover form. Of course the smaller the better, or a decent book in pocket book form. Anything elevating and portable and that doesn't cost thousands to get out here. Don't forget to cut those articles out of *Lloyds* each week. Especially that article on Ideals. Forgive me for worrying you so very much, won't you dear.

Re green envelopes. We are given one each about every week. I'd write every other day with a green envelope if I could get them.[47] I bought a green envelope from a fellow in order to write a decent letter to Johnson. I expect you will soon be hearing from Western's. Let's know when you hear, won't you. While I'm out here I'm getting, if I want it, 20 francs a fortnight (or thereabouts). That's not my full money and so far I've drawn 20 out of 60 and next Wednesday I shall draw 5 leaving 15 on my book and so I should have quite a decent sum by the time I come home, help to swell my bank account a bit. By the way how did Mother take the news of my going away when you told her on Sunday 7 weeks ago? Once again don't forget to <u>heartily</u> thank the subscribers to my last parcel.

I was wondering the other day if you ever use my photo as an apology for the purpose of xx. You won't take the polish off it, will you, otherwise you'll give the game away. If you have asked me any questions and I have not yet replied to them just set them out in a list and I'll do so.

---

[47] Green envelopes were introduced in March 1915. The letter writer had to sign a certificate to the effect that the contents of the enclosed letter referred to nothing except family and other non-military matters. They were not routinely censored, but were still liable to be checked at random.

PS. . . . When I wrote to you re French Lessons <u>all</u> I wanted was for you to buy (if you have not already one) a French book and in each letter copy a sentence from it and send it me word for word. I fully realise you are frightfully busy. So please don't trouble. But you can send me a 'French' book in your next parcel if you like.

<u>9th May</u>
3.50am orders received to move to Béthune to prepare College de Jeunes Filles to receive wounded.
8.20am Arrived. Building prepared for reception of wounded.
11pm Wounded received. All officers and men worked all night.

<u>10th May</u>
9am up to this hour 177 men received. All evacuated during the day . . . except cases too serious to be moved. Five men died.
War Diary.

15th May 1915
Dearest,

Thanks for your letters especially the lock of hair. You say you don't know why I should want it. Don't tell fibs. Why did you ask me on one occasion for the same thing. The whims of <u>women </u>are <u>artful</u>. The scent was nice too. I can wave it in my face, close my eyes and imagine - - - . How nice! Scrumptious!! Foretaste of coming glory.

I have now some news for you. Last Friday morning about 4.30am we were all suddenly called up. The guns were sounding terrifically and the whole place shook. One constant roar. The men were soon marched off in full marching order and I stayed an hour or so cooking breakfast for fatigue party left behind clearing up and finally left in a motor ambulance for a rather large town about 3 or 4 miles from firing line.[48] The bombardment was heard plainer there. Like Hell gone mad. Something big seemed to be on. We

---

[48] Béthune.

stopped at a very big school equipped for a hospital and I had to stay on night duty. About 10 o'clock the wounded began to arrive and presently they poured in. I and the other cook on with me had to go like mad to keep up the pace.[49] Hundreds of wounded came in. The first time I saw a wound was that day in the operation room. I can't describe some of the sights I saw. Suffice to say I came away not fainting as I anticipated but trying to imagine what God must think of so-called Christian countries. Daisy, it was awful. I was absolutely disgusted with the world. You at home can't properly realize what things are like out here. Some of the cases were horrible. Ghastly. Poor fellows swamped with blood. Some of the men were so hellishly mutilated that it made me cry. Some had legs blown off, the whole face smashed in, many blind for life, these are mild wounds compared with some I saw. Many died here. Every man was a hero. Those who lost fingers and had arm and leg wounds, although in great pain smiled because they said they were lucky. I only heard a few moans. One poor fellow had gone mad and asked repeatedly for his mother and girl. It quite touched the fellows looking after him. Another touching incident was when a Black Watch arrived and was asked by a chum how things were going. 'Jock' he said with tears in his eyes 'The Company's gone, the Company's gone.'[50] One fellow I was holding a conversation with a week ago I saw dead yesterday. No wonder he said to me 'I wonna come back.' I little knew how true his words would be. There's no mistake about it we've got some brave chaps in our army. I like the Scotch best. I can't write any more just now. Let Mother and Dada know how I'm getting on. Read parts of the letter to them. Let's have Mr Mander's piece of poetry, 'How did you die?'[51] Don't forget to let Dada and Mother know how I'm getting on and when you see Mr Mander thank him for his letter to me and tell him I'm really too busy to answer it.

---

[49] 'Experience teaches that wounded men (who have already received first aid) need their stomachs filled and a bed to rest on before all else.' *The Tale of a Casualty Clearing Station by a Royal Field Leech.*

[50] The Commonwealth War Graves Commission records 23 Black Watch killed from 10th to 12th May 1915. Seven are buried in Béthune.

[51] *How Did You Die?* by Edmund Vance Cook of Canada.

PS. . . . Dearest, when they sing at Twynholm *Hark my Soul* think of me. It's what I hum all day, my favourite.

> *May 16th 1915*
> *Beautiful sunny day, not so cold as yesterday. Attack began about 3.40am. Visited 5th and 6th LFAs, both had about 100 wounded at 10.30 am. In afternoon again visited both FAs. The total wounded up to 9pm, from 9pm last night, in 5th and 6th FAs was 585 of whom 217 remained. During the night Béthune was again shelled by field guns, 6 at midnight and about a dozen at 3am.*
> **War Diary of Assistant Director of Medical Services (ADMS)**

Monday 17th May
My dear Daisy,

Thanks for your many letters. I have made another shift and am now in an Advanced Dressing Station 1000 yards from German trenches. About a dozen of us. I have been in our trenches. Our billet is at the entrance. The trenches are named according to familiar London streets. Harley St, Hertford St, Piccadilly Circus, etc. More exciting here. Several batteries just near here and they're not particular as to the hour they choose for firing. However, I like it here. I'm still in good form.

Thursday 20th May
My dearest

I've just got your parcel and as you will see I'm making use of your pad. I expect you have had my letter informing you of my present duty in an Advanced Dressing Station.[52] I don't want you to get at all anxious about me but I'm going to just tell you all. I'm sorry to have to tell you first, we've had 2 casualties in our

---

[52] Pont Fixe or Harley Street Advanced Dressing Station.

Ambulance one killed[53] and one wounded. Both occurred at the other Advanced Station. We have 2 Advanced Stations, each have a dozen men. The remainder are in a large town some miles back, which often gets shelled. The last night I was there, about 3 o'clock in the morning, we had to get up from slumber and resort to the basement.

Although I'm in the Advanced Station I'm the cook and I can tell you I don't venture out much. Shells fly all round here and at night rifle bullets 'ping' all round the place. We have two stretcher parties of four who take it in turns to go out at night. They can't carry some cases along the trenches and have to come across open fields with stray bullets hissing all round. I'm glad I don't have to go out. It's a jolly dangerous job. Last night a bullet came over the wall and through the shutter and struck the wall the other side of the room. We sleep in the basement and are not allowed above the ground floor (General's orders). It's very warm here. I can tell you as I'm writing I can hear hundreds of bullets striking the walls here and the noise of the artillery is awful: shakes the whole place. Goodbye for now. I'm off to bed.

Friday

I've just aroused enough courage to try your cakes and really I like them immensely. If you make them as good as that when we are - - - I'll have no complaints to make.

Just been given to understand we are leaving here today and returning back to the remainder. Another Ambulance is going to carry this show on. One fellow's had to return owing to nervous breakdown and I think the Colonel considers it's too much of a strain for all of us here. Any rate none of the others seem anxious to take our place.

A piece of shell hit the step a few feet away from me this morning and two days ago 3 of us were out in the garden and the nozzle of a shell just missed the other fellows' heads and struck the

---

[53] Pte John W. Edwin died of wounds 18th May 1915, aged nineteen. The War Diary records that he was mortally wounded at 3.30am whilst collecting wounded close to the firing line at Festubert (working out of Tuning Fork Dressing Station). He is buried in Béthune Town Cemetery.

ground within arm's length of me. All the houses round here (except ours for some unknown reason) are smashed to bits. But I can assure you I don't go out when shells are flying about, in plain words I 'hop it'. My duties confine me to indoors.

Last night there was a bombardment about a mile off and we watched the shells bursting over the trenches. It was like a huge firework display. We also watched an aeroplane attacked by shells. I've seen some awful sights here. I hope you don't consider I'm venturesome, I'm not. Although not nervous I'm very cautious and I don't risk much. My object's to get back home to you safely. If it's God's wish for me to return you may rest assured German shells won't alter matters and I know it is His wish. Something compels me to believe this.

Dearest, I'm longing, craving, eagerly anticipating the time to come for me to return. When peace is declared I shall go mad. The excitement in our Ambulance I know will be terrific. We are all looking forward to that day now. It seems a long time coming, but it must come some day and it's a consolation each day to know I'm a day nearer England. England, England, England. As soon as a man is wounded the first question is 'Shall I go to England?' In fact if a fellow has anything short of his head blown off it may be a smashed leg, broken arm, fractured skull, or other wound, he's envied because he may go to England. The very name is Heaven to us. Can you wonder at it. The Front, so foolishly yearned for by the new recruits, is Hell without a doubt. As I'm writing half a dozen fellows have just passed the door with the dead body of a pal. They're going to bury him in our garden, which is more of a graveyard. One of the many unknown heroes of the War. There's no ceremony about it, no parson, no coffin even, but the bare heads and gloomy faces truly express nevertheless sincere sorrow and so passes away one of England's brave sons and the child of some poor mother murdered by a so-called Christian nation. Our chaps here are just about to make a rough wooden cross to put over the grave. I have to brace myself up sometimes and whistle or hum and sing, otherwise I should have to cry all day. The sights I see are beyond description. I really can't go into details. The enclosed flowers I got out of the garden.

Thanks for parcel. The book I've read, but as you say it's worth reading again. Re Mander. I'll write him <u>if</u> I get time. But when I do get a moment I write to you. It sounds easy to write one person a line but in my present position it can't be done. I have at least 20 letters unanswered. Explain position to him and kindly don't <u>worry</u> me about writing people. When one is up sometimes night and day spare time is useful for sleep. Everybody's asking me to write to such an extent that I'm sorry sometimes to see the postman. It's really getting on my nerves. Every day's a working day to me. Just got orders to pack up, full marching order <u>at once</u>.

Sunday

I am now right back about 10 miles behind trenches. I packed up and retired 3 miles to a little town behind firing line.[54] We stayed a night in a school[55] and had a very bad time. We were shelled and 7 men were wounded (not our Ambulance) on 2nd floor and one killed just above, in fact the plaster came down on me, it was awful. There was no basement and we had to try and shelter ourselves behind the thickest walls. I then came back to the large town referred to above for a moment or so and then with the rest of the Ambulance we have come right back to a lovely spot and no fear of shells here. Whether we are sent back for rest I can't say but we are resting. At the moment of writing I'm laying on the grass, Sunday evening glorious weather (although a storm last night). I've seen enough of war now and I'm simply craving for peace.

Just got your letter. I wish I could return home and see you, especially as I hear so much about your garb. So dearest I must admit I've had some very dangerous experiences and in a few days shall return to danger zone again, but keep smiling and pray night and day for my safety and you need not fear. One with God is always a majority and something (I should say 'Somebody') convinces me I shall come home safely. Have faith in God. I am Yours always

---

[54] Chateau le Réveillon. According to Daisy's notebook, Will described his time here as the 'best days in France'.
[55] At Labeuvrière.

Wednesday 26th May
My dear Daisy,

How I long to see you. Do you think I'm asking too much if I say I'd like some more photographs of you in your new get-up. It wouldn't cost much for just one or two. Just postcards you know. I'll pay. Not for circulation but just for me only so you only need get one of each in different get-ups and positions. You know what I mean. I'd like a few photos of you. Different ones. I'm awfully glad you're sticking to your music, you know how keen I always was on that. I'm anticipating something good when I return.

Thursday

I've read your letter and the answer to those questions of yours are certainly very appropriate. I understand from Mother you went with Harry and Annie on Monday. I trust you enjoyed yourself. Next Whit Monday I hope to take you out, but what I'm longing for is our first walk après la guerre. When do you reckon it will be? I think and hope next autumn. What is the general opinion at home? If you have time and can conveniently manage it would you just 'phone Curtis and let him know how I'm getting on. Tell him I've just returned from firing line, our casualties, the shelling casualties in hospital where we stayed a night, and generally how I'm going. You know how to tell a tale.

By the way I have something very important to tell you. The first night we came for a rest we slept in a barn and well I knew it. Next morning the whole Ambulance was ~ ~! A clean vest of mine was so swarmed with them that when I went to put it on I was smothered. Not in ones or twos but whole battalions. So in your next parcel let's have some Keatings.[56] Now, don't you consider that important news?

I have no further news. I've just returned from a long march where we have our shower baths, jolly nice too. I've been for a swim in a pond twice a day since we've been here. I'd like to stay here till the end of the war.

---

[56] Keating's Powder was a pyrethrum-based insecticide powder.

Advertisement for Keating's Powder from RAMC Depot Magazine of 27th October 1916

My dear Daisy,

First of all I had better inform you that owing to an accident with a tin I have a poisoned finger and my right arm in a sling. However, it comes in handy. I've been able, with difficulty, to write a few letters including one to Mr Mander. We are still resting and haven't the slightest idea when or where we are moving. We have been given new respirators and some suggest Ypres or a dozen other places including England. You'd be surprised at the absurd rumours.

You say in your letter that for one or two reasons you at first decided not to send me some photos. Might I ask the reasons? When I'm dreaming of you it seems much more real when I can look at a photo of you. You can send me 50 if you like as long as they're all different or even a young cinema. I enclose 10 francs. We can draw 20 every fortnight if we choose. Most do. So far I've drawn 45. 10 of which are herein and 10 in my pocket and so since I've been out here I've only spent 25. The rest is to my credit. So you see I don't squander much. If you can bank this paper money to its full value I'll draw it and send it home. It's dark now and the stars out and I can't see to write any more tonight in the open, so goodnight.

Thursday
Good evening
    I am lying on the grass still in the same place. We might be here hours, days and possibly weeks. Before I go any farther might I ask you to send in your next parcel: <u>1</u> an English dictionary (the one I left at home if you can find it or a facsimile will do) <u>2</u> a compact simple French book (neater and smaller the better) and <u>3</u> some leaflets from the Churches of Christ book department. I suppose you are aware that from the C of Christ you can obtain gratis or for a 1d or so leaflets on subjects as Baptism, Communion and so on. They would come in handy just now being no trouble to carry and very instructive. Don't you think so? One at a time will do. By the way do you cut out the articles from *Lloyds*? My people have *Lloyds* and you can cut them out of their papers after done with. And for some unknown reason (I think through a misunderstanding) you don't send me a *Lloyds* now. I think I said <u>you</u> could arrange with the publishers and <u>they</u> would send the current paper each weekend. I <u>believe</u> this is possible. If you could arrange this for me I should be ~~highly obliged~~ I mean glad (mustn't say 'highly obliged' may I).
    As I have my brassard sewn on my arm it's rather a long job to unstitch it and resew it when it requires cleaning so if you would send me some white 'blancs' (that pipe-clay stuff I used to clean my belt with) I think it would save trouble (and send me tooth powder and lemonade powder).
    Dearest, I'm so glad you are working hard on your music. I'm sure you'll never regret it. The songs you intend buying I simply adore, but I'm a little surprised you're not including '*Somewhere a Voice is Calling*'. However, we'll buy quite a crowd when I come home. Might I suggest how the dumb-bells are going on. You must keep fit you know.

Sunday

I expect you will be awfully surprised to hear at a moment's notice we had a 'Sports Day' yesterday and so I entered the 440, 100 and 220. Seeing I'm training for an elephant I wondered how I should get on. Several fellows 'funked'. One fellow who won the 100 yards City of London Championships last year and also 2nd Kilda Sports and another fellow who is a Poly Harrier and won scores of prizes. I bought a pair of shoes and with a vest and short pants I look 'hot'.

My first race I got the Poly man in my heat 100 yds. I had a bad start and he beat me by inches after an exciting race. He won the final easily beating the City of London man. My next race 220. Won the heat easily and in final lost again by inches after a good race. He had inner course and I lost at the bend 3 yds. However drew up in the last 50 yards and the general opinion is that if it had been a few yards more I would have won. I beat the C of L man. My last race was the quarter. Ten started off including Poly man and C of L. I won this easily by 35 yards in very fine time considering grass and roped bottom shoes. My time was 50 seconds. The world record is about 48 secs. So I came home quite satisfied. In fact I surprised myself in the quarter mile. My prizes were a large tin of tobacco and a cake. So although I seldom go on marches with the others and haven't run for 3 years I take it I must be in good physical form. Anxiously waiting photos (which I hope are numerous).

PS. . . . Finger is much better and my arm is not now in a sling. I am laying on the grass a beautiful spot. I do wish you were by my side. Ever seen a picture like this? xxxxxxxxxxxxxxxxxx Is it shorthand? Can you interpret it?

Wednesday 9th June

My dear Daisy,

I expect you will be surprized to hear I'm in hospital. This is my 3rd day here. I came in with a temperature of 104.2. Yesterday my temp. was 100 in the morning and 102 in the evening. This morning it's just below a hundred and so you see I'm rapidly improving. I've been on milk diet since I came in (or rather supposed to have been, but as a matter of fact I couldn't eat anything). This morning I've made a big improvement and can sit up and write a letter which was right out of the question yesterday. I don't suppose I shall be allowed out for another week yet. I believe it's a sort of fever I've got.[57] So you'll excuse short letter.

PS. . . . Keep smiling. I expect you'll get 2 green envelopes at once.

Friday 11th June
My dearest,

I am still improving and when the doctor comes round today I expect he'll allow me to get up for a while. I am quite happy here lying on a stretcher in the top room of a nice chateau. I'm well looked after. Yesterday I received your parcel and letter. The chocolate could not have come at a better time. Please thank Ivy for me for her portions of the gift. I had a letter from Ivy yesterday in which she said that the war was 'curing her of her silly prejudice against fellows'. She insinuates she didn't like fellows before the war, sour grapes methinks. Eh?

Re your question about photos. I like the recent one best I think. It's not such a 'pretty picture' as the locket, but it's a better photo. I understand that you have broken your glasses. If it is essential for you to keep to glasses you had better get them repaired at once and if impossible buy a new pair at my expense and don't be afraid of getting good ones. Let me know your opinion. In reply to your question, we get English *Daily Mails* here a day old for 1½d each. At Béthune we could get other English papers.

I had a nice letter from Alex yesterday. In one of my green envelopes I said I enclosed 10 francs which I omitted. I think I shall wait and get a collection of them and then get our postman to change them into into a postal order. However if you think it is any use sending them direct to you (5f notes) I will do so. Now about yourself:-

1   Are you in good trim?
2   Do you methodically use the dumb-bells?
3   Have you made any increase in figure, weight etc since I left?

---

57   'The health of the troops has been good but several cases of a mild form of influenza have occurred.' **War Diary summary for June 1915**

4   What is your exact weight now (no exaggerations)?
5   Do you do much walking?
6   If you do exercise daily, have you got an exercise book, or do you know now enough to work upon?
7   Do you ever consult Harry on any little queries re music?
8   Do you intend following up swimming this summer?

I should like you to answer these questions. I want you to take the greatest interest possible in yourself.

PS. . . . Send me a copying ink pencil please.

Monday 14th June

Dearest,

Thanks for parcel and letters. Before I forget also send me in your next parcel:- lemonade powder, Cascara[58] (as I bought at Boots) a pair of braces, boot laces, looking glass. It is Monday evening and I am still lying on a stretcher. I came in last Monday with a temperature of 104.2. Last Saturday the Doctor said I could go down stairs, but by Saturday evening I had fallen back again with a terrific temperature and since then I've been on milk diet and not allowed to move from stretcher for anything. I'm waited on 'hand and foot'. Tonight I'm feeling much better and am thus writing a letter. But I don't feel very grand you may guess. As a matter of fact I should not be sitting up writing, but I know you think I don't care if you hear from me or not. At least you said so. And so I'm trying to alter your mind.

I hope you won't worry about me. I'm very comfortable and the Dr seems to take extra interest in me. (Just came in to enquire about me.) It's very quiet here and I find it very restful after the blood and thunder at the front. Of course I can still hear the guns rumbling. I wish you were my nurse, I'm sure I'd progress more favourably don't you? Wouldn't it be topping. Of course there would only have to be one patient in the room. Eh? However, when I come home we'll make up for lost time.

---

[58] A tonic and laxative.

Friday 18th June 1915
My dearest,

I am now up and getting on well and expect to be discharged from hospital tomorrow. We have not shifted and there appears no likelihood of it yet, I'm glad to say. I believe this is my 14th week out here. It seems more like 14 years. Won't I jump for joy when peace is declared. As the days pass I always think, a day nearer England. I'm looking forward to the time when we can renew some of our old walks, the Bridle Path especially, Kingston way. After the war before I go back to business we must have a holiday together. The best time's coming, isn't it.

I'm gradually getting on with *Ben Hur*. The book I should have liked best I think, is the book I've often spoken to you about, Gordon's *'Quiet Talks on Power'*. I think it would have been an ideal book to send me. Don't send it now I'm bunged up. Re the tobacco I won. I'm giving it to a friend of mine on the understanding he gives up playing 'Poka' a gambling card game.

Tuesday evening 22nd June
My dear Daisy,

I have returned to duty and am in good form again. We are still resting 10 miles from firing line and there seems no prospect of moving.

It is suggested that there are too many Field Ambulances out here and I believe there is a fair amount of truth in it. Consequent on this surmise many rumours are going round. 1 That we are going to split up and form Advanced Dressing Stations. This is possible. 2 That we are going as regimental stretcher bearers to infantry regiments. A frightfully dangerous job. I haven't much faith in this, but it is possible. Owing to heavy losses stretcher bearers are certainly scarce. 3 That we shall be asked or compelled to join other regiments. Some believe this but until conscription comes in it is not possible to compel a non combatant unit to fight. 4 It's all over France that the 2nd London Div and all territorials are going home soon. You ask me if this is at all likely. I'm very pessimistic as to rumours as a rule, but on sound reason I certainly can make a very good case for this last rumour. Don't place much faith in it, yet personally I wouldn't be surprised if it came off. I can't say more.

I'm still anxiously awaiting the arrival of these photos. I expect I shall get something extra special after all this time. The enclosed blades kindly get sharpened <u>quickly</u> and return to me. In the next parcel will you please send me some sauce. We are getting plenty of 'bully beef' now and a little sauce would make matters go a little more smoothly.

Might I venture to ask you how you spend your Saturday afternoons and evenings now. When I return home I wonder whether you'll be too shy to take my arm or shall we walk yards apart?

Wednesday evening

Just received a letter from you with a white rose. Before reading the letter I thought of the song '*Flight of Ages*' at once. I'm going to keep it with your photo. How peculiar, a fellow is just passing whistling 'Until No Rose in all the World' etc. I often hum 'Absent', 'I hear you calling me' and 'Somewhere a Voice is calling' and other of our favourite songs and I imagine all sorts of nice things regarding us two and long for our meeting. I'm absolutely craving for the time to come when we shall once again behold each other. My Word, won't our hearts beat with excitement! In fact the anticipation makes my heart throb. 'That will be glory for me.' By the way, dearest. Are you going to accept my offer re glasses. You haven't told me yet?

Where we are stationed is a lovely place. I'm bivouacking out with two fellows, one from Lancs and the other from Warwick. They are very nice chaps. We lay down at night with simply the waterproof above us in the open and more often than not our conversation is about our various holidays and the <u>great</u> subject of fellows' 'girls'. It's ripping to get one's thoughts away from war.

Tuesday
My dear Daisy,

Thanks for your numerous nice letters. I should say thanks <u>awfully</u>. Not having your letters by my side I cannot refer to your questions, if any. First of all re your beautiful voice:- I always was of the opinion that you have an exceptionally good voice and I have frequently told you. If Mr Thingamebob had said anything to the contrary I should have not believed him. All you want is (you know) which I expect, in fact I know, you have acquired since I've been away.

Dearest, I can say no more. I'd give pounds to hear you sing to me now. I simply adore your voice. I would suggest my paying to have it trained, if it were not for the fact that you were practising the piano, which I consider far more important. It would not be much good having a trained voice if you have no one to play decent pieces. I can't. Whereas if you learn to play the piano nicely, you will certainly be able to sing. As far as a professional singer is concerned, I wouldn't entertain it for one moment. The temptations are nearly as great as those of an actress.

I can't say I liked the idea of the actions of Mr ~. From his last visit and from what you have told me about his previous visits I should rather be inclined to think he took liberties. He may be middle aged, but I know of many men who at 50 have not altered in sexual desires. And the 'kiddy' business I object to also. If I were there when he used the term I'm sure you wouldn't think it in order. You're 22 now not 2. If you like the name 'kiddy' I'll also call you by it, but it seems to me absurd to call a young lady of 22 a 'kid'. Dearest, you know what to do in future. I hope you don't think I'm ratty. I'm not. It's now dark and I'm to bed.

Wednesday 30th June
Good afternoon x

Dinner is over and I'm sitting on a tin box in the sun. It has been raining but now it's drying up. The last few days we've had plenty of rain. Now re the 'lesser evil'. If you could have seen what a boon a 'fag' is to wounded soldiers at our hospital I don't think you would term smoking 'lesser evil'. Give a British Tommy a 'fag' and you can almost take his leg off without a groan.

Do you know last night I was having a cup of coffee in a nearby cafe and the young lady told me I had 'a beautiful face'. This is the second time in France a young lady has passed this remark. I shall soon become conceited. Do you know I think I must be good-looking!

Thursday

~~I have just been ordered by my Captain to replace my clasp knife which I lost months ago. So will you please get one for me and send it as soon as possible. It must have a tin opener.~~ (Now have one). Re parcel. Thanks very much. I only have one complaint and that is the pencil. It's a 'dud'. It breaks a dozen times in one letter. So please send me a better one. The enclosed letter to Mr Curtis both you and Mother can read and then seal it up put on the address of Westerns and send it off. I think it will be interesting for you to read. Still smiling. Keep grinning.

8th July 1915
My dear Daisy,

I've just received your letter written last Monday. Re Mr Cox. You say you are astounded at my last letter. From what you said in your last letter it would certainly give one the impression that Mr Cox, the 'gentleman' referred to, took liberties. I still think so. The mutual promise made at St Albans has nothing to do with the matter. It's a matter of discretion not fidelity or trust. I still trust you. Please don't even insinuate that I don't. Everyone is apt to be indiscreet. And re the 'kiddy' business. I'm absolutely positive you told me he still calls you by this name, which is very out of place. While on this subject of liberties I well remember <u>more than once</u> certain relatio<u>ns</u> of yours taking liberties with you (not kissing) which you permitted till I objected. Absolute liberties. I didn't question your fidelity towards me then, but, nevertheless it was very indiscreet. I expect you know what I refer to. All your people more or less have the habit. A certain action when one is not in an upright position.[59] What do you mean by the sentence re trust 'As I was mistaken <u>nothing matters now</u>'. The context of the paragraph is to the effect that you were living in the belief that you were trusted? I'm anxious to know what this sentence is meant to imply. Dearest, I meant no 'insult' by my letter. You must have misconstrued it. Re the word 'liberty'. What one person would term a liberty another

---

[59] Being patted on the behind.

wouldn't. Re 'insult reflected on Mr Cox. He is a gentleman'. He may be. Apparently by your letter I'm not.

Re pencil. Thank you. You say you are no critic. Have you ever known a lady that wasn't? Ask Myra. I wrote Curtis instead of Johnson this time. Re 'numerous nice letters'. I really mean what I say. Re Kiddy again. Doll for a girl sounds infinitely better and more sensible than little 'Kiddy'. Re fags. Your reply is in exact harmony with my ideas. Nevertheless, I ofttimes long to smoke again.

I expect you are longing to hear what I think about the photos. Candidly speaking they are very moderate. The sitting down one is the best of a bad lot. I've come across worse. They don't compare with the one you first sent me. A case of almost sublime and ridiculous. You look as if you were trying to pose for a photograph. Not natural. And as I've said before black and low collars suit you much better than white and high collar business. Your glasses seem too big. When you get your new glasses get smaller ones if you can. And it's not what I meant. I said different positions and different 'get-ups'. For instance you could have had one taken with your hat and coat on. What you have sent me are almost exactly alike. When I suggested different positions I didn't mean moving an inch or so. I hope, dearest, my severe criticisms won't hurt your feelings.

We have not shifted yet, but may do soon, within a day or so. Things are very quiet on this front. Extraordinarily quiet. A lull before a gigantic storm.

In one of your letters you said you'd give anything to lie on Wimbledon Common with me now. My Word! Wouldn't I. I dwell day and night on our old outings. Won't our first <u>spoon</u> after I come home be ripping. What! What!! Shan't we make up for lost time. The best time's coming. Be patient. 'Patience is a virtue' confined to women. I know I'm getting desperately anxious.

Monday 12th July 1915
My dear Daisy,

We have not made a move yet and there seems no prospect of doing so. In reply to your last letter. You seem to be under the impression I've heaps of time. An army cook is always more or less busy. Excuse my curiosity, but I should be awfully obliged if you'd let me know the answer you gave the 'impertinent enquirer'. I know what answer I should have given. Re Bert Coward. I have not seen him since the first week I came out here. Might I ask to see Mr C's letter to you. The cartoons you sent me were very good, but I'd already seen them. Dearest, I should like you to take about 2/- out of my money and buy something for Basil's birthday. It will be from both of us. I believe his birthday is near. I don't know the exact date. Will you please send me a pair of football boots. Get Harry to buy me a pair size 8 about 7/- or 8/-.

Tuesday

I've just received the parcel. Thank you very much. All your spare time must be taken up looking after me. Why I don't write much oftener than once a week is **1** I only have one green envelope a week as a general rule **2** I can't write anything much in an ordinary envelope. Writing occasional long letters to Curtis and Johnson, Mander and to Mother, Alex etc. I'm not left much leisure time, which I sometimes spend reading or playing an occasional match for our team.

The front is still very quiet. I understand that our Ambulance is being held in reserve at the present time. I hope you don't think the apparent infrequency of my letters is due to slackness. Dearest, I'm passionately waiting the time when we shall be together again. It is now 18 weeks since I left England. It seems 18 years to me. Every day to me is exactly alike. There seems no Sunday no Saturday. In fact I often lose count of the days. We often ask each other what the day is. However, I'm happy. If you could see me I'm sure you wouldn't say I'm wasting away.

I'm writing this letter in the little farm house where my section's billet is. A barn. The old lady and gent here have just heard that their only son has been killed in action. It's a house of sorrow now. The poor old chap is especially cut up about it and after the day's toil he sits down before the little French stove and cries. It's also extremely hard on the son's fiancée, a nice humble girl, who has a little baby only a few months old.

Monday 19th July 1915

My dear Daisy,

The parcel you forwarded me was excellent. Thank your father for the cucumbers won't you. You are sending me some remarkable news lately. The Kinch business absolutely surprised me.[60] Give him my ~~congra~~ sympathy.

Mr Mander is happy now, I guess. Don't you wish you were in Mrs Mander's position?[61] However, all good things come to those who wait. As I have said before, every day, nay every moment brings us a little nearer to the day of my return. Eighteen weeks today since I landed in France. Although it seems a long time since I left England, the days and weeks seem to pass very quickly now.

In your last letter you said you didn't feel very well. I sincerely trust that you are quite alright again. What sort of sickness were you suffering from 'love-sickness'? I expect you find it rather dreary waiting, waiting, waiting & wondering how I am and what I see. I heard from rather good authority that I shall not be moving for weeks yet. Where I am now[62] is as safe as Wimbledon Common. If you were here I couldn't half take you for some ripping walks.

I hope you won't be disgusted but just lately I've had an almost incurable longing to smoke and I venture to suggest to you to forward my pipe. Please don't criticize me too severely. You don't know how monotonous it seems sometimes out here. No Saturdays, no Sundays, to me as cook every day is exactly the same, no change whatever. However, I keep surprisingly cheerful, always brightened by the happy days which lay before me. Tobacco you need not send, I get heaps of it.

In my last letter I enclosed £4 and the previous letter £2. £6 in all. I hope you received it safely. Do you know this time last year I was in Belgium at a place called Arlon. I'm getting quite a traveller. I understood you to say you were buying Gordon's *'Quiet Talks on Power'*. When you've read it, will you please let me have it? Do you know that ofttimes I dream about you, such lovely dreams too, and when I wake up I feel so 'ratty'. Are you ever as silly as that? What do you think of the postcards?

---

[60] Arthur Kinch, of Twynholm Church, had become engaged to be married.
[61] William and Mary Mander became parents of a baby girl in June 1915.
[62] Le Réveillon.

Monastery of Labeuvrière from a postcard in the editor's collection

Monday 26th July 1915
Dearest,

Yesterday we made another shift a little nearer the firing line in a different direction. We are still well out of the danger zone. Our billet this time is a monastery.[63] I'm sleeping on a stone floor, but it's quite alright. Today I'm leaving the cookhouse. I've asked for a rest for a month. I expect I shall return after the month is up. The Front is still extraordinarily peaceful. Whereas, formerly guns were booming all day, now we go for days without hearing a gun.

Kitchener's Army seem to be coming out here fairly fast now. I've seen many Scotch regiments and batteries of artillery and physically they leave nothing to be desired. And my word, aren't they confident. Of course we are quite veterans out here now and can spin quite an 'old soldiers' yarn to them. Wait till the time when we are squatting on the grass over on Wimbledon Common and I'm spinning a few yarns to you. How long is it going to be now? When *is* the war going to end? However, it must end some time and every

---

[63] 'Removed to Labeuvrière and established hospital in a monastery and in tents in the courtyard.' **War Diary 25th July 1915.**

day we are fast approaching it. Nearly 20 weeks now since I left St Albans. The last 8 weeks have flashed past to me.

I understand you are soon going on your holidays. Let's hope you have a good time. In one of your parcels a pair of braces were sent me. Like the pencil they were cheap and no use. They are now broken. By the way in your next parcel please let me have some more bachelor's buttons. I'm gradually getting on with Ben Hur. When I consider his trials and mine and his long separation from loved ones I come to the conclusion mine are very trifling. At the present moment I'm in hospital again. I've been queer the last 2 or 3 days. Today I reported sick. I'm an up patient. I expect to come out tomorrow. Have just received your letter. Very nice one too. I don't see why you can't send the chimney[64] separate.

Friday 30th July 1915
My dear Daisy,

Have been discharged from hospital today, and I'm feeling quite fit. I received the parcel. The cakes were very nice, and 3 of us soon demolished the chocolate cake in one go: 3 active service chunks. The boots look all right. I haven't tried them on yet. I found the contents of the boots. The two songs you mentioned in your letter are very good I should think. The words of the first are highly appropriate at the present time. I mean:

> 'Watch as I go my weary way alone
> Keep Thou me still since I am still Thine own
> <u>Pray Thou for me before the great white throne</u>
> Till I shall come to Thee'[65]

It's my position quite. I think these words very fine. In your next parcel please send me bachelor buttons, 1 small rough towel, laces, International Sunday School lesson book after finished, safety pins and packet needles.

---

[64] Pipe.
[65] *Dear Love Remember Me* by Charles Marshall and Harold Harford, 1903.

Your suggestion re my birthday is excellent. I'd like to have one or two of Gordon's works. By your letter you seem to suggest that things are rather hard at business financially. I should have thought as far as female labour is concerned now ought to be a 'golden age'.

Saturday 31st July 1915
My dear Daisy,
   Tomorrow I'm going to get some photographs of myself and so I'm keeping this letter back. If only I were in England, I expect we should be together. But this time next year, eh! It's too dark for me to write further.

Sunday
   Don't be surprised to hear of my going on leave any week now. We are expecting a large percentage to start leave soon. It may be next week, it may be 6 weeks hence, but I think it's coming. What think you of photo. Of course they are only novice work. Forward letter to Alex. Give Ada a photo, also Harry.

Will with a suspicion of a moustache, July 1915

Sunday 8th August 1915

We have made yet another move, just a few miles back.[66]

I'm glad you like the photo. They were so very dirty I had to clip it off the edges. The 'suspicion of a moustache' is really a poor likeness of the actual thing.[67] Being fair it does not show much. You seem to suggest something extraordinary in your letter. It's your imagination absolutely. My dearest, surely you must know I wouldn't correspond secretly about you. I can't conceive how you got such an idea into your head. That sort of thing is quite alien to our friendship, always has been, always will be, why suggest it now? However, I'll forgive you: put it down to 'suspicious woman'.

I'm sorry to have to report I've lost my locket and chain. I miss it immensely. Whoever found it could have returned it as my identification disc was on it.

Now I'm out of the cookhouse I have to do police duty 2 hours on 4 off commencing 6.30 pm. It's a job where one's thoughts naturally wander: a good opportunity of dreaming of home, especially when on a lonely spot between 12.30 and 2.30 am. However I like the lonely night duty, to me it is restful and very fascinating.

In your next parcel let me have some <u>tooth powder</u> and please dinna forget the International Sunday School Lesson Book and *Joyful Tidings*, not *Lloyds*, also a small rough towel. All the latest news you'll find in my letter home. I really have no more to say so I must bid you goodbye.

PS. . . . My Motto: Keep smiling. Your Motto: Profound hilarity!

My dearest,

I'm sorry I've not written before. They haven't given us any green envelopes till now. Before I go any farther I want you to read the letter to Dada and Mother. Dearest, I can quite understand you getting depressed occasionally, I'm glad you do in one way for it's a sure sign of deep affection. <u>I</u> do at times, very much and have to

---

66   '11.30am. Received orders to clear monastery by 3pm and move to Lapugnoy.' **War Diary 6th August 1915.**

67   Although widely ignored by this date, military regulations still required the upper lip to be unshaven. The order was finally rescinded in 1916.

strive hard to keep it off. However, you're six months nearer seeing me then you were when I left you at St Albans. That's a lot you know. And I don't think it will be long before you see me again on 7 days leave. My word!

If at the worst it is another year before the war is over, it will soon pass and then we shall be together for always.

> *'There's a silver lining*
> *Through the dark clouds shining*
> *So turn the dark clouds inside out*
> *Till the boys come Home.*[68]

Thank you for JT and the parcel and please don't forget to thank your mother for the pickles etc. Thanks for the explicit Balance Sheet, I hope to send you some more money next week. How is Beethoven getting on? Slow but sure, eh? It's a ripping change being out of cookhouse.

Daisy's Mizpah brooch

---

[68] *Keep the Home Fires Burning*, Ivor Novello 1914.

Thursday 19th August 1915
MIZPAH[69]
My dear Daisy,

First of all will you please send me <u>per return</u> in a letter some nails for my boots for Divisional Races. As I have to wear boots I want some nails or rather studs so as I can get a grip on the grounds. I want you to use your own judgment. Not too big so as to be heavy: perhaps cricket shoe studs would do, this shape I believe they are ▼. A nice sharp point. <u>Don't</u> send flat pancake things ⬬. On the other hand don't go to the extreme, I don't want a bayonet. If you can get proper running spikes to fit in my boots do so. If it is possible to get proper spikes to fit in don't get big ones, for they <u>might</u> be noticed and I should get disqualified. By the way don't get anything I can't fit in. Now, darling, after my elaborate explanations perhaps you know what I'm after. (What are you smiling at?)

How are you getting on by now. Let's hope you are well and happy. Do you know it will soon be 7 years since a certain event happened. How time passes. Do you remember one Monday night, I think it was 6th October, after Ivy had been drilling, my asking you if you'd like 'a certain person's photo' and then the following morning at Mansion House Station. And my first visit to Forest Gate was quite an event wasn't it. I remember Mile End Station well. Have you forgotten the way from Forest Gate to Mile End yet? What a picturesque walk it was. Truly Love is Blind. Wanstead Flats weren't bad though. By the way have you forgotten a certain event on a certain site in Bishops Park. One of our nicest walks was one Christmas time when the snowballs followed us in Roehampton Lane. Remember it? Do you know I can go right through the time from when we first met: right through the whole 7 years. We've had some happy days in the past, haven't we. But even better times await us in the future. Six months nearer home than when I left you at St Albans.

---

[69] MISPAH or MIZPAH. *'The Lord watch between me and thee.'* It was often used on brooches and rings given between lovers. The family has a gold Mizpah brooch which belonged to Daisy. It is just 1.5 cm wide.

A SPORTS MEETING AT THE FRONT

Sir, No doubt it would interest a few of your readers to know that, although we are engaged fighting for our King and country, we find time to have a sports meeting behind the line 'Somewhere in France'. We held a meeting on the 25th in a field chosen for the purpose. The weather was glorious. We had two bands in attendance and it took away the monotony of war . . . for that particular afternoon. First of all there came the high jump and it was well contested, the winner jumping 5ft. Next came the relay race and some fast times were recorded. Then came bomb throwing . . . there was also a long jump, steeplechasing for officers and a prize for the best turned out motor ambulance. The finish ended in a mile flat race and bare-back mule riding, which was rather funny. All the prizes were cash.

Driver Lawrence Close,
6th London Field Ambulance.
The Daily Mail, Tuesday August 31st 1915 (abridged)

Friday 27th August 1915
Dearest,

Thanks for your letter received yesterday. Yesterday, we made another move ten miles towards firing line near French lines.[70] We are now 3½ or 4 miles behind firing line in a quaint little village, or a dirty little hole. I don't think this place is ever shelled, but in a few days I understand we are going farther up still and we shall once again be sending out Advanced Dressing Stations. I may have to go up to the Advanced Dressing Stations and I may not. I'm still cooking for transport and our transport doesn't go up, so I might not. Even should I not go up to Advanced Dressing Station and we should move to the next town and there carry on Main Dressing Station as we did in Béthune, I shall be in what you would term 'danger zone' as the town is frequently shelled. However, I'm not

---

[70] From Allouagne to Houchin. 'Will slept under a school shed by himself near the cookhouse fire and drew water from a nearby well. The church was crammed with wounded after the Battle of Loos' – from Daisy's notebook.

in danger yet. The Front is fairly quiet, although the big guns kept me awake somewhat last night. I think some big move is coming on soon and that is why we are concentrating here. Don't worry: simply pray that in the event of my getting into the danger zone I shall be kept from all harm. After all I've been out here 6 months and have only been in danger zone at most 3 weeks so I've a lot to be thankful for. Many battalions if not in the trenches are billeted in the 'danger zone'.

Now with regard to the Sports.[71] I came in 4th out of 8 in heats. Not much good, you see. I was only allowed to run ¼ mile. Nevertheless, all the fellows in my heat had running shoes and proper running dress and they told me they knew about it 6 weeks ago. I prepared a pair of boots as in Brigade Sports and as luck would have it took a pair of slippers in case of being allowed to run in them, which I used. I knew 6 days beforehand and could not practise as I sprained my left leg in Brigade Sports which I just got in fair form after plenty of embrocation for Div Sports. However, when you come to consider that every man who took part in his particular distance was the best of his battalion (1,000 – 1,200 men) you may guess it was very 'hot stuff' running. There were some amateur champions present including Walker (the South African champion sprinter)[72] who pulled off 100 yds. Hutson,[73] the fellow you saw at Poly sports win the 3 mile and a few weeks after he ran in International Sports, would have run, but for a wound. The Sports were 1st class. Contrary to my usual style I ran last, 8th, and in the last 150 yds made a terrific effort to pull up and get a place, but I only managed to just get in 4th. Let Dada know this news re Sports, as I don't want to have to yarn another long letter with exactly the same wording. Comprenez Dear?

---

[71] Divisional Sports at Lozinghem.
[72] Reginald E. Walker of the South African Infantry. He had won South Africa's only gold medal in the 1908 Olympics for the 100 metres.
[73] Will has misremembered who ran. George W. Hutson did indeed run in the Polytechnic Sports at Stamford Bridge, 20th June 1914, winning the mile, but he had been killed in action on 14th September 1914. According to the *Daily Record* of Monday 22nd June 1914, the three-mile race was won by A. H. Nicholls.

It is now getting very dark and I can hardly see. Well! Good by for the present.

PS... Re your letter. My Word! Don't I wish I were there again just after you had washed your hair.

> *'Loose flowing hair give me, before all the chicaneries of art*
> *Which take mine eye, but not mine heart.'*
> Dr Johnson[74]

PPS... I heard from Esme and will write him soon.

This time next year. What? What!
Wednesday evening 1st September 1915

My Dearest,

How are you getting on now, still cheerful I hope, patiently waiting. If you will read the letter home you will get most of the current news. In your last letter you ask what song I would like you to especially practice for when I come home. I suggest the song which runs thus:- '*Watch as I go my weary way alone etc*'. I simply adore the words of that song.

In your next parcel please send:- **1** English Dictionary (I've lost the other one) **2** Tooth powder **3** Another book if it doesn't cost too much to send **4** a razor strop – no – I've got an ordinary razor now, it's much cheaper **5** Chocolate **6** er, er, er I suggest some cake.

Friday night

My dear Daisy,

I'm continuing this letter not having the former parts of it with me, it's in my tunic just down the road. This may explain its disjointure here. We are having terrible weather just now and our bivouacking ground is simply shocking, an awful quagmire. We are up to our necks in mud and swamped out. The ground is piles of mud and pools of water. By far the worst conditions under which we have slept. Words can't describe it. I believe I told you I don't sleep in

---

[74] '*Robes loosely flowing, hair as free; Such sweet neglect more taketh me, Than all the adulteries of art, They strike eyes but not mine heart.*'

my bivouac. I sleep under a shed under a bench and so my sleeping place is dry.

However, the officers have been searching for billets today and 90 of us have been fixed up: my billet is a sort of cow shed affair, but it's dry. Tomorrow the officers are making a further search and we shall be all fixed up in time. If they're not quick about it all the corps will be laid up. I couldn't put a dog in some of the bivouacs, the ground is swamped and the water-proofs leak. As above-mentioned I don't sleep in my bivouac, I'd sooner be shot at dawn. So don't worry about me. Necessity is the Mother of Invention and I always manage to wangle a nice dry sleeping place.

The cooking conditions are very poor and we have to cook in the open and so you can guess how <u>easy</u> it is to keep a good fire with wet tree wood and the rain coming down heavens hardest. Oh! It's glorious. Every now and then we snatch a minute to get in under a shed. Nevertheless, we get used to it more or less and so long as I can keep my fire going and dinner's up in time I'm satisfied.

But I'm not miserable yet and if you could see me <u>now</u>, washed, shaved, hair-parted, sitting in a nice dry place writing this letter in candle light, I'm sure you'd say I look happy cheerful and well. So, my dear Daisy, don't get down-hearted, I may be a long time coming home, but in God's good time I shall see you again and then My Word! Won't we make up for lost time. All good things come to those who wait.

Thursday 9th September 1915
My dearest,

Thanks for parcel. Thank the various subscribers for me. How goes it now. Getting 'fed up' eh? Never mind it won't be so very long now before we are reunited. The longer we are separated the more glorious our meeting, and as I've said before won't we make up for lost time. The best time is coming undoubtedly. This is my 26th week. Time flies along to me now. The last 3 months have simply flown. Your last letter to me I think was very nice. There are two handwritings I always look for among the letters, yours and Mother's.

You will see I've enclosed £2 which please bank. On receipt of this letter go to the nearest shop and buy a razor for Dada's birthday.

I wish I could have told you before. However, darling, get it as soon as possible for him, won't you. I have no more to write just now. Next letter I'll write you I'll try and write volumes. Mr Black wrote me today. I understand he has another son. Goodbye for now, Yours ever

PS. . . . Keep Smiling

14th September 1915
Dearest,

Today being my birthday I felt it incumbent upon me to endeavour to write you a nice letter. When I sailed away to France I fully expected to return in time to celebrate my 23rd birthday at home. Unfortunately my anticipations were not realized and today finds me in a tiny French village 6 miles at the rear of the trenches.[75] My billet is a barn, and as I'm sitting here writing, I have mingled feelings of depression and happiness. I have seen 6 months of foreign service and I have no doubt many more months of similar experience are yet before me. I'm beginning to wonder how and when this war is going to end; sometimes I think it won't finish until at least another year has gone, and on the other hand I consider it highly probable that before many winter months have passed an agreement will be come to. Perhaps it depends largely upon whether our next move comes off this autumn or is delayed till next spring. We have been told officially that a terrific bombardment will soon take place, but nobody knows when. We expect it any day now. When it comes off it will be nothing short of Hell.

Now for something a little more cheerful. Sunday six fellows went home on leave. However, in reply to your last letter I expect at the earliest my leave won't come before 'the dark days of December'. That matters little to me as long as it comes. In fact we can spoon better in the dark. At any rate as long as I return safely to you that's everything, isn't it? As I have said before we'll make up for lost time then. My Word, not half.

Every letter we get out here now mentions about the 'Zeps'. They seem to have done a fair amount of damage too. I've never a seen

---

[75] They are still at Houchin.

a 'Zep' out here, but hardly a day passes but what a Taube passes overhead followed by bursting shells. I've never seen one brought down yet. Yesterday one passed right over our parade ground while the troops were on parade. Of course the falling pieces of shrapnel from the bursting shells are very dangerous. Instant death if anything like a piece struck anybody.

I had a nice letter from RWB in which he gave me all the Twynholm news. Yesterday I went to a large town near here (which is under fire occasionally) and had my photo taken and so in my next letter I hope to send you another photo. I also bought the enclosed postcards there. What do you think of them? How many have you got now from me?

Goodbye dearest for now, Yours affectionately

> *'God is our sun, He makes our day*
> *God is our shield, He guards our way*
> *From the assaults of hell and sin*
> *From foes without and foes within'* [76]

Saturday 18th September 1915

My dear Daisy,

Thanks very much for the cake. It was ripping. And as to the cards, I'm afraid you will have to thank the various people for me. I really couldn't find time to acknowledge them individually. And I must especially thank you for your cards. I wonder where I shall spend my 24th birthday. Let's hope it's in Angleterre. When the war is over I must bring you out here and show you the places of interest – my bunks for instance and all the places I've stopped at.

Things are a little more exciting now. A party of men go up each day digging trenches and working on sandbags. Sometimes they get it pretty warm. Two days ago one of the party got a smack in the face with a small piece of shrapnel. It had lost its velocity and fortunately only caused a scratch. Of course shrapnel wounds vary very much, some wounds are very slight and others are ghastly. Tiny fragments are harmless, but the large chunks inflict most

---

[76] Psalm 84.

unsightly wounds. When you see the wounded in London they look very comfortable: nice clean uniform, more or less spotless white bandages, but in our hands totally different. We see the wounds freshly done, bandages, yards and yards of it soaked in blood, uniform smothered in blood and mud; stretcher draining it off as the patient is carried along. I didn't think there was so much blood in the human body. However, I see very few wounded now. Ours is a sick hospital at present.

I expect you wonder how we get on for baths. We keep 6 baths going for patients. When we are near mines we go there where they have properly fitted up shower baths; sometimes quite 500 of them going and a beautiful spray of hot water too. Where we are at present we can get a fine shower bath. We go once a week 5 miles each way. It's a long walk but it's really worth it. When I was in training a few weeks back I had a hot bath every day. Although working under adverse circumstances we always strive to keep clean. As a medical unit it behoves us to uphold cleanliness. The trenches are, as I suppose you know, teeming with lice. I understand they line them up in battalions and get them to shift sandbags and occasionally 15 inch guns.

We have a fine phonograph, which one of the officers gave us, and we've clubbed together and bought a fine selection of records. Last night I went to one of the bivouacs where they had the phono, and spent a glorious time sitting down on the ground listening to such records as *Somewhere a Voice is Calling, I Hear You Calling Me, Nirvanah, Spring Song, Songs of Araby, Holy City, Adeline, Just a little love a little kiss, Love is a story that's told*, banjo solos, marches etc etc, and the stars above, our only light a candle, made it most impressive. It made me think of you and home more than ever.

Tonight I'm night cook in the hospital. I finish at about 11 o'clock and have to keep things going in case of a sudden rush. I have the next day off. I sleep by the trench on this job if the weather is fine. It's ripping lying down by a coal fire in the open field and gazing up in the myriads of stars dreaming of you.

PS. . . . A group of us are standing by waiting to go to a dangerous Advanced Dressing Station.[77]

Thursday 30th September 1915
My dearest,

I've just arrived back from trenches 6 miles now, quite, behind firing line. First of all re your audit. It's rather unfortunate that the error occurred, but it's just as much your loss as mine. The account is <u>ours</u> not <u>mine</u>. Don't be so silly as to worry about it dear, please, and as for your making good the loss, that's absurd, I wouldn't think of it for one moment. Surely you didn't think I was going to make a fuss about it. Now forget it and cheer up. In your next letter tell me that you are smiling again. Look in the looking glass and make sure that you are really and truly smiling. Understand?

Now for my experience. After posting my letter to you I got in a motor ambulance and approached a small town near the line. Here we got out and had to walk in ones and twos up a road which is very heavily shelled.[78] The houses on each side are masses of ruins. Our guns were booming something terrific. I felt awful. It was like walking through the 'Valley of the shadow of death'. We trudged down this road for nearly two miles till we came to a garden city, a Heaven turned into Hell. Shells were flying over at this time. Here we halted and went into cellars and dugouts surrounded by sand-bags and I began to feel safe again, although a heavy shell smashed into the next house but one. By this time I'd got a shocking headache and turned in and went to sleep. Next morning I fixed up a range[79] and was much cheered by our captain telling us that 'our boys' had advanced 5 miles. In the afternoon the excitement began. Our party were called out and one of the men being unwell he asked me to take his place as stretcher bearer. I didn't like the idea but I couldn't do otherwise than volunteer. It was pouring with rain, we

---

[77] Battle of Loos 25–30 September 1915. The War Diary notes that 379 men were admitted to hospital through the 5th London FA's casualty clearing station from 25–30 September.
[78] South Maroc Advanced Dressing Station.
[79] 'Made the fire in a cellar, supplying tea to stretcher bearers bringing in the wounded.' – Daisy's notebook.

had about ¼ mile to trenches through masses and masses of ruins, passing many German prisoners on the way.

We got to the trenches and marched across the open fields across barbed wire and mud mud mud, then we got in trenches again for a yard or two then over the old parapet. We've no sooner got right out in the open than a machine gun was turned on us and we had to lay flat down. We got up and the gun was turned deliberately on us again, down we got again. It seemed to me idiotic to keep out there and so I rolled over in the trench, the others followed. We went along trench again slop slop slop in mud right through German trenches just taken. Shrapnel was flying about among dead Germans' skulls and skeletons, blood and massacred men. We crawled out over parapet and brought in the wounded. And so we went to and fro in the pouring rain sometimes in trench, sometimes in open, bringing in the wounded.

After 5 or 6 hours of this we went back to our cellar swamped and covered with mud. Some went back and worked all night facing rain, mud, shells and snipers and what is more they went cheerfully. I haven't been out since, I've been cooking. But our men have been called up in the middle of the night and gone out cheerfully in the pouring rain. Last night they had a very bad time stumbling over dead horses etc etc sprinting here and there out of the way of that machine gun controlled by a concealed sniper. They came to a place where they were stopped because of heavy shelling. The 4th and 6th [80] wouldn't go on, but our boys, the 5th, pushed on and got to the wounded. When they returned they were congratulated by the 4th and 6th who had refused to go. We've earned a name over our work. Our boys are simply grand. I'm proud of them. We have had no casualties except one or two got a little gas.[81] Excuse my rough description. I must now turn in.

PS. . . . What do you think of the advance. I told you it was coming. You'll find more successes yet. We've got guns and shells now. Lloyd

---

[80] 4th and 6th London Field Ambulances.

[81] The War Diary states that three of them were severely gassed and had to be carried in.

George shells. If you want your head knocked off run down David to a Royal Field Artillery man.[82]

> *"I estimate that the number of wounded carried in by my subdivision was 60. Most of the cases had to be carried about a mile. There was a certain amount of firing on the bearers by the enemy by shells, snipers and a machine gun which was turned on to the entrance of Trench 25. There were no casualties."*
> **Capt. Whitehead RAMC, report in War Diary on 25th September 1915**

> *To Officer Commanding 5th London Field Ambulance*
> *I return to you herewith the reports of the work done by the subdivisions of the unit under your command, when acting under the immediate orders of Capts Sandilands, Jordan and Lt Matthews during the period 25/9/15 to 30/9/1915. I have read the reports with great interest and satisfaction. I consider the work done by these subdivisions worthy of the highest praise. Such work not only reflects highly on the unit to which they belong, but the cause for which they work. Please convey to them my appreciation of their work and my thanks for the help rendered.*
> **Letter in the War Diary from J D Ferguson ADMS[83] 47th Division**

Thursday 7th October 1915

My dearest,

Since I wrote you, I have moved a few miles back for a day or so and have returned again. Now in some village about 6 miles behind line.[84] You will be interested to know I have been made officer's cook. Let me have a cookery book next parcel and once again

---

[82] David Lloyd George was Minister of Munitions in 1915 and had managed to speed up greatly the delivery of ammunition to the Front.
[83] Assistant Director of Medical Services.
[84] Houchin.

Eucryl. Re franc notes. We are paid in 5f notes. Now a 5f note is worth out here about 3/9 thus 5 × 3/9 = 18/9. You lost 1/- changing. You should have got 18/9. I think it must have been an error on the part of counter assistant. What do you think? It is very late and I'm tired. Goodnight, dearest, I'll write again in a day or two. What do you suggest for Mother's birthday, Oct 16th?

Friday 22nd October 1915
My dear Daisy,

Thanks for your many letters, and I hope you will excuse my not writing before. Mother asked me to send her a letter all to herself hence the waiting. With regard to a letter of yours re Eucryl, I'm sure I've asked for it many times. Three months since I had the last. However, I'll coincide with your request and make complaints direct. Have you forgiven me now?

We have moved our Officers Mess today. We were in a private house attached to a school, a nice person (for a change). Why we shifted I'm sure I can't say. Of course same town. Maddison's ambulance is somewhere here.[85] I get very little time now to myself, start at 6am finished 9pm or thereabouts. I cook for 10 officers. Breakfast: eggs, bacon, toast and tea; lunch salad, beef & potatoes, milk pudding and coffee; tea - tea; dinner soup, perhaps a pie, potatoes and peas, sardines on toast, apple charlotte and custard, coffee and hot water for rum. I do absolutely all the cooking myself. Really hard work; always working Saturday and Sunday of course as well.[86]

Saturday 23rd October 1915
I have just a few moments and so I continue. By the way I have sent Mother a little acknowledgment of her birthday and also Irene.

---

[85] William Maddison, a fellow clerk at Western's. He had enlisted on the same day as Will and served with the 6th London Field Ambulance.
[86] On one occasion while Will was cooking the officers' supper by candlelight, he noticed that one of his tallow candles was missing but thought nothing of it. Later one of the officers said that the meal was very good but they all felt a bit queasy after the soup as it was so rich, delicious but very rich. When Will was cleaning the pan he found the candle wick at the bottom.

I believe in Mother's letter I omitted an enclosure and so if she mentions anything about it you can explain.

Thirty two weeks since I left home, or rather, Angleterre. I shall have soon been away a year. Our Colonel went home on leave <u>again</u> yesterday (lucky beggar). The ones who do least, get it. By the time leave starts for 2nd Lon Div there'll be only about ¼ of originals left, the other ¾ have either been killed or wounded. However, après la guerre, I shall get leave and then by gum! Won't we make up for lost time. <u>Perhaps</u> I shall be too shy to sp~~n. Don't you think so? Will you? Just answer me this question. When you next see me within a yard or so of you, what do you think you'll do? A nice little puzzle. Wait and see, eh?

Well! I have no news. I'm in good form, but could do with some leave. All I can tell you is that men and guns are here now in abundance and I'm positive Fritz will never do any more advancing on this front. I enclose 20f note and a few 5f notes which please change yourself if possible. 5fs is worth about 3/7 now. Goodbye, mignon.

Wednesday 27th October 1915
Dearest,

I expect you think I am rather lax in not writing quite so frequently lately. But really I have practically no time at all for correspondence. As you suggest it is about time I wrote to Westerns again and I'll certainly try and wangle time somehow for this purpose as soon as possible. I should think I have at least a dozen people I ought to write: Mr Black for one, he occasionally writes me but his last letter, weeks old, still unanswered. However, dearest, I'll do my level best to write you perhaps a little oftener.

No doubt you are wondering when I am coming home on leave. I wish it was within my power to tell you, it seems as far off as ever. Never mind 'all good things come to those who wait'. Won't it be ripping to see each other again? How I long for the time to come, and more so the end of the war. But I really consider this time next year I shall be with you in civilians again. It seems too good to be true, doesn't it, nevertheless I'm sure it won't be long before we resume some of our old walks. Bridle Path eh? What does it remind you of? I know. How's the ring? I hope it won't be long before I give you another ring. No not a telephone ring, although I don't think you'd mind me ringing you on a telephone. 'Home on leave, leave business and meet me at once.' That wouldn't be bad would it. I mean a simple plain ring. I'll let you guess the rest, My Word!

I've been humming and singing today *Absent* and *Somewhere A Voice is Calling* etc. It does make me pine for you, you know. Dearest, how are you progressing with your music. You must have made some progress. But the music I long to hear is the music of your voice. Just you speaking to me, you know.

By the way won't it be nice to one day be sitting on the sofa reading this very letter. Of course I should be on the sofa and you'll be on my ~~. You'll be holding the letter and I shall be holding ~ ~ waisting time. How delightful. Well, it's time good boys got to bed. So goodnight.

Saturday night
Dearest,
Just finished work 9 o'clock. Started 6 this morning. Tired. I'm just off to my barn. As requested I enclose hat badges. It's not the one I came out with, but it's seen plenty of service. Hat badges are very hard to get. But as luck would have it I had one given me yesterday and so I send you the old one.

Sunday 11th Nov 1915 [87]
My dear Daisy,
Before I go any farther might I ask a question before I forget. You say in your letter that you know where you would like it to be and what would happen, referring to our meeting. Where? What would happen?

I enclose 20frs. I don't think it is necessary to go right out of your way to Charing Cross, surely any respectable Post Office will change them. If you find it too much of a nuisance to change the money, please dear, let me know and I'll try to see what I can do.

---

[87] This is what Will has written. However, 11th November 1915 was a Thursday.

Thanks ~~awfully~~ (I'm sorry) very much for your offer of knitting, but I don't think I shall require it. I've had a good cardigan, scarf and gloves issued. By the way are you wearing your fur yet?

I've just had my photo taken with the other two fellows in the Officers Mess, the waiters etc, had it taken in the garden of the house I'm cooking at.

How is Beethoven getting on? I shan't have a look in when I come back, you'll be so expert, no mistakes, absolutely charming, eh? We had a little harmonium arrive here yesterday, bought by one of the officers for the boys. It's quite a treat to have a play after such a long time. Nevertheless I haven't forgotten *Flight of Ages* and *Somewhere a Voice is Calling* and a few other songs.

Friday 12th November 1915
Dearest,

I enclose a letter which please read and if time Mother and Dada also, and then forward 'tout de suite' to Mr Curtis, c/o Westerns etc. Let me know exactly what you think of it. I think you'll find it interesting.

PS. . . . Keep letter clean and nice as 'bosses' will read it.

The Mairie at Auchel. Part of it was used as a hospital.

Thursday 18th November 1915
My dear Daisy,

Thanks for parcel. I don't know what you sent, all I received was a handful of crumbs. I salvaged a few grapes and some fragments of chocolate. I could not read the letter, it was soaked in grape juice. Never mind, next time a wooden box or cast iron, or to be absolutely certain, armoured plate.

On Sunday we moved about 12 miles back to a very nice place,[88] not been here before, but very near. The people here are splendid. We have all got nice billets. I have a fine range and most obliging people. I sleep in the kitchen on straw, jolly fine, nice and warm. Lot of children here and one of them is my 'petite fiancée' a ripping little girl of 8. She clings to me all day. I took her to have her photo taken with me today. You won't be jealous, will you. She calls me 'Villiam'. Some more fellows went on leave a few days ago, 7 of them, so my turn is coming. It may be before Christmas, it may be after and it may be 'après la guerre'. However, keep smiling. We shall see each other soon. I suppose by now you have received my letter to Westerns and your reply is on its way. How I long for home again. I wish the war would soon end. I dream about you nearly every night, such ripping dreams too. When dreams are realities, won't it be fine. I suppose you don't miss me much now, do you? Getting used to my absence.

I am glad to hear you are persevering so much with your music. I can foresee such happy times when I come home, can't you? Have some nice walks and talks, my word, What! What!!

When is the war going to end? Do you know I believe the war will end where it began, in Serbia. This time next year I hope I shall be in 'civvies'. The trenches out here owing to rain and snow are in an awful condition. Where I am now, the father has 3 brothers and one son prisoners in Germany and the daughter about 20 has had her fiancé killed, isn't it awful. Sometimes after work I take a stroll in the dark down the garden and some of the things I've seen and know make me cry. You don't understand the term 'War' in England.

---

[88] Auchel.

'Though the mills of God grind slowly,
Yet they grind exceeding small
Though with patience long he waiteth,
With exactness grinds he all' [89]

PS. . . . Turn the dark clouds inside out. Till 'your boy' comes Home. Remember me to all at home; Your love.

99 Engadine Street, Southfields, SW [90]
18th November 1915
Dear Mr Stocker

I am much obliged to you for your very full and interesting letter which certainly shows that you have seen much active service and been in some very tight corners. Certainly from what you say, you deserve a holiday and it is unfair that the man with the soft bed and soft job should get all the good things in leave when so many have to rough it out there and no sort of compensation is given them. We are going along quietly in the office. Not pushed too much of course but there is enough to keep us going. The two girls are keeping your job warm for you.

I saw Parker on Sunday. He is still kicking out his heels doing nothing particular. His brothers who enlisted a long time after him are out in the trenches and one of them has been home wounded. Maddison wrote about a fortnight ago. He seems to be having a quieter time than you just now. But he has had some hot work earlier in the war.

Mr EYW was so interested in your letter that he took it home for his wife to read. He told me to say he was very interested in your doings. Young Creasey, the searg. of our Tuesday night Training Class has been

---

[89] Friedrich von Logau translated by Longfellow.
[90] This is the only letter sent to Will which is known to have survived, most likely because he forwarded it on to Daisy. Alfred Curtis was the secretary of the London Association of Churches of Christ. He also worked with Will at Western & Son.

killed in France.[91] This makes two we have lost. He was a promising lad.

As you say Lloyd George is our man. Morris still looks on him with suspicion. However there is a great difference in the Tory press towards him now. Churchill is coming out to you. I hope he will be able to win back his name. He seems to have suffered through Antwerp and the Dardanelles. Serbia looks rough doesn't it. I hope things will soon go better there and that we may see the end of this terrible war. Food is increasing in cost and of course, the poorer classes who have no increase in their income are feeling the pinch although many of them are getting now much better incomes on munitions work etc. The latest Zeppelin raid came near enough to our office. A bomb dropped in the Law Courts Yard and another on the skating rink in Kingsway. But I suppose this is nothing compared with your experiences. I expect you won't be sorry to get back again. The streets at night are almost dark and it is very miserable out of doors but the Zeps seem to have forgotten or lost their way as a consequence.

Mrs C sends her kind regards. I also send kindest regards and hopes for your speedy return and the best of luck.

I remain, yours sincerely
Alf J Curtis

---

[91] LCpl William Creasey, East Surrey Regt. Killed in action 13th October 1915, aged nineteen.

Will with his petite fiancée in Auchel. Despite an appeal in the local paper L'Avenir de L'Artois, no one has been able to identify her.

Sunday 21st November 1915
My dear Daisy,
 I enclose photograph. What do you think of it? Also one for Mother, Ada and Harry and send one to Alex. I forget his address. The letter you may read and seal for Harry. Don't you think she is a nice little girl 'my petite fiancée'? I also enclose a letter from Mr Curtis. 'EYW' is our senior partner. I am glad to see he took it home. He was evidently very interested in it. I have no more news, except that the guns are booming terrifically again.
PS. . . . I had to laugh about the coal box.

Friday 3rd December 1915
My dear Daisy,

Thank you for your letter. I'm glad you like the photo. So R.W.B. thinks I'm getting fat does he? Perhaps he is right. Do you think so? Fancy Bert on leave. We are sending 7 a week and there are 175 to go still, so I may be some time yet. All good things come to those who wait. However, time soon passes. I have now been out here 38 weeks. But when I do come home, we'll make up for lost time, won't we? Yesterday afternoon I felt rather tired so I had a nice little nap and I dreamt you came to me and I heard you laugh and it woke me up. I was disappointed.

Monday 6th December 1915
My dear Daisy,

Thanks for your letter received today. Can I guess this ambition of yours. Is it a nurse? If not you must tell me when I come home. 'Am I any nearer home yet?' Of course I am. The war can only last a certain time, and each day is 24 hours nearer the end of it. Thirty eight weeks today since I landed in France. The time has passed fairly quickly to me, although in another way it seems as if I've been out here all my life. You say you long to see me again. I'm sure that you don't long for me more than I do for you. I look back upon the past only to have on impatient desire for a speedy repetition. This time seven years ago. Do you remember Forest Gate etc. We little thought then that today I would be a soldier in France. Why it will soon be 2 years since a certain April 21st. Do you know that quite a number of our fellows who have been home on leave have got married. Sounds amusing doesn't it? By the way only a few moments ago I heard that an officer had married a girl out here. I should reckon he <u>must</u> have wanted a job. Nasty lot of girls out here.

I enclose 25 francs which please bank for us. And I expect you will soon be hearing from Westerns. Regarding Ernest. You of course remember my lending him £10, now just over a year ago. I want your advice. Shall I ask him (in a nice letter) if he would now start to pay me say a few shillings a week. Or shall I wait till the end of the war before even suggesting the matter. At any rate I think I ought to write him and Ada suggesting 1. Some little arrangement or 2. Telling them not to let it enter their heads until after the war or lastly make them a present of it and I forget it. If you like ask Mother quietly about it, tell her I asked you to. You know I should not like Ernest to worry about it.

Thursday 16th December 1915
My dear Daisy,
See to enclosures for me please, dear: brooch is for Basil. Got parcels safely and letter. Thank you all very much indeed. Write you a nice long letter next time. Very very tired.[92]

Thursday 23rd December 1915
My dear Daisy,
Nearly Christmas. Have not had a letter from you for a day or so, naughty girl. You may not have much time, but I'm certain you have more time than I. Not even Sunday do I get a rest. I write to several people, you write to one. I don't suggest you ought to write oftener, but you know, dearest, I wouldn't say no to a few more letters from you. Isolated as I am from home I do not have anybody to talk to in the way of kinsfolk to the absent one.

Well dear, 8 more went on leave today and my turn must therefore be a little nearer. Blair has returned. I have an idea it is coming soon. So 'keep smiling'. We'll have a ripping time when it does come. You must get a programme ready for us, but I think I know what it will most likely be.

I have disposed of a portion of your parcels. Very nice too. Just reminds me. You must buy yourself a Christmas present and put it down to my account. If you like send me a list to choose from. Two of our boys have been mentioned for bravery in the trenches. I should like to see a few medals in the corps. Shifted to another Mess yesterday, a better house, same town. Well it is now 11.45 and I'm off to 'bed'

---

[92] There are no letters for ten days. On 7th December the War Diary notes that eleven men of the 5th LFA were in hospital, one with chickenpox. On 11th December the entire unit moved from Auchel to Noeux-les-Mines.

Friday

Today is Christmas Eve. Its message is 'On Earth Peace goodwill towards men'. How well the Christian countries are carrying it out! But let's hope that 1916, before it is very old, will bring the end of the war. I believe it will. Won't it be glorious for us to be together again. No more separation. However, it's coming. I have been spared nearly 10 months and have been led safely thus far, I know that I will be led right on to the end. After all my job is not an over dangerous one now. I'm cook to the officers and as some officers stay in the hospital while others are in the trenches I'm always wanted behind the line. Of course the towns get heavily shelled at times in the danger zone, but not since the bombardment of the trenches. If I keep my present job I don't suppose I shall have to go in the trenches again. So you see I am not in a very dangerous position. And greatest of all if God intends to keep me safe till my return no power on earth can alter it, so keep cheerful. Hoping once again the New Year will give you the reward you so patient waited for: My Safe Return.[93]

---

[93] The Christmas card from Will to Daisy is an embroidered silk card. Will has written 'A Happy Xmas, Will to Daisy X'. In Daisy's handwriting at the bottom is the terse comment *'What hopes!'*

1916

1st January 1916
My dear Daisy,

I'm glad to hear you had a fair time Xmas. Perhaps next Christmas I'll be with you again. I don't think there is very much doubt about it, although one never knows. Basil's remark rather amused me: 'Be sure your sins will find you out.' You say you are impatient so am I. Who isn't? Well you know they say anticipation is better than realisation. I'd sooner have realisation though wouldn't you?

It has just struck me that it is 6 months since I had your photo. If I don't go on leave soon I shall ask you to send me another photo. A photo, not a~ ~. It is now 11.30 and I've to be up early tomorrow although it is Sunday so Goodnight. x. I am sending on 55 frs which please change and bank.

7th January 1916
My dear Daisy,

Thanks for your letter which I received today. You say you are still waiting for me and so am I waiting for leave. It's a long time coming isn't it. After the war I shall have plenty of leave. You seem to suggest that when I go on leave we shall practise something, not music. May I ask what?

Re your compulsion for saving. 'What do I think fit?' Nothing. I don't know where you get your conception of this business from. Was it John Bull or Comic Cuts.[94] Was it the journal that suggested stopping wages and proposed issuing monkey nuts?

'How long after the war are you going to stop on the clothes line?' Is this an insinuation as to when am I going to get married? Oh! I see now, this is leap year. Ladies proposal. Answer. According

---

[94] *Comic Cuts* was a weekly comic costing a halfpenny. *John Bull* was a popular weekly newspaper costing a penny. Although highly patriotic, it took an anti-establishment stance, championing grievances of the troops during the war.

to circumstances. I should like to know if my assumption is correct. Don't swank, tell me honestly. <u>Don't forget.</u>

If I am not home within a fortnight from today I want you to send me (at my expense) another photo of yourself. Only order 1 or 2. Don't order a photographers, will you.

PS. . . . What does this hieroglyphic mean, X ?

Wednesday 12th January
My dear Daisy,

Thank you for your letter which I received Monday. You say in part of your letter that Westerns wrote asking for news of me. As you know, I wrote them November. If in future you get a letter from W&S mentioning anything otherwise than my allowance, let me see the letter please. If you have the letter you refer to let me have it. Make observations if you like as well. You also remark upon my changing. The moustache makes me smile. Only a few weeks ago I shaved off what little I did have. I don't think I have grown much taller, if any. I may appear a little more elephantine. Personally, I don't think I have changed but very little outwardly. At any rate, you have a recent photo of me. <u>What do you think</u>? Can you discover a moustache. Would you like me to change in appearance and would you like me to change in personality also? I should be very interested to know. Don't forget to answer will you?

When are we going to have a walk along the Bridle Path again? Let's hope very soon. How I long, sigh, crave, to re-traverse some of our old walks. When the war is over won't we make up for lost time. If the war should end summer time we'll go away together, won't we. I shouldn't care where it was so long as we could both go. So you are gradually progressing with your music. That's good! You'll never regret the time and money spent, I'm sure.

My turn for leave hasn't arrived yet. The 'leavites' go off every Friday night. Only four are going now we are up the line. When we go back again 10 will go again. There are 150 more of us to go.

Wednesday 19th January 1916
My dear Daisy,

    We made a move Monday a little more behind the line.[95] Now about 6 miles I should think, from where we were last September. Our billets are wooden huts in a muddy field. Of course the officers have a good billet in a large house standing in its own grounds. I have a nice little stove in one of the outhouses. I sleep in one of the rooms of the house. Tiled floor, carpeted walls, electric lights. I am writing this sitting up in my bed, 3 blankets, fur coat, and my clean underclothing forms a nice pillow: nice and warm. I wish you could see me. In fact, I wish you could be with me. Don't you? How delightful the thought.

    Tomorrow, Thursday, 4 more will go on leave. I don't know who they will be. When we go down the line again 10 will go at a time. We are still considered up the line as we have a party in the trenches and Advanced Dressing Station. If I had a good excuse for leave I believe I could soon get it. Otherwise I may have to wait a long time. It may be weeks, it may be months. However, as the time passes we are gradually getting nearer the end of the war, which I reckon will be some time this year, but not as your friend at business suggests, not February.

    Now for some of the remarks in your letters. In your last letter you mentioned something to the effect of my having a poor opinion of your modesty. Where do you get the notion from? Why should I? Why aren't you modest? What makes you think I have so poor an opinion? And the part which made me smile: 'and having got this idea into my head not likely to alter it.' Would you mind explaining matters. Well, dearest, it is getting late and I must say goodnight hoping to meet you in dreamland.

    Yours ever xxxx

PS. . . . Note the hieroglyphs. You must close your eyes and have vivid imagination to get the real effect.

PPS. . . . I enclose three 5 frs notes. If I'm not home by when I said don't forget the photos. <u>Urgent</u> Please send me weekly or monthly a

---

[95] Houchin rest camp.

book called 'Knowledge', this is an Astronomical again.[96] Send this as soon as possible, don't wait until you have a parcel to send. Also, some more Sunday School Books or any book calculated to educate. <u>And bachelor buttons.</u>

Sunday 30th January 1916
My dear Daisy,
    I am still borrowing paper. If you cannot get pads at one shop try another. Have not had a letter from you for days. I have not been able to write before as had no paper. Not keen on everlasting borrowing. Did you get my letter asking for 'Knowledge' and one or two other things? and enclosing 15 frs. Haven't had a letter for a fortnight from anybody. Some girls write daily to their friends abroad, some forget. **Forgotten**

4th February 1916
My dear Daisy,
    Thank you for your letter. I expected that my letter would get a hearty welcome and apparently my surmise was correct. The paper you sent me to get on with went in one evening when I wrote to Mr Mander, Black, Home and you.
    Re 'proves the shallowness of my affection'. If you say so, well I suppose it is so. As to my excitement and newness etc. Thank you. If working every day from 7 in the morning till 9.30 or 10 at night is not monotonous, what is? And if you term frequent and prolonged visits to 'the line' exciting, where reigns devastation and blood, thank the Lord our opinions as to 'excitement' differ. Now for your 'sacrificed pleasures' for a 'cold sitting room' and in return an 'unkind letter'. A peculiar sacrifice. I reckon you have a handsome chance of learning music which many would be glad of. However, I'll see if I can get you inserted in Foxe's 'Book of Martyrs'.
    Act 2.
    First of all forget Act 1. I received 'Knowledge' thank you. Get February's also. It's dearer than I expected so finish after February. I hope to be home this month. Now you're beginning to smile. Yes,

---

[96]   *Knowledge* was an illustrated science magazine.

I really and truly think I shall be home this month. I have made application. No elaborate excuse, merely 'an application'. The officer in charge of the mess smiled and put it in his pocket when the 'waiter' handed it in. The fellow who handed it in is willing to bet me 5 francs I'm home in a fortnight. Now I know you're smiling. I can hear you. Sorry! I'm mistaken, it's a Naval gun. When I come home do you think it will be possible for you to get a portion of your summer holiday. It would be great if you could arrange it, wouldn't it? However, if you couldn't I could take you to business and meet you coming home in the evening, my word! Foretastes of the coming glory.

It is now, 10.30, Saturday night, if I were in England now under normal conditions we should probably being xxx at your house gate. What shall we be doing next year at this time. What do you think of the enclosed card? Rather pretty, isn't it? When I come home I've several very interesting subjects to chat with you on.

Thursday 10th February 1916

My dear Daisy,

Thank you for your letter received today. So Don is getting married is he, or rather just got married.[97] Silly chap! There's no knowing the depths of human folly. One of my friends went home today to get married. Such a lot of people are asking for trouble just now. Tonight, nine more went home on leave and <u>perhaps</u> you might be interested to know I may be home on Friday if my turn is Thursday. I think you can reckon safely on Thursday or Thursday week. I got a letter from Alex and shall be glad if you'll send him the enclosed. I am sitting up in bed writing this so please excuse clumsiness. But my letters are always clumsy so really an apology is not necessary.

---

[97] James Donald Sutherland 'Don' Munro was a friend of Will and his brother Harry. He married Sister Clara (Clare) Latham, one of the nurses who had cared for him when he was invalided back to London from Gallipoli. Will's brother Harry was the best man. For a full account of their story, see *Diaries of a Stretcher-Bearer 1916–1918 – L/LCpl Edward Munro MM, 5th Field Ambulance AIF*, edited by Don's nephew and namesake, Donald Munro.

Don Munro and Clara Latham on their wedding day

Monday 14th February 1916

I have just received my green envelope but before posting I thought I'd write a little more. I have received another letter from you and you say that if you have a holiday it will be at your own expense. If you are sure that by your having a week you will not influence your position at business, and if you will allow me, I will give you 25/- so that you will not lose anything by staying away. It would be ideal if you could arrange it. Have a good try, won't you dearest. We could have such a fine time. You won't forget now, will you. Thursday or Thursday week. Don't forget to get the band out.

Sunday 20th February 1916

My dear Daisy,

Thanks for your two letters which I received on Friday. I have them before me now and as I see no question requiring an answer, I'll get to business. Oh! I see you want forgiveness for omitting to write. I'll pardon you with a severe caution. It's remarkable, however, how speedily we discern our own faults in others, by the way. Now I must ask your forgiveness: reciprocity (Hem!).

I am now about 10 miles behind the line, just a few yards off the mess, where resides my 'petite fiancée'. You know to whom I refer. This is a very nice mess, one of the best we have struck. I am sorry to have to inform you that our leave was again stopped on Thursday, but recommenced last night, only 3 going instead of 9 or 10, so I shall be put back a little. We shall not go on Saturday until some other alteration is made. I don't know how long we shall stick to 3. Of course I may go next week, quite likely, but I really can't say. I know that my name is down and very near the top of the list. It's rather rotten isn't it. One consolation, the weather improves daily and the days grow longer, so cheer up. I understand you have a large programme for me. You must appear in every item, you know. Regarding Mrs Barber I can't say. If the busses run we may go, but if it means wasting precious time in a train, it's out of the question. Visitation can be knocked out of our programme. Uncles and aunts won't stand a look in, unless it's by accident. My motto:- 'When I go home, I'm going home'. After the war will do for relatives. My time will be spent with you and my people and of course Twynholm.

I have not received my BS yet. I'm **we** are getting quite rich aren't **we**. I have nearly 200frs[98] due to me in my Pay Book also. So I don't waste much.

KEEP SMILING

Friday 25th February 1916
My dear Daisy,

Last night three went home on leave, and this morning all leave has again been stopped. So I can't say when I shall be home now. I felt very disappointed yesterday, but now I'm not, must take things as they come. I received a letter from you yesterday and also today. The brass band business made me smile. And as to your 'greediness' so-called, I can assure you, you will have your request granted. So you are still unwell are you, perhaps it's a good job I'm not coming home this week, I might make you worse. You are having your

---

[98] Just over £7 at that time.

photograph taken are you? That's good. I have been anticipating it every week for the last few weeks. Well, I must now bid you adieu.

Friday 3rd March 1916
My dear Daisy,

Just received your long letter. I am sorry I disappointed you regarding leave. I was not reckoning on stoppage and the cutting down of passes, it hasn't restarted yet and so I can't say now when I shall be home. Today we had our football team photo taken and so I hope to send you a print in a day or so.

5th London Field Ambulance football team, Auchel, 3rd March 1916
Will is seated front right of photo. He has noted on the back:
Killed in Action: A. Smith, W. McFarlane, E. Austing, W. McPherson. Wounded: Barnet, Col. Rutherford and W. Stocker.

I have now been out here nearly a year; a year since I saw you. I little thought when I saw you last at St Albans that it would be a year at least before I saw you again, did you? I thought then that the war would be over by now, but now my humble opinion is that, at the earliest, it won't end before the autumn, although I saw in today's paper that the Kaiser is supposed to have said the war will end on April 15. How are you really getting on? Do you manage to keep happy. Your letters are quite obscure on this point. I expect you feel despondent sometimes. It seems a long time to wait, doesn't it? But you've gone well over half way now and after all, time really passes very quickly. Perhaps you're feeling old, nearly 23. If the war finishes this year and it's almost sure to, we shall be again united at 23: still nippers you see and perhaps after a year or two, greater unity (you know what I mean). I shall leave the army better off financially than when I entered it and I hope physically stronger and I've gained more than lost in the way of education so our future is really very bright, isn't it. So 'keep smiling' and look after yourself 'till the good time comes'.

PS. . . . Enclose a bottle of chutney in your parcel please.

Tuesday 14th March 1916
My dear Daisy,

Thank you for your letter. On Sunday we approached the line a few miles and in a few days we are going right up again.

By the way you know the ring you gave me, I squashed it in the pump, finger and all. After a struggle I got it off and now wear it on my little finger. You don't mind, do you? Now don't go and do the same with your ring will you? Do you know it is a year tonight since I came to France. It does seem a long time. Fancy a year since I saw you. I used to think a week a long time: I little knew we were going to be separated so long. However, the war will end this year for certain. So keep smiling.

In your letters you talk about giving somebody a 'bit of your mind' possibly at your concert. I hope you are not a suffragette now. Excuse my venturing to suggest that it is hardly a ladylike expression and I am surprised at your using it.

What do you think of the team photo? I think it is very good but not great of myself. Perhaps you will recognise Arthur Sturt. The other photo is of our cooks, you will find somebody in there you know.

Now behind the front recently taken over from the French. We have now an 80 miles front. When I came out we had 35 miles. In a sequestered spot now. A farmhouse and 2 or 3 houses. I like it, it's very pretty.[99] Please, dear, excuse my delay in writing I've been very busy fitting up kitchen etc.

24th March 1916
My dear Daisy,

Thank you very much for your nice letter. Four more men have just gone on leave and so you see it has been re-opened, my turn is therefore a little nearer. But you know I think I would sooner wait now till your birthday. Wouldn't it be ripping to get leave on your birthday. Nearly as good as two years ago. Some day eh? So you think I am getting 'plump', do you? They are always telling me that here; they won't take my word that I am wasting away. 'You're easily 12 stone' they tell me. At any rate I'm quite fit. I am eagerly waiting for your photo. Let's hope it is a good one.

Saturday

Today is Saturday. A day we look forward to out here (I don't think). We used to in civil life, didn't we? This time, next year, we will eh? I was wondering, you know, whether I shall be too shy to catch hold of your arm when we first meet. Do you think so? But I can assure you this that when we go for our first walk again if I do not hold your arm I shall be 'waisting' time.

Last night I had a peculiar experience. I made the officers a plum 'something'. After it was cooked and I had served up five portions, I cut off a piece for myself and the first bite I bit a stone, as I thought, which turned out to be my ring. Lucky an officer didn't get it. Ring of many adventures, eh?

In your next parcel please send me:- writing pads, baking powder (for officers) say price.

Sunday 2nd April 1916
My dear Daisy,

I have really good news for you this time. I told you that leave had been re-opened. Well! We understand that all leave is to finish within a month before the big attack (which by the way may finish

---

[99] Fresnicourt-le-Dolmen.

the war). At any rate since I wrote you four lots have gone on leave, making about 30. When leave is on we send as rule 5 or 6. Now we are sending 20 a week, six more go tomorrow (I'm not in that 6) and another lot on Wednesday and Thursday (which I may be in). That's good news isn't it? So I may be home next Sunday, but I won't promise anything.

I am in the fields writing this at one of our Dressing Stations about 6 or 7 miles behind line.[100] We only have a few here, about 60: a nice hospital in the open fields. It is glorious here now, for the moment it doesn't seem like active service. We had dinner today at 1 o'clock and so I've no dinner to cook this evening and I feel very free.

Just got your letter from my pocket and trying to find out your puzzle:- A.M.T.H.G.F. Got it after a ½ hour hard work. Absence makes the heart grow fonder. (Hear hear). Post is just going so Goodbye,

Saturday 15th April 1916
My dear Daisy,

Sorry I have not written you before, I've been working hard and the last few days indisposed with a bad arm. Not quite fit yet, hope to be soon. Thank you for your photo. It's not bad, but not so good as your first, which I'm sorry I have lost, much better than your last three which I have torn up. But I'm satisfied with it. I am sorry to say I have lost my ring. I treasured that you know.

All leave has again been stopped. It has been going alphabetically and when it restarts I stand a good chance, 'St' nearly last.

Very tired, Goodnight

Sunday
Please, if you can, let me have the things I asked for per return, razor etc, dictionary. Please dear, when I especially mention things let me have them as soon as possible. You keep me waiting an awfully long time as a rule, don't you. Now there's a good girl let me

---

[100] Cabaret Rouge at the end of the Cabaret Trench, Souchez.

have as soon as possible the following, apart from what I may have mentioned before: - <u>Urgent</u>

1. Razor
2. Dictionary (Eng) as before
3. Toothpaste
4. A smock. <u>Dark</u> blue (black preferably) overcoat affair like Ernest's butcher's overalls. Use your judgement as to size. Get it to fit Harry, buttons at front. I think you know what I mean now.
5. Power's book on Doctrine[101] (ask Harry)
6. A pocket Bible.

How are you going on now. Fed up. Eh? It's rotten about leave, isn't it. But, you know, I think, (and many out here), the war will end this summer. The Germans are fast going to the wall. You must be getting used to my being away now. But I suppose you are like me being buoyed up by the hope of being re-united. When you see me the first time after the war. My Word!!

Yesterday I had occasion to go to the next village shopping and you'll be surprised to know I went on horseback. A friend of mine had to take two officers horses (full saddle) to the village and I rode one. He gave me a tip or two. We had a firm canter and then a trot, it was good. I got on rippingly.

Friday 21st April 1916

My dear Daisy,

As today is your birthday I thought I would write you a letter. As you know I expected to be home today, but there's no luck. Leave has again been stopped and so there you are. I expect you well remember the event of two years ago.[102] I do. I should have very much like to have been home to celebrate the 2nd anniversary of it, but when my leave does come you will be glad that you have waited and what is more it will make the time shorter before I see you again. 23 today. Aren't you feeling old, almost ancient, you are not grey yet are you? I wonder whether this will be your last birthday

---

[101] *Bible Doctrine for Young Disciples* by Frederick D. Power.
[102] Will and Daisy's engagement.

without me. Hope so, eh? Long time the war, isn't it? Be over this year though easily.

Raining here very fast, had poor weather lately, it was a fine day when I woke up this morning too. In your next letter please let me know what Harry is doing[103] and also in your next parcel (or if it has already gone, separately) send me on any old football boots which <u>may</u> be at home. Ask Harry to see. If you find a pair have them re-studded and forwarded to me quickly. If you cannot rake up a pair please send me some of the studs (iron) you sent me in August last. I must really apologize for troubling you so. I am sure it must be inconvenient to you. In one of my recent letters I asked you what you would like for your birthday. Please send me a list (a long one). By the way when you send me a parcel and it costs a lot for postage let it appear in my bank statement. Might I be inquisitive enough to ask if you spend much time of a weekday at my home. I am only curious to know. Now time for officers tea so I must 'knock off'.

1st May 1916
My dear Daisy,

Thank you for your parcel and letter. Everything was quite good except razor which is useless. Penny Bazaar may do for tin tacks but not razors. The smock is fine.

Today several more go on leave: we are now down to the Fs and so I'm gradually coming on. I am very sorry I have failed to write more often. As a matter of fact I've had nothing to write and no time to write it in, we are very busy now working hard for coming offensive. Say you'll excuse me won't you? I started a letter a week

---

[103] **Tribunals – A Straightforward Plea from Twynholm Hall**
Mr H J Stocker, aged 24, teacher at Millbank School, Westminster of Waldemar Avenue, Fulham said he belonged to the Church of Christ, Twynholm, Fulham Cross and spoke on Sunday morning and evening meetings. He had two brothers in the RAMC who both joined immediately on the outbreak of war, both leaving good positions. He was advised to finish his course of three years' study at Kings College, and endeavoured to join the same corps on release, but it was closed. His present objection was only to combatant service. Applicant was recommended for non-combatant service.
Fulham Chronicle, March 17th 1916.

ago to W&S and have not been able to finish it yet. I hope you won't think I'm forgetting you. I think about you all day and ofttimes dream about you at night and long, nay, yearn for our reunion.

Although we have been disappointed about leave I'm sure when it does come we shall be more than glad that we have had to wait. My Word! Just fancy seven nice summer days and evenings together. I often wonder whether I shall see any difference in you and you in me, in nature as well as appearance. Do you think so?

Thursday
Received parcel and have cooked and tried chicken. Only one fault, being in an outlandish show I could not get any stuffing and so had to cook it just as it was, but it was quite alright and I thank whoever sent it very much.

I note what you say about 'studs'. As a matter of fact I most particularly wanted them yesterday; playing in ordinary boots on grass I slipped up so often that I'm not on good terms with my knee and have had to attend hospital for treatment. In a few days we are playing a return match with this team which we have just beaten 1-0 and as it's about the most important match we have yet played please send (if it means searching London and the suburbs) some studs. <u>In the next few days please</u>. When I ask for certain things I don't care a hang what you put in the parcel as long as I get things mentioned.

Friday 12th May 1916
My Treasure,
Must begin with usual excuse, sorry I've not written before. However I start with good news. It's about leave. We are now down to P's and if leave continues at its present generous rate I should be home some time next week. To show exactly how we stand I may say that there are now 32 only to go on leave out of our roughly 250 odd. During the past few weeks 17 have been going per week and I am just in the next 17. So providing the usual number go next Thursday I shall be among them. When I arrive at Folkestone I shall probably telegraph and when at Victoria I'll 'phone. That makes you smile doesn't it. Let's hope you can have the week off when I do come home.

Thursday 18th May 1916
My dear Daisy,

I expected to start today on leave, but at the last moment eight were knocked off after the passes were made out. I am now 7th on the list and we are hoping to go on Monday next. If I do I shall arrive home Tuesday afternoon. We seem very unfortunate but it is all for the best. I am given to understand that eight per week are going to be knocked off now. As we have during the last few weeks sent 20 or more a week it now leaves you see 14 a week and so as I am 7th I should go for certain next. But for all I know it may stop again. However I'm exceedingly hopeful so cheer up.

8th June 1916
My dear Daisy,

Arrived back last night[104] after a very stormy voyage on 'Golden Eagle' and a day at Boulogne Rest Camp waiting for the train. How are you feeling. Not hilarious eh? I must confess I felt, especially last night, right down in the dumps. I am not in the mess so far. I was on a digging job today, draining land and all the time I was humming *'No more to leave you etc'* and *'A little bit of Heaven'*. I think you sang the former song well when I was home and I can imagine I am hearing you now, you sang that so prettily. My leave seems like a beautiful dream now. Let me know please, dear, how Mother and yourself were after I left you. Try and keep cheerful dear, won't you? I think some time this year the war will finish and then it will be a case of 'no more to leave, no more to roam' 'All good things come to those who wait'. I can hardly see now the light is fading.

10th June 1916
My dear Daisy,

It is very kind of you to write me so frequently: I do so much appreciate your letters. I think I'll first of all try and answer your questions. You say I do not answer your questions, as a rule I suppose it is due to the fact that I never keep your correspondence for long. It's awkward to carry about and I should not like to lose it

---

[104] To Monneville.

and have a stranger reading it. Sometimes of course I have to keep one because it contains something special and it remains in my pay book for months.

The solution to C.Y.K.A.C. is Consider Yourself Kissed and Cud---d. Got it? Imagination (so we are told) goes a long way. Re the Bottom Drawer. It all depends how big it is and what you have in it. Tell me what you have in it and I'll be able to judge (hem!).

Friday

I have just had my dinner (bully beef and potatoes). I am not in the Officers Mess now, nor Sectional Cookhouse. We are up the line but are not running any Advanced Dressing Stations. You will be interested to know that in our recent action on Vimy Ridge[105] three of our Ambulance have gained Military Medals which ranks next to VC.[106] Jolly good, isn't it? And in a few days some of our officers are also going to be decorated.

Have just received your parcel for which I thank you. As for your sickness I have a remedy but I must bring it with me personally.

I am on a building job this afternoon (jack of all trades and master of none). We are billeted in a little mining town and several of us are in private billets, such as they are. Mine is a small outhouse and badly wants whitewashing. Next door they have an empty back room and six of our boys are there; hanging from the low ceiling is an old dusty lamp shade and on this shade some house martins have built a nest, the older birds fly in and out of the window all day and seem quite tame. It's really very quaint. I'm quite interested in it. I must now get off to my job. I should say the architect must proceed with his plans.

Saturday

Have just been paid and enclose 35 francs. As I am not in the mess I find myself buying a lot of extras. But as I wish to be thrifty I must go steady. Things are very dear out here, for instance a tin of

---

[105] 'Festubert near Vimy Ridge. Dangerous to show head above ground.' - Daisy's notebook.
[106] Edmund Holness, John Barker, and Percy Stevens.

peaches 2 frs. However, don't send parcels with dainties in as I think it is a very dear way when one considers postage. When I wrote for an overall I thought I was going in the mess.

Went for a nice walk with John Blair last night in the woods at the back of the town. It reminded me of our walk over Wimbledon when I was on leave. I cannot think of any more questions you require answering. If I have missed anything let me know.

19th June 1916
My dear Daisy,

Many thanks for your letters. I have one in front of me dated last Thursday which contains a song. I do not know the song but the words would suggest it is a good one. You say my eyes are blue, are they? I didn't know they were any particular colour. I am told I sometimes give a black look. However, I expect you know, girls take note of things like that. By the way what think you of Russia, some 'biz'. If she continues, as she has done the past week 168,000 prisoners and I suppose inflicted as many casualties, the guerre bientôt fini. I shall be glad to know if you have been made 'boss' of your department. Some boss.

Wednesday 21st June 1916
Dearest,

Have just returned from a paper chase 'hares and hounds'. Johnnie Blair and I were the hares and I suppose there were 50 hounds.[107] A 3 mile run through thick woods. I lost John and the course too and returned home after a 5 or 6 mile run smothered in mud and cuts. My idea was to set a false train in some bush entanglements and meet John later. The hounds who followed my course came back in a fine mess too. I met some of them later in the

---

[107] Paper Chase (or Hare and Hounds) is a racing game played outdoors in woods with any number of players. At the start of the game, one person is designated the 'hare' and all others are 'hounds'. The hare starts before everyone else leaving a trail of paper shreds behind himself. After a set time, the hounds start and attempt to catch the hare before they reach the finish line. The paper shreds can be blown around which makes the chase more difficult (Information from **Wikipedia**).

evening hobbling about on sticks. When I got to my billet the old lady seeing my knees covered in blood and my face scratched and ornamented with mud asked me if the officers had been punishing me. Although I tried to explain she failed to see pleasure in a game like that.

It is now 9.30 and the bugle has just blown 'lights out' so goodnight. Let's hope I dream of you.

Sunday 25th June 1916
Dearest,

Today is Sunday. I have been trying to write to you for the last two or three days but I am busy now, or rather I have been busy. I am in the section cookhouse again John Blair is my 'boss'. I should say Cpl Blair. At the moment of writing I am in a bivouac with Johnnie a few yards behind town. It is 9.30, time we were in bed, the bugle has just played 'lights out' but as we are isolated and John is interested in the same job as myself we are not turning in yet. We have Daylight Saving in France now so it is fairly light. By the way thanks for your letter today containing rose etc, it's very pretty. I showed it to John, he thought the same. 'Do you think you'll be the same after you are married?' he said. I answered decidedly in the affirmative. Of course we will be the same to each other, won't we? In fact if it's possible, greater unity greater love. Regarding the bottom drawer. I think we are coming on.

Thank you for the smock, it will come in very handy after all. I suppose you wore the bracelet today?
PS. . . . MBBFAL. My best boy friend and lover <u>is it</u>?

Wednesday
Dearest,

Have been inoculated today, a large dose too and have been given two days off duty and so I take another opportunity of writing you. Your letters seem to suggest a slight depression. Cheer up! I shall be home probably before Xmas for good. Had any rain in England? We are getting flooded out here. Rain, rain, rain every day now. I got washed out of my 'bivy' last night.

Friday
Dearest,

Have been training for our sports this evening, so you can guess my arm is fairly well. We are still a few miles behind the line running a Sick Hospital and Rest Station. The weather here seems to have made a change for the better and I hope it's come to stay. Am keeping quite fit and trust you are the same.[108]

Sunday 16th July 1916
Dear Daisy,

Thank you for your letters. First of all I might tell you we are not issued with green envelopes now. Regarding your query as to address. Letters will reach me quite safely if you leave out the Division and Brigade. I wrote a day or so ago commenting on the photo, but apparently you have not received it. I consider the likeness excellent, extremely natural, and the best you have had taken and thanks very much for it. I have nothing sensational to report. I expect you find the daily papers quite interesting enough just now. We are moving up the line tomorrow.[109]

29th July 1916
My dear Daisy,

Thanks for your letters. Things are just about the same out here and so I've nothing very interesting to report. I was very pleased to

---

[108] The following day, Saturday 1st July 1916, was the first day of the Battle of the Somme. The 5th (London) Field Ambulance was running a rest station behind the lines at Barlin. Will recalled that although things were quiet work-wise, there did seem to be a lot of messages coming in and out of the unit. The War Diary simply states 'Weather warm. News received of British Advance'.
[109] To Quatre-Vents.

meet Alex two days ago, but as we are on the move I'm not likely to see him again for some time.[110]

Sunday 6th August 1916
My dear Daisy,
   Thanks for your letter. I am going on quite well. The weather is very warm. I'd prefer it somewhat cooler for marching. We are still trekking and are now in a pretty village a good way from the line.[111]

Saturday 12th August 1916
My dear Daisy,
   I happen to have had this green envelope given me and so I send it straightaway. This is not an issue and I expect you will have to put up with ordinary letters for some time to come, perhaps until after the war.
   I am now about 40 miles behind the line. We trekked here, why, I don't know. We've passed some lovely little villages on the way. But my Word! Hasn't it been hot. Full pack in boiling sun, open country. We are now staying at a small and pretty village for some days. This is about our 10th day and yesterday we held our Sports. I did fairly well. I won all I went in for 100yds - 1st, 220yds - 1st, mile - 1st and my team won the relay. As all the running was done in the evening I had a very busy time. I ran all my lot within 1½ hours. It was like a race-course for 'bookies' and in the mile it was 4 to 1 against my winning. Some of the bookies had to pay out 80 frs

---

[110] Will's brother Alex went to France in June 1916 with the 2nd/6th London Field Ambulance remaining there until the end of November 1916 when the unit was transferred to the Egyptian Expeditionary Force. On 27th July 1916 the 2nd/6th LFA was at Haute Avesnes while Will's unit moved to Divion from Estrée Cauchy, about 6 miles from Haute Avesnes.

[111] '. . . started marching southward (to Gapennes) on August 1st. We had hot summer weather for the journey and started early each morning from our billets to get our marching done before the heat of the day – a pleasant rest during the afternoon and evening in a quiet country village, a night under the sky in a green orchard, breakfast at sunrise, and on the road again."
The History of the 47th (London) Division 1914-1919.

over my winning the mile. This race I won in 4 mins 50 secs. Ten started.

For each race there is 10 frs or 15 frs for first prizes so I have about 40 frs to come. With this money I have to buy a prize or prizes and show to the officers. I will get the money at our first concert. What I propose is this: For you to buy a watch worth about 30/- to 40/- equivalent to my prize money; have if possible an RAMC badge engraved on the back and inside something after this style:

On Active Service
5th London Field Ambulance RAMC
Sports August 1916

In the corner something after this style

Pte W Stocker
1st 100 yds
1st 220 yds
1st 1 mile

Ask Dada to get the watch. One suitable for engraving, double case affair. I should think you could get a fairly decent silver watch for 35/- about, exclusive of engraving. This would be a good souvenir of the war, wouldn't it? Until you hear again from me you can keep your eyes open for a suitable watch. <u>Don't buy anything until I send you orders (hem!)</u> I'm only giving you, I hope, lucid instructions what to do. So when I write again I shall have to use an ordinary envelope and therefore be very curt and perhaps inexplicit. Comprenez?

By the same post you may receive some money in a registered envelope. This is <u>not</u> prize money. It's a little more for our joint account and when you have entered it up and also W&S's money I shall be happy to receive Balance Sheet. I forget since I have sent the last green envelope all your questions. I couldn't in an open letter answer some of them. Perhaps you would like to know I am now not sectional cook but solely hospital cook except when I have few patients and then I help the sectional cooks. I must now close as

I have a lot to do. Thanking you again for the ripping photo you sent me.

PS. . . . Excuse, dearest, this ragtime letter.

Will's prize watch

Saturday 19th August 1916
Dear Daisy,

Thanks for your letter. Will you please get my watch done now and send it to me when finished. The engraving I should reduce a little. By the way send with it some sort of dust-case. I'm keeping fit and hope you are the same, still trekking to 'somewhere'. Sorry to hear about Walter Hall, let's hope it's not serious. Remember me to the folks at Home.

PS. . . . Will you please send me a shaving brush and a pocket mirror.

Friday 1st September 1916
Dear Daisy,

Thanks for your letter. Glad to hear of your promotion at business. I suppose, like most 'bosses' you'll have a 'snip' time now. It wouldn't be a bad idea to take an armchair and half a dozen novels to business now. We are having just about the same kind of weather as you have been having, only it's a little more inconvenient out here.[112]

Friday 22nd September 1916
My dear Daisy,

I have received your kind letter. At the moment of writing I have just returned from the line (by the way I am now a stretcher bearer).[113] I have not had a wash and shave for 5 days and about 3 washes during the last fortnight. We have been very hard worked in a warm zone in abominable weather; now perhaps you will excuse my delay in writing. We are now having by far the hardest time since we joined the army and I shall not be sorry when it's over. You might explain to others why there has been a lull in my correspondence. Letters are out of the question. It's hard enough to steal time to sleep.

I was glad to hear about the watch, it sounds rather good. I should be glad if you would let me have a parcel next time you write

---

[112] The War Diary notes rain and thunderstorms.

[113] On 4th September the 47th Division was sent up to the trenches near the tree stumps which were all that was left of High Wood. At dawn on 15th September, the division attacked High Wood. By mid-afternoon the wood was taken but there had been 4,500 casualties in the 47th Division alone, of which nearly 1,500 passed through the 5th London Field Ambulance assisted by the 4th and 6th London Field Ambulances. Eight hundred of them were stretcher cases. During this time, Will had time to send only two field service postcards. They had been working out of the ADS at Bottom Wood and Flatiron Copse. On the 15th September 1916 the War Diary noted that 800 stretcher cases at Bottom Wood ADS had been fed and evacuated after having had their wounds dressed. 'Everyone worked very hard and very willingly.' There is no mention of the visit to the field ambulance by the prime minister, Lloyd George.

me containing some of the cakes you sent me some time ago of your own make and some chocolate.

Saturday 23rd September 1916
My dear Daisy,

Now that you have aroused my curiosity I should like to know all about the trouble referred to in the first paragraph of your letter. I've received your postcards two days ago and thank you very much for them. The clock business is rather interesting but unless you are particularly keen on the idea I should let it pass. Should I follow Walter's footsteps it would be useless.[114]

Might I ask you to drop the 'good books' business. I'm not very fond of having my leg pulled on matters like that. April 21st two years ago should be enough. I am keeping fairly fit and hope you are the same. Remember JTs motto for this year.[115]

25th September 1916
Dear Daisy,

Thanks for your letter and photo case. I like it immensely. Rather singular, it's exactly what I expected. You could have sent me nothing better. At the time of writing we are a little distance behind the line resting and in the near future I expect we shall go back to the same part again. Let's hope the next birthday will be spent in England. I really don't think there's much doubt as to that.

Will you please obtain for me (early) a small pearl pen knife about 2 inches long and with four small blades. It's to replace one I have lost belonging to a friend. Sorry to trouble you.

On the 2nd October 1916, a fire broke out in the kitchen of the Cough Drop dugout Advanced

---

[114] Twynholm Church member Arthur E. Walter of the Middlesex Regiment, killed in action 1st July 1916.

[115] *'Be of good courage'.*
Twynholm's Motto for 1916 has been chosen to suit these dark days of trial and tribulation. 'Have not I commanded thee? Be strong and of a good courage; be not affrighted, neither be thou dismayed: for the Lord thy God is with thee whithersoever thou goest' Joshua 1–9. **Joyful Tidings, January 1916.**

Dressing Station due to 'someone mucking around with a primus stove'. This event is mentioned by Richard Capell in the papers of the 6th London Field Ambulance at the Wellcome Library in London. Will told his son Bruce about it many years later. No one was injured but a large quantity of stores and cooking equipment was destroyed, mainly that of Will and John Blair. A few days later a senior officer came to investigate what had happened. He asked John if they had lost a certain valuable piece of equipment in the fire? John told him no, he had never had one. Their own officer was horrified by his answer. After the visitor had left, he rounded on John and remonstrated that he, John, had 'dropped him in it'. John just said, 'Sorry, sir, but it's the truth. I won't lie for anyone.' Will remembered that he was very impressed by this. The missing piece of equipment may have been a field cooker. The War Diary mentions in December 1915 and February 1916 that they had tried to obtain one without success.

John never mentioned the incident to his own family: 'Dad never mentioned anything about a Cough Drop dressing station fire. He seldom talked about his time in France. I think it was too full of blood and gore and he no doubt wanted to forget it.' (Letter from Dave Blair to Editor).

Unfortunately a single sheet of the War Diary of the 1st/5th London Field Ambulance is missing and with it the first ten days of October 1916 and so we do not know what it had to say about either the Cough Drop fire or the death of Captain Clark. Neither event is mentioned in the War Diaries of the 4th or 6th London Field Ambulances. The War Diary for the Assistant Director Medical Services (ADMS) of the 47th Division records for the day in question: 'Cough Drop dressing station was accidentally burnt out last night. CAPT. S. CLARKE (sic) 5TH LOND AMB killed in action today.' Padre David Railton of the 20th London Regiment, wrote to Mrs Clark after her husband's death. The letter was printed in the Suffolk newspaper, The Bury Free Press, on Saturday November 4th 1916.

There is a good account of the 5th London Field Ambulance's work at this time in Maude's History of 47th Division – chapter VI pp. 75-76 and appendix A.

11th October 1916

My dear Daisy,

We have just come out of the line. I had my first wash and shave for a fortnight this morning. Our Division has advanced considerably since we went in, but at a big cost. We had our share of casualties including the death of our CO.[116] Hoping now to go to a different part of line where they're not 'pushing' and still yearning for the end of this hellish business they call war.

PS. . . . Got both parcels. Write longer later

18th October 1916

Dear Daisy,

Thanks for your letter. Rather interested to hear about Esme. I admire his pluck.[117] Harry acquainted me of the fact a week ago and is of the same opinion.

Regarding Western's. Maddison is on hospital duty miles behind the line and consequently has more time at his disposal than I have. I should rather like to see this 'annoyed letter' from W&S. By the way how about the BS. I received your parcel and also the watch. Needless to say I did justice to the parcel especially the chocolate.

---

[116] 'We regret to state that news was received on Tuesday of the death in Action in France of Captain Sydney Clark, MD, MRCS of the RAMC who will be remembered by a host of patients and friends as the popular doctor of 630 Fulham Road. He was mentioned in despatches last December and was to have been gazetted as Major later this month. . . . On one occasion he rescued eight wounded men under fire when four others had refused to go out.'
Fulham Chronicle October 6th 1916 (abridged).

[117] Esme Howard of Twynholm Church had both married and joined the Grenadier Guards.

I consider that S. Bros[118] have made a splendid job of the watch, beyond expectation. Re the knife. Please buy a pearl handled one so as to be as near as possible a facsimile of the original.

21st October 1916

Thanks for your letter received today. I am now on a totally different sector just behind the line.[119] Glad to hear of Harry's success and I was somewhat amused by Myra's letter.

Wednesday 25th October 1916

My dear Daisy,

I am writing this in anticipation of a green envelope and so I hope to write you a nice long letter. First of all let me say I am writing W&S a letter which I hope to finish by the time I receive the green envelope. I want you to read it as I am sure you have had no idea what I have been doing the past two months. In this letter I try to explain the experiences (or rather some of them) which I have passed through. Suffice to say ofttimes I wondered whether if after all I should see you again. All the time I have been out here has been child's play compared with our recent work. Ofttimes, I never expected to come out alive. Time after time with perspiration simply pouring down my face through high tension of the nerves, expecting to be blown to atoms at any moment have I breathed the prayer 'Father lead Thou me safely on'. We have had many casualties but few compared with some Ambulances working in this part. Calcutt, who you know, is severely wounded. Capt. Clark, one of our officers who lives in Cheselton Road, Fulham, was killed and many of our stretcher bearers were wounded. I was a stretcher bearer. When you turned in at night I wonder if you have ever thought of us out in the pouring rain soaked through and through knee deep in mud struggling desperately to bring in some poor fellow to a place of safety over miles of shell-swept and flooded country. On one

---

[118] Stocker Bros, of Long Acre in London, the family firm of silversmiths.
[119] The 47th Division had moved up to the Poperinge area in Belgium. According to the War Diary, the 5th LFA had arrived at Caestre railway station at 1 a.m. on 18th October and then marched, about 8 miles, in driving rain and gales via Steenvorde to Vancayseele-Sohier Farm, arriving at 4.30 a.m.

occasion after a long desperate struggle streaming with perspiration and fatigue soaked through and through I collapsed at the Dressing Station and they found it necessary to revive me with brandy.[120]

I do not wish you to be anxious about me. I am now behind the line on a very quiet front. I don't expect we shall go to that front again for some time. No constitution in the world could stand much of it.[121] As a matter of fact, I am at present very fit again and none the worse for my experiences. Now you can perhaps understand why I have not written frequently lately. Do you know, dearest, that once when returning from the line weary and worn I received a letter from you telling me that other girls' fellows write oftener than I do and that if I did not want you to write, say so. I knew that you did not understand. If you had seen me reading that letter unshaved, dirty, heavy eyed covered with mud absolutely 'done up' you would, I know, have cried. So please in future never doubt my fidelity (you know you have no reason to) and always send letters of inspiration and encouragement. Do not dwell on what I've just written, I know you did not understand and I understand you.

The news about Esme is interesting I hope he gets on alright. But he seems to me to have started too early. I must now bid you goodnight.

PS. . . . The last few days I have been cooking for the sergeants.

---

[120] 'The Somme fighting of 1916 offered the most severe test to which the divisional RAMC was put during the whole time the division was in France . . . the men were physically tired before the attack on High Wood took place. The difficulties of transport . . . were enormous. A system of bearer reliefs as was customary, was at first organised, but the number of casualties among the troops was so heavy that the men had to carry on till they dropped from exhaustion.'
The History of the 47th Division – A. H. Maude.

[121] "Those September and October days on the Somme, 1916, seen in retrospect, are to the average 'bearer' little but one black nightmare of what seemed almost futile effort and brutalising fatigue . . . neither before nor after did we have such desperately exhausting toil . . . the next year when we were getting ten times as much shelling and the joys of gas as well, no-one wished he were back 'on the Somme'."
Richard Capell, abridged from *Stretcher-Bearing on the Somme*; Papers of the 6th London Field Ambulance (Wellcome Library, London).

Sunday night

Just received your letter and also a letter from home. I'm very sorry to read about Ernest.[122] Today is Sunday. How I wish I could spend it at Twynholm with you. Surrounded as I am by such environments I ofttimes feel I need a change of atmosphere something which will invigorate the 'better man' and assist me to fight more manfully the good fight. You know what I mean, and so if you have anything likely to elevate let me have it. Everything out here seems so superficial and wicked, a little depth and spiritual comfort from you would be very much appreciated. You understand me Daisy, don't you? I had a letter from home today. I understand that Don Munro is now Flight Commander in the Royal Flying Corps.

30th November 1916

Dear Daisy,

Thanks very much for parcel and letter. The book I understand is good and the other things I think will be alright. The 'shoes' I <u>hope</u> will prove useful. I admire your business instinct but not your conception as to the size of my feet.

7th December 1916

My dear Daisy,

Thanks for your letter. So Harry is acting as your trainer is he? I guess from what you say that his criticisms are about the same as mine. You say you wish it were I aside of you, no more than I do. I'm beginning to get jealous you know. However <u>when</u> I do come home I must make up for lost time. I'm a long time coming home though aren't I. I suppose one day we shall meet for good never again to be separated. Over two years I have been in the army. It seems two hundred. But after all I've a lot to be thankful for. The book you sent me is jolly good. I am getting well on with it. Have you read it? I comprenez now why you were so eager for me to read it. When I have finished it you can send me another. Makes me homesick though when I read a book after that style or is it love sickness?

---

[122] His brother-in-law had been injured.

Do you know the night before last I had a sort of dream, and I saw you plainly standing by my little bed in the corner and I sat up and awoke to find it wasn't true. I did feel disappointed. A few days before I dreamt I waited and waited for you at your house and then somehow I missed you. How I long for this war to end so that we can again enjoy each other's companionship. However we mustn't get downhearted, must we. We shall shortly enter 1917 and the Year of Peace. I really think we haven't long to wait now and when we do reunite how we shall appreciate it after such a long and anxious absence. I must now bid you goodnight.

Sunday

I've been playing football, on a Sunday too. What do you think of me. This is not the first time either. All days seem the same to me out here. We won 11-0. Had our new togs on, red shirts and white knickers. We've got a good club now. My boots are too big. I exchanged for a smaller pair.

Christmas we are having a good turn out. Our boys have made a stage and the sculptors and artists etc have decorated it. The figures etc painted on the thing are really fine, no novice work, and it looks great. Drape curtains etc, a work of art. All the officers who visit here are shown it. I'm enraptured with it myself. I don't suppose there's another Ambulance in the BEF that has such artistic talent. I got parcels, pudding etc, thanks. Your dream amused me. I wished I'd dreamt the same. However it will come true one day, won't it. You might be interested to know leave has started but I don't expect my turn for some weeks yet. About March or April. I'm hoping the war to be over by then though. Fancy my coming home being on April 21st 1917 for good. How my heart leaps with joy at the thought.

I read some more of *The Harvester*[123] last night. It makes me want to go home and follow his example, you know. Did you hear parts of my letter read on Thursday[124]? If so what parts were read?

---

[123] *The Harvester* by Geneva Stratton-Porter. It is a story of a man building a log cabin for his wife in the Limberlost area of Indiana USA.
[124] At the Twynholm Church evening prayer meeting.

I believe I told you that the Westerns took home my letter for their wives to read.

PS. . . . Can you guess my new title for you. Something to do with *The Harvester*.[125] Got it now?

19th December 1916
My dear Daisy,

I have your letter before me now, thanks ~~awfully~~ sorry! very much. Feeling very fit just now, having returned from our baths 'all poshed up and nowhere to go' and so I thought I'd write to my er er – don't blush, my beloved. My friend opposite me says 'tell her you are sitting by a nice big fire where there's room for two'. Now for a letter. I understand you are not very well. Got a bad influenza cold. How's that? You must look after yourself you know. Now what are you going to have for an Xmas present. Do you want one? What's that? Would like two? Don't want any? Oh yes you do, and I <u>know</u> what you would like. A heavy winter coat. Good guess eh? Don't blush, you know you asked me for it. You didn't! Oh yes you did! You're rumbled! Well, you had better get one and let me know how much it costs. By the way are you busy now? I don't think I get quite so many letters. Not the one I'm answering at the moment but some of your recent ones have been very brief too. I tried today to have my photo taken but the light was too bad. Would you like another photo of myself or have you enough already?

I have read *The Harvester*, I like it very much. If you have not read it lately I think it's worth re-reading. I enjoyed it immensely. Very elevating. However when you send another book I'll have a change and come back to the Limberlost Tales again later on. Any book with a manly character in it I always appreciate. Nothing too dramatic, I get enough of that out here.

Once again Christmas is drawing close and I am separated from you. This is my second Christmas on active service and I am almost positive it will be the last. Next Christmas I shall, I feel sure, be with you. Our separation I believe is nearing its end. I can see peace dawning. It's in the air. I am eagerly watching events just now, if you

---

[125] Dream Girl.

are too you'll understand why I am so very optimistic. Did you see today a suggestion of a Peace Conference on January 15th? I hope it comes off. However, although I have had experiences galore which a year or two back I should have considered it impossible for me to stand, I have much to be thankful for. So far I have been kept safe and free from harm and my prayer is daily that I shall be further spared until the grand old days of Peace return and I come back to you. Wishing you (if not too late) a Happy Christmas.

Yours for ever

26th December 1916
My dear Daisy,

Thanks for your letters and card. The design on the front is very appropriate, it reminds me of the second card I gave you. Next Christmas I shall hand you a card personally. I'm looking forward for this year to go quickly.

I suppose you are anxious to know how I got on Christmas. I very much regret to say, that although our dinner and especially our evening concert were very fine, a dark cloud hung over us. On Christmas Eve our Ambulance had a catastrophe.[126] Our Dressing Station up the line was blown in and four of our boys were killed and six wounded.[127] Johnnie Blair had a miraculous escape. He was in the room when the shells crashed through. It was only a small place and how he escaped God alone knows. You remember young

---

[126] 'The kitchen of Railway Dugout ADS destroyed by high explosive shells. Four killed, one officer and seven other ranks injured. Reinforcements sent.' **5th LFA War Diary.**

[127] The Advanced Dressing Station at Railway Cuttings was a series of dugouts dug into the embankment beside the railway line near Zillebeke approximately a mile south-east of Ypres. A handwritten memo from the medical officer at the ADS, Captain Charles Whitehead, lists those killed as L/Cpl Walter MacFarlane, L/Cpl Arthur Smith MM, Pte George Bird and Pte John Walker. They are buried in adjacent graves in Poperinge New Military Cemetery. Those injured were Ernest J. Barnett, who suffered a spinal injury, and Leslie J. Davies, who suffered a severe compound fracture of his right arm. Both were discharged from the army a few months later. The others were Sidney C. Neale, Charles W. Restarick, Archibald V. Young, John N. Blair, and William G. Bond.

MacFarlane who came home on the bus with us from a Chelsea concert, he was killed. I cannot go into horrible details, but when you've played football with two of the 'promoted' time and time and in the greater game have been surely into the very gates of Hell and Valley of Death, you may guess how I feel. But I'm glad, yea joyful, that JB is safe. Let's drop the subject and pass on.[128]

Have you got your coat yet? Don't you think I'm good at thought reading. I'm just waiting to receive a letter telling me off. I wonder if I shall be disappointed. Ivy wrote to me a day or so ago. She isn't half a rib. I don't think I've ever laughed so much over a letter before. By the way she told me that she disagreed with you on the subject of Love. You say the love which exists between man and woman is different from love for a mother, father or sister etc. Please explain to me why, will you, and also the differences? Nice little job you've let yourself in for, or rather Ivy has.

I am very glad to hear of your lessons in music. I'm expecting great things when I come home. Don't forget the piano though. Wait

---

[128] 'I might be able to fill in a little more detail with regard to the Railroad Dugout: About a mile or so behind the trenches there was a railway overpass and since the trains were bombed out there was no rail traffic. The first aid gang to which dad belonged decided that they would set up a dressing station on the road under the rail line in a cave-like dugout. They used some of the rails to block off the ends and were busy sandbagging the roof and sides on which they devised a white cross to indicate it as a first aid station. Just after noon they saw a German observation plane pass overhead but gave little thought to it since it was acknowledged that a dressing station identified by the white cross would not be a target. At around 4pm in good British tradition they put on the kettle on the tin stove and were taking a little time-out for tea. As yet, since they were setting up the station no wounded were brought in. Dad got up to make a cup of tea when one of the other lads stepped in front of him saying, "I'll get you the hot water" and at that moment, what Dad referred to as a Howitzer 5/9 artillery shell, came through the roof and exploded. Dad was knocked out and as he regained consciousness realised that he had no feeling in his legs. As it turned out the explosion had brought down a rail from the roof and it had fallen across his legs cutting off the circulation making them numb; thankfully both his legs were OK. The chap who had stood in front of Dad took the force of the explosion and was literally blown apart.' **Letter from Dave Blair to editor.**

till the time when you can play and sing to me in <u>our</u> own home, or play while I sing, my hand resting on your shoulder. My Word! What days! Everything in the future seems bright, doesn't it? Once the war is over and then, won't we have a good time? How I long for the day of peace. So let us pray that it may come soon and that I may be spared to Come Back to Thee.

The graves of the men killed in the Railway Dugouts Advanced Dressing Station on 24th December 1916. Poperinge New Military Cemetery.
L-R – Walter MacFarlane, Arthur Smith, George Bird, John Walker

1917

1st January 1917
My dearest,

Thanks awfully for your letter, apparently my suggestion for your Xmas present was appreciated. I should very much like to see you in your new garb. And as for the hug, don't I wish I could come home and receive it. Now you have promised it, when I do come home it will be the first thing I shall want from you. Don't forget, will you now, and of course you know what must go with it. Something the Harvester longed for.[129] Got it? Now, don't forget.

I'm feeling very stiff today. I played in a hard game of football in the rain and mud. I was in my glory you may guess.

Now how about your New Year's Resolutions, made any? What are they? I <u>know</u> you have made some. Please tell me. If you haven't made any it must be because you don't need improvement. May I guess:-
1 ~~To play the piano perfectly~~
2 ~~Get married soon~~
3 - - -

Can't think of any more. I'll give up and wait for your letter. I might add that I have made ~~some~~ one. I will tell you perhaps if you tell me yours first. I have felt fed-up today, pessimistic, depressed, you know, the sort of humour you love to see me in:- want to go home and can't. Lovesick and Homesick and feel stranded. I expect I had the expression on my face which would have called forth the remark from you, 'What's the matter?' 'Nothing' 'You seem very quiet'. You know what I mean, don't you? I'm just going off to a concert by our boys and will continue when I come back. Wish you could come too.

---

[129] A kiss.

2nd January 1917

It was too late last night to write any more when I got ~~home~~ (I don't think) back. I have just received your letter telling me all about Boxing Day. And also what do you mean about writing to 12 boys. Harry asked you if you had. I don't quite comprenez. So you confess your letters are short. Well! The one before me is a nice long one so I'll let you off. As for resting. I am behind the line because I have got a sort of staff job but we have some up the line. I believe I told you in my last letter about our ill fortune up the line.

While I am writing I am trying to solve what CYMaFO means. Haven't got it yet. By the way did you solve mine, what was it? The CY I believe I've got. 'Consider Yourself' and now I'm stuck. M. What is it?

<u>1</u> Mine <u>2</u> Married <u>3</u> Mad (thanks) <u>4</u> Missing. I give up. Still can't think what MaFO means. What is it?

Re the photo, I will have it done when I get time. I've been twice and each time it has been too dark to sit. Perhaps they funk taking me and offer the above as a plausible excuse.

Thanks for the promise of another book. You say you daily yearn for peace and for me to come back and you wonder if there has been any change in our affection since I have been away. Do you think there has? And you want me to come home quickly and tell you all you want to know. What do you want to know, perhaps I can tell you in a letter. Can I? It is now tea time and I must stop. I'll finish later.

You say I do not write very long letters. My Word! I'm going to make you waste some time reading this volume. Now about leave. I expect it will be a long time before I come home again if I have to wait for leave. A friend of mine, one of our footballers and concert party, has been waiting some time to go home and get married and not even such a catastrophe as that permits him to go out of his turn. If the war has not ended by May I expect to go home on leave but I am afraid that it will not be much earlier. But of course it <u>may</u> be sooner. Anyhow, dearest, we must patiently wait. A fellow who has just come back from leave was telling me that all he can see is a Hopeless Dawn, of course he was naturally depressed coming back from leave. I can tell you dearest, it's an awful feeling coming out here again after leave. But my dawn is not hopeless nay, I can already see a faint light on the horizon; the glorious sunshine of peace is not far off. This is the Year of Victory and Peace. Next year may be the year of something else if my ambitious are realized.

The fellow here working with me has just been telling me that his sisters are earning very high salaries just now owing to war prices. Do you know that I should have thought that your firm would have almost doubled your money owing to terrific war prices. Man labour is so scarce. From what I can see Liberty's[130] are sweaters. If you really are as useful as Manley was, you would now have his salary. The argument that Liberty's is permanent is feeble. You don't want a job for life, do you? This must be the Golden Age for young women, I'm convinced of it. If Liberty's don't pay you nearly as much as Mr Manley you should demand it. If unsuccessful, keep a sharp eye open for something better and I'm confident you'll find it. I know if W&S don't give me a substantial increase when I return I shall push off. Excuse me, dearest, touching this subject, won't you but I've often thought about it and I shall be more than interested to have your reply. Nothing's lost by trying and so because *I* ask you – try.

Now this is a long letter isn't it. I expect you now wish I had cut it shorter especially the last part. Aren't I a rotter, eh? xx. I must now bid you goodbye. Wishing you a Happy New Year.

6th January 1917

Dear Daisy,

Thanks very much for your letter which I received yesterday. I also got one from home telling how you spent your Xmas. I sincerely hope Alex, Ernest and myself will swell the company next year. You won't forget to send me the book you promised me, will you. I wrote home a few days ago for W. Hardy's 'Degree'. Perhaps you can help them in the matter. We are still in the same district.

9th January 1917

Got your letter today. Thanks very much, I feel happier today now, a little nearer home, you know what I mean. And as for the

---

[130] Daisy was a clerk at Liberty's Department Store in Regent Street, London.

hug I'm going to keep you up to that. Do you honestly mean to tell me you do not know what the 'something' is which must go with it. What's a full stop in shorthand? Your new resolutions are very good. I do not think you could have had better. Now you say you want to know mine. Singularly enough your first embodies part of mine with this addition 'gratitude for the past by fuller devotion in future'. The concert I mentioned was our own. It is a very fine one. I wish you could hear it. Nothing vulgar as most concerts in France. Fit for a lady.

Thanks for the interpretation. Thanks very much. Now my enigma. If I tell you the last two words I think you can guess the rest C.Y.K. 'many times'. Shut your eyes and let your imagination loose – any sensation? No? Try again. Now getting late so I must bid you goodnight.

Will, photo of 12th January 1917

Friday 12th January 1917

I had my photo taken this afternoon. Happy now? I purposely took off my cardigan in the shop so as not to appear so big. So in a few days I will send you them.

Regarding our affection I agree with you and as for that, or rather those, things you would like to know, when I come home remind me. Now for my ambitions and that which might happen in the latter part of next year. If we have saved enough (and I do not see why by then we should not be near the £150 mark or more) and if my future is bright and I am earning a <u>good</u> salary – enough for two – er, I'll leave you to guess the rest. Don't make me blush with your reply. I must now bid you goodnight.

> *Unfortunately a letter has been lost here, there was a torn corner scrap held between two others in the pack of letters. The war diaries of both the 5th LFA and ADMS record that on 16th and 17th January 1917 the divisional laundry at Hopoutre accidentally caught fire with the drying and mending rooms burned down. 'The baths were saved by the prompt action of RAMC personnel. Bathing and sock issue uninterrupted.'*

30th January 1917
Dearest,

Today I have been handed a green envelope and so as usual I will try and enclose in it a nice long letter. You know you oft-times ask me questions which I do not like answering in an open letter and so if I sometimes reply curtly you will understand. These 'posers' I generally try to answer in a green envelope, that is of course if I can think of them, I don't usually keep any letters hanging about me for very long. In reply to your question as to what we may be doing in December 1918. I hope it will be closely connected with 21st April 1914. It all depends on how I get on, 'the heart is willing, but the money is weak'. By then I hope it will be fit. Quite a lot of our boys are going home to get married lately. Corporal J Blair is on leave just now, but I think he will return still a bachelor. How is Esme getting on? Is my brother Harry after anybody to fill up the gap Annie made?[131] I've got an idea he is. Of course I have been away nearly two years and am not acquainted much about Twynholm young folk.

So your Aunt Ada does not like my photo; neither do I. Six I had done, but I funked sending home the others, not because of the pipe, oh no! But because it was not a very good photo. As for the 'secret' I don't mind anybody knowing I smoke, only if you do tell anyone make it clear you have known all along. My people already know. In fact Dada wanted to know if he could send me any 'ammunition' for it. As for Mother's surprise, I told her when I was home on leave. I received '*Caged*'[132] thank you and am very pleased to hear you are <u>trying</u> to get me a Shorthand Magazine.

I hope you are trying just as much with the piano still. I have no love for a mandolin whatever. It might come in useful when you sit by a cradle and play a baby to sleep, but your ingratiating voice would do that better I'm sure. I mustn't poke fun at your mandolin, it's nasty of me isn't it. It's not bad really but not like the piano. Got me? No! Well you will when I come home. I do not know when I will come home on leave, but most of our old boys have gone and of course I shall have my turn before the new ones. It's just struck me. I've got a good conduct stripe. So you see I'm not such a bad boy after all, bit of a nuisance though – got to sew it on! I don't like sewing, like to earn a ½d? No! I'll make it a penny providing it keeps on for a week.

Having any cold weather your way? It's shockingly cold out here. Do you know that while I am bringing water from the well to my 'engine' it freezes on the way. Really! Everything in my little larder freezes and that is inside in the hut where I sleep. The mustard, vinegar, salt, freeze into blocks, pots and pans freeze to the floor as there's always a certain amount of dampness in the floor boards. It's too bad. I have to march about with a hammer smashing up mustard and salt. If I wash anything up it sticks to the table before I can dry it, in a matter of seconds too. My gloves froze this morning on my

---

[131] Harry's fiancée, Annie Black, had died from tuberculosis, on November 5th 1915. She was twenty-two.

[132] *Caged! The Romance of a Lunatic Asylum* – Headon Hill, London Ward Locke, 1900 – is a melodrama about a stolen diamond and a woman unjustly imprisoned in a lunatic asylum.

hands and in thawing them I khakied them.[133] Reminds me of a young lady who used to buy gloves too small for her and oft-times in church they'd split. Know her? She's a nice girl for all that. Can't write any more now, just going to bed. Xxxxxxxx

31ˢᵗ January

By the way have you sent me a bank statement for Jan. I don't quite remember it. It's interesting to watch our account growing, isn't it. I hardly spend anything on myself out here you know and now I have about £10 credit on my Pay Book. Of course I've been lucky having a cook's job, that has helped me. We have really posh dinners in the Sergeants Mess and so I have no need to buy extras and when I was in the Officers Mess the same applied. I always smoke issue tobacco and so I don't waste any on smoking. Awful miser, am I not? What is Harry doing in the BRC[134] now? Could you tell me? I should like to know.

Saturday

I went off to a town last night, or the remains of one, for my photos which I promised you, but they are not done. I believe and hope they'll turn out alright, head and shoulders. I know I have a sort of a grin on because while my chum was 'posing' for his I was playing the fool and poking fun at him and so when my turn came to sit he had his own back. Why I have not sent this before was because I was waiting for the photos so you'll excuse delay won't you.

I received your letter yesterday and today. As regards the subject of nicest girls marrying etc. Of course I agree that the fellows spot the best and marry them. As for approaching a girl 'on a basis of friendship' because of her goodness; 'friendship' if deep and true must involve love and the two concerned must of necessity be therefore lovers and lovers have an object in view – marriage. I think your comrade is mixing up friendship with flirtship. Now what are you going to tell me.

---

133 He means he made them so dirty that they matched his uniform.
134 British Red Cross.

I have some more bad news for you. Two days ago another of our boys was killed up the line and another badly wounded and awful shell shock. We are having bad luck just now. Both the unfortunate fellows were 'old boys' and chums of mine. One had been wounded once and had not long returned from England.[135] It gets me down to hear of my own chums going under. I can't write any more about it, I wish the war would end. But Dearest, thus far I have been spared and trust in God that I shall come through safely to the end. So may your prayers at home be sincere and earnest, and your works deserving of your long cherished hope, our reunion after the war.

February 1917

Dear Daisy,

Have received your letter. Merci beaucoup. I had a letter from Harry yesterday and with it he sent an extract from JT by Alex.[136] Have you seen it? If you have not, I suggest your reading it: it's very good. And as regards the vacancy, I suggest K. Black.[137] Are you of the same opinion?

By the way ask my father what the Royal London are doing in the War Loan, perhaps he can put you on something good. Re the War Loan. How about getting £50 of the 4% through the PO. If you agree, get some before you are too late. Shouldn't touch the 5%. Let me know exactly what you have done in your next letter. If, however, you have any objection, leave it alone.

---

[135] Private Horace Nicholls was killed in action on 1 February 1917. The War Diary records that the Railway Dugout ADS had suffered another direct hit at 11.40 p.m. on 31st January. Two 5.9 shells had entered Transport Farm billets, killing one man and injuring three others. Horace Nicholls had only recently returned to the unit after suffering a bullet wound to his shoulder in March 1916. He is buried in Poperinge New Military Cemetery.

[136] See Appendix Four.

[137] They are wondering if Will's brother Harry will get together with Kathleen, the sister of his late fiancée Annie.

20th February 1917
Dearest,

Received your letter today. Thanks awfully. I think you acted wisely under the circumstances re the War Loan. Perhaps it is best to leave it alone. So you are taking up theory are you. You'll be able to teach me something when I come home.

I do not know in the least what made me suggest Annie's sister. Instinct I suppose. I know he always had a fair regard for her.

I was showing my photo of you to some chums of mine. And they like them very much. They are good photos you know. I mean the last two. The one with the flowing hair, my favourite, they reckon is beautiful. Do you know every time I look at it I yearn to get home again, it makes me feel quite riotous. The photo I enclose of myself is, according to general opinion, poor so don't advertise it, tear it up when you have had a good look at it. You know my policy with poor photos, don't you. By the way this is not the photo I promised. The one I promised is awaiting mounts and is worse, so when you receive it likewise tear it up. You'll be quite busy tearing up for the next few weeks, won't you. The next one is a better class of photo than the previous rubbish.

Regarding the blouse. What sort of a thing is it. Is it like the one in the photo (with the long hair) a V-necked affair? If it is not, please alter it for my special benefit and you must put your hair one evening (for my special benefit) like it is in the photo and you can guess the rest.

The reason why I have not asked for any more books is, I have had one or two good ones lent to me; when I have finished them I will let you know. Leave has not restarted yet and so I have some time to wait. When we go behind the line again, a generous number will go a week and I shall not be long coming home. But the war may end before then. And when the war does end, won't we make up for lost time. I am longing to meet you more than ever before. It is now getting late, dearest, so I must say goodnight x.

26th February 1917
My dearest,

Once again with pen in hand and no notion of what I am going to write, so I sit on a wooden form in a little hut puffing at my pipe for thoughts. First of all about the photos I have enclosed. One I wish you to forward to Alex. Do you like it? Most of the boys seem to think it very good. I didn't when I first saw it. What do <u>you</u> think?

What do you think of this chorus? It's of a song we had at our concert. The fellow who sang it, a friend of mine, has just got married. Very appropriate. Awfully pretty tune too.

> *You know that I love you, and you love me*
> *And we both love each other you see*
> *I've got a mortgage on some happy days*
> *Now that I've got wise to your loving ways*
> *Our ideas just seem to harmonize*
> *My heart for you is nearly twice its size, dear*
> *We don't care what other folks say*
> *Don't care what they do so long as*
> *You've got me, hug me closer, dear*

Well! We are nearly at the end of February and shall, I suppose, soon be looking forward to the spring and summer. I wonder whether we shall be able to have a holiday together at the end of the summer. I wonder whether the war will be over in time. Wouldn't it be fine, ripping. My Word! However when I do come home, dearest, as I have said before, we shall be able to make up for lost time. And absence makes the heart grow fonder. Separation is the best proof of affection, it has certainly displayed the depth of our love, now hasn't it? Oh! for an evening stroll on Wimbledon Common, the Bridle Path its sweet reminiscences. Do you remember the stile, the intrusive moon, the stars, a ring, you and I. We shall appreciate each other's company more than ever before when I come home. 'I've got a mortgage on some happy days' I can assure you. How is the ring and the bracelet getting on.

I see there is a big strike on at Krupps,[138] I hope it keeps on, it would be a good way of ending the war. I want to get home now. Well, my dear, I really have no more to say and so keep smiling and never cease praying for my safe return and our reunion.

March 1917
My dearest,

I received your letter today and also one from home. So apparently you are not particularly struck with the souvenir photo. I agree with you that the lower part of the face spoils it. I like the toothache simile. Thanks. Don't forget to tear it up. So you like the hair, forehead (hem!) and eyes. As regards your hopes on the reappearance of 'side pieces'. I don't know as I shall revert to the old idea. The present arrangement is much easier to do. Just 'chuck' it back and it flops into position and there you are (lovely).

'Am I really as fat as in the photo?' Don't say 'fat'. No I'm not fat. I may be a fraction taller and a fraction broader.

Wednesday 7th March 1917
Now about this 'V' necked blouse. So you say I am not to call it a thing. So sorry! I most humbly apologize. However, apparently it is not a bad er – blouse. As far as the replica of the photograph, you say when I come home you'll have to see, and so shall I. Comprenez? I like the 'Bridal Path' referred to in your letter. Do you think it will be better than the other Bridle Path? Après la guerre there'll be some good times for us. Bust the War! I wish it would end. 'Take me back to dear Old Blighty'.[139] By the way you'll soon be 24 years of age. Do you remember what I gave you for your 16th birthday? Shall I come home and buy you something for your 24th birthday, or would you sooner get it yourself? I wonder whether I shall be home in time for your birthday. Some Hopes!

Leave has been stopped in our Division, been stopped for some weeks. However, I'm not reckoning on leave, the end of the war I'm hoping will come first. By the way, will you please in your next letter

---

[138] German armament manufacturers.
[139] *Take me back to dear old Blighty* by A. J. Mills, F. Godfrey and B. Scott, 1916.

send me a John Bull fountain pen. About 2/6 they are. The weekly paper John Bull advertises them. And also (don't laugh) ½ dozen cherry wood pipes with mouth pieces, not wholly a wooden stem. They are about 4d or 6d a piece for quite posh ones. They are not all for me and don't forget to state what they cost. Don't make a mistake and send clays. I think if I were you I'd put Harry on that, I can just imagine you tripping into a shop: 'Half a dozen cherry woods please'. 'Er, er, beg pardon?' 'Half a dozen cherry woods please.' 'Sorry miss, ain't got none. What's they for, blowing bubbles?'

Thursday

I'm somewhat 'fed up' tonight. A passing cloud I suppose. However I must not let it get me down. It is now two years since I landed in France. It seems longer. How I yearn for peace and the good old days. Do you ever sit and dream of our past, right back to the Forest Gate days on and on through lovely scenery till at length we enter the present black tunnel. Unfortunately, it's not a tunnel you can 'spoon' in. Never mind, cheero, we are going full speed ahead now, we shall soon reach the other end.

I don't know if I told you, but when Johnnie Blair came back from leave I asked him if he got married as I advised him. No, he said but I wish I had taken your advice. Fancy me advising a fellow to get married - always getting somebody into trouble.

How is the music going on. Are you really 'hot stuff' yet? My Word! I'm expecting great things from you when I come home. When you think you can beat Harry easily please let me know, perhaps you can already, can you? By the way the selection of songs you sent me the names of, which you're learning, are, I think, too much of a muchness. What's the idea of learning all Scotch stuff. I can easily guess Harry is your tutor. By the way I heard a song the other night which I've been humming ever since, the chorus runs:

> And they built a Heaven in that land
> And they called it Dixie land
> They made a summer breeze to keep the snows
> Far away from Dixie land
> They built the fairest place I know

When they built my Home Sweet Home
Nothing was forgotten in the land of cotton
From sugar to the honey combs
They took an angel from the sky and you're her heart to me
They put a heaven in her eye just as blue as blue can be
They put some fine spring chicken in the land
And taught my mommy how to use the frying pan
They made it twice as nice as Paradise
And they called it Dixie Land[140]

14th March 1917
Dearest,

Two years ago today I was at Southampton waiting to embark on the 'Viper'. At this particular moment, 6 o'clock, I think I was listening to an open-air service. We sang hymns, about 5,000 of us quite, 'Stand up for Jesus' 'Abide with Me' 'Fight the Good Fight' and 'Onward Christian Soldiers'. I shall never forget it. I was in a very pensive mood at the time and did not sing, I could only listen. I was wondering what I was going to and if I should ever come back. Since that time much has happened, very few of the Division who set sail that day are left, but thus far I have been spared and hope I shall see the end. However, I enter upon my 3rd year in a spirit of optimism. Now as regards your letter. The marriages are interesting. I hope they all turn out happy ones.

Thursday 15th March 1917
Dearest,

I'm awfully obliged for your letter, 'over parts of your letter I was very cross with you or sorry for you, I don't know which'. Ha! Ha!! 'Sorry!' For me' Pourquoi? I must really apologize for making you cross. It takes a lot to make you cross, doesn't it, so I must have committed an awful crime. Please forgive me I feel quite a fiend now - - - Forgiven me? Yes? Thank you. xx. If you find that writing additional letters would entail dropping some of your studies, carry on as usual, but dearest, if you could manage to squeeze a nice extra little

---

[140] *They called it Dixieland* by Whiting and Egan, 1916.

letter occasionally I'll - - well! What can I do. Oh I know. I'll give you an extra kiss when I come home. Is that any attraction? No? Well, I'll give you some extra <u>kisses</u> when I come home. Agreed? Regarding 'any suspicion between us' When I said 'you write to nobody else I believe', no suspicion arose in my mind whatever, I cannot possibly imagine any infidelity. I have the greatest faith in you and I can assure you that you need not think otherwise of me. Now, let's drop a silly subject.

Now referring to your former letter. I'm very very curious to know what you have an especial longing for, that which you are going to whisper in my ear when I come home. I wish you would tell me. I've got an idea, you know, it's not a sudden fancy is it? <u>May I guess?</u> You have not said definitely about the lace. Let me know won't you?

Friday 16th March 1917

I could not continue yesterday as in the evening we had a feast on to celebrate our 2nd anniversary in France, and I hope the Ambulance's last on foreign soil. So I know you will forgive me for not posting this letter before. I had a piece of wedding cake yesterday and was told I had to wish something. Can you guess my wish? Quite simple – 'I wish this wedding cake was mine'. I understand leave has reopened but the number per week is small as we are still in action. I still think the end of the war will come before my leave. However, one never knows.

I must now finish this letter as if I do not I shall never get it posted and you'll wonder why I have not written and I shall get the 'bird'.

Saturday
Dearest,
Have received your lovely long letter and am sitting up in bed writing; it is very quiet just now. I wish you were here with me. With regard to 'going for a stroll and no addresses'. No headings for addresses. Now do you comprenez?

By the way what was the last tune 'homeward bound' from Hope Hotel. And also what was the conversation about the first evening I met you from business on my leave. Why did it make you blush? I completely forget, so just tell me some of my remarks.

You mention in your letter something about a new dress for summer. By the way you mentioned it in your list of birthday presents. Do you really want one? I don't know what they would cost, if it's reasonable say £2 odd and you don't mind, how about having one for your birthday. I'm sure I don't know at all how much a costume or dress would cost now, but if you can get what you want from something near that figure get it. And regarding the lace I'll get some narrow lace for 'underclothing of smaller kinds' if you let me know how much to get.

With regard to your question 'Do you still trust and believe in me or are there moments when you doubt'. In short I have absolute faith in you. That covers all. I should be very obliged if you would let me know how Harry has upset you. Don't forget to tell me. Dearest, I don't like the way you talk of the future. Please don't strike any mournful notes. And you talk about not being qualified for a fiancée, <u>why</u>?

I am sorry to hear you are not quite so well. Look after yourself you know. If you wish to buy any expensive extras don't be afraid to ask me. <u>You are mine now, you know</u>. Always remember that. You say you sometimes dream of me. Let me know some of these dreams. My Word! I do get 'fed up' now out here sometimes. It's a rotten unnatural life. Well, it is now very late and so I must bid you goodnight.

PS. . . . Sunday. Have just been ordered 'up the line' – the trenches. I don't suppose I shall be able to write very frequently. I hope you will keep me well supplied though.

25th March 1917
Dearest,

Thanks for your letter. I wondered if you had forsaken me. I think this is the first ~~letter~~ note for a fortnight. I believe it is the longest you have kept me waiting since I came to France. Consider yourself – well! What shall I say – kissed. Next time I shall – I'd better not say, let's pass on. How are you getting on. Are you well and happy. I hope you are. I am not particularly fit myself, got a bit of a cold. I want a change, you know, ten days leave would soon put me right, don't you think so.

I got your parcel safely thanks. The pipes are very good. Which one blew the biggest bubbles? Thanks for the heather. Don't talk of

Wimbledon Common, it makes me feel lonely. 'Bust the War', I wish it would end, right now. Nine months since I saw you and two years and half of separation from you. How much longer? But I think it will end this year, I hope it's in time to have a summer holiday together. Some hopes! If however, I should get leave first you must arrange to get your summer holidays at the same time.

By the way if you were here at this present moment you would think the world was coming to an end. A continuous and heavy bombardment is on on our front about 6 miles from here. I suppose a few hundreds of guns are firing. Some life this. I can't write any more just now so I wish you Goodnight.

Monday 26th March 1917

I am feeling fairly fit again today. Hope you are too. (Excuse writing my pen is awfully scratchy). Herewith I am sending 60 frs which please change. Our account is gradually growing, we shall be rich some day, won't we.

Do you ever think of what we shall do after the war. Really I don't think I shall want to stop at Western's long. Can you really see me a foreign missionary? I should like to know your thoughts very much. Do you really think you would like to be isolated from nearly every white being in a mission field? I often plan and scheme for the future. Do you? Don't smile will you. Sometimes I imagine myself at a first class seaside resort with a really first class confectioners shop and afternoon teas etc arrangement. Quite a swanky, posh little affair you know, with a miniature boarding establishment. Temperance hotel idea you know. No dinners. Hang that. Then I imagine myself stopping at W&S and living in private. Sometimes a commercial traveller enters my head. I have some ideas in my noddle. Before I finally 'knock off' I want to ask you such a funny question. Have you ever put your lips to any of my photos? If you have, I should like to know which one, or (hem!) ones. When you tell me, I will tell you something.

31st March 1917

Thanks for your letter received yesterday. Regarding the 'Bridal Path', you say "unlike the Bridle Path the more successful it is, the more the onlookers". I've got my doubts about that. What's the idea of a crowd. I think a midnight elopement is more after my style. Something secret, you know!

2nd April 1917

Have received the pen as beautiful writing denotes. So you quite expected a 'talking to' for not writing. I'll let you off severely cautioned this time. I wish I could get hold of a few green envelopes and I would write you much more often. One cannot write with ease when one's letters are censored by one's own officer. I am writing this letter in the anticipation of a green envelope. I am glad you came out so well in your examination. Accept my heartiest congratulations on success. You say you occasionally build castles in the air which soon tumble down. What castles do you refer to? I think your remarks regarding Missions well put. I, or rather, we, shall have to settle that question sooner or later. You pass no remark about my other castles. Not worth considering, eh?

Now regarding the photographs. Why I asked was because while looking at one of your photographs (the one with the beautiful hair), I had to (you know). Nothing like the real thing though, is it? But as I have said once or twice before when I come home we can make up for lost time. How I long and yearn for that time to come. However, it is fast approaching so cheero and then. My word. By the way, do you remember once upon a time you were saving your hair for a chain for me. How is the collection getting on. I hope you haven't thrown it away. Have you?

A lot of our boys have left us for commissions and yesterday two more of my chums made application for commissions in the R.F.A. which is considerably better than the infantry. They have about six months training in England including a month's leave. Do you know I am thinking of asking J. Blair to make application with me. What do you think. This is roughly why:-

1) A change
2) A month's leave and training which might out see the war
3) A good recommendation after the war. 'Late R.F.A. Officer'.
4. More pay and useful experience.

What do you think?

Wednesday

The last few days we have had some very wintry weather, quite a bizzard – sorry blizzard. This pen writes jolly thick, it's got a tendency to run away with me. A bad workman always blames his tools. This evening is very nice, makes me wish I was home just about to go for a stroll with you. Remember our ride to Epsom, the ladder and the obliging station master, the woods (Hem!), the ride back? You know I ofttimes think of the past happy days. One of my old habits often amuses me now. How I used to make for the door after a cinema show as if I were about to catch a train and leave you about twenty yards behind. Remember! Impetuous bounder sometimes wasn't I? No not impetuous, enthusiastic sounds better, although perhaps the former is more true. The headings of addresses. My word! I did used to get fiery. I smile over it all now, nevertheless, I am still 'Will S', although when I come home I hope to abolish some of my little eccentricities. (What are you smiling for, don't you believe me?). I wonder whether I shall abolish the habit of 'sp-----g' hope not. What do you say? I'd like to come home and see if I had forgotten the habit. (Did I really hear you say 'I hope you haven't') What do you keep smiling for, if you are not careful your aunt will ask you what you are laughing at and then you'll have to tell her --- a fib.

How is this blouse of yours getting on. Is it finished yet? You know I'm looking forward to this ~~thing, arrangement~~ garment of yours. Is it an evening dress affair? I suppose when I come home I shall see. Leave opens again this week. I expect my turn will fall due about June and I hope the war to be over by then.

PS . . . Parker of Southfields has just come to us with some reinforcements.

18th April 1917

My dearest,

I am sorry I have not written before. I hope you will forgive me. Many Happy Returns of your Birthday and I sincerely trust that on your next birthday I shall have the pleasure of being with you. I don't think there is much doubt about that. So you are twenty four today (I presume you'll be reading this on the 21st), feel any older?

You are as old as I am now. I remember when you were celebrating your 16th birthday. I can picture you now, lovely long hair flowing down your back. Makes me wish I could come home now and see a real and live facsimile of my favourite photo, I wish I could come home right now. This time next year I wonder where we shall be and what doing. My Word! Some happy days are in store, aren't they. Just a few yards away from my billet a 'posh' little hut has just been built, varnished outside, it's a treat. I was imagining us living in it in some quiet retreat. It would make a ripping bungalow.

Now how about your birthday present, what you going to have? You can either wait for me to come home or if you have a particular fancy you can have it satisfied. What are you going to do. If you have a long list of things forward it to me. I suppose you don't want another winter coat or any other 'coverture'? If you would prefer anything now don't be afraid to say so, if you would prefer to wait till I come home, right oh.

Referring to the commission I haven't done anything further in the matter. I haven't definitely made up my mind either way. Do you ever read the papers? If so, you will notice that we are doing splendidly on the Western Front. On my particular section there is no push so far. However I expect to be in some severe fighting ere long. I am standing up at a table writing this and I can assure you it is not very comfortable. Thoughts are beginning to get slow and so I'm going to turn in now.

I have received your letter. Merci! Do you really consider you are old to be single. I think 30 is a good age to marry, don't you? Regarding John Bull's wager – he's daft. Do you read John Bull?

I haven't received a bank statement. You will let me have one soon, won't you. Have we reached £100 yet. I enclose 80 francs which please change and I hope to send another 80 in a fortnight's time. Have you seen this month's 'Watchword'?[141] It contains Kipling's 'If'. It's not a bad booklet you know.

I scribbled out a piece of poetry the other evening, when I find it I'll send it to you. I've lost it somewhere. I keep on changing my

---

[141] A magazine for the Defence of Bible Truth and the Advocacy of Free Church Principles.

writing, one of these times I shall be able to write, it's a long time coming though. What do you say. 'Yes' of course; you seem awfully keen on making me write. However, I score in one thing. My letters are longer than yours. That's one home, isn't it?

22nd April 1917
Dear Daisy,

Enclosed please find postal orders for £3. Thanks very much for the eggs, you must thank your aunt for me. Unfortunately they had a very rough passage and arrived very unhappy. I had a letter from Ada yesterday and was very sorry to learn that Ernest was wounded at Vimy Ridge. However, from what I can gather neither of the wounds appear serious, although I expect it will be many months before he will be fit to come out again, if at all.

Saturday 28th April 1917
My Dearest,

I expect you have by now received a registered envelope with £3. I think you are quite justified in complaining to the Postmaster about the delivery of your letters. However, the individual who opened the letter must have known the letter was not for them and if the letters go missing again let me know and somebody will sorely regret it. Even now if you can trace who had the audacity to tamper with my letter, I'll write him or her with a severe caution. Now regarding the B.H.T.C.H.N.E.L. I'll solve a part of it for you 'But H to change H name ere long'. Got it now? I like your particular fancies. What do you want a diamond ring for and what is the idea of another bracelet and silk dress indeed? Re the wedding ring for 6d. It might save me a shilling one day. When and what age do you really hope to get married? Don't blush now. Tell me honestly. I shouldn't have asked you if you had not tried to pull my leg 'about 45 – 50'; what do you mean? Now you've properly let yourself in for it, haven't you. Ha! Ha!

Perhaps you are right about the number of letters you send me being altogether longer than my few 'long' letters. But I only get few green envelopes, every letter you write as far as secrecy goes is as good as a 'g e' and you have an unlimited supply. Comprenez? By the way they have changed our numbers, mine is now 536373, please don't forget 536373.[142]

You will see I have enclosed my poetical attempt. What do you think of it? Your birthday presents are very good. What is the tea cosy for? And also the pickle fork. Might I enquire who the would-be suitor is who married last Xmas. And this 'knight' of yours. If a person followed me twice, I'm afraid they wouldn't the 3rd time.

Re our account. I never forget the 10s. I knew it was something over £70. I often think about it and look forward to the day when it will be £700 and later on £7,000. Your 3rd birthday without me and as you say the 4th and ever after with me. Something to look forward to. You can rest assured the war will end this year sooner or later. Russia won't and can't go on over, <u>if as long</u>. The Western Offensive has only begun. Do you know I often dream of you, almost every night. It proves I must think of you a good deal during the day, doesn't it?

By the way, out here I can buy real Belgian lace (order it and see it made) it's very dear, about 5 francs a yard I believe. I suppose you wouldn't like any for your birthday? Personally I'm awfully keen on lace especially on underclothes (excuse me, but you know what I mean). If you think it's too expensive and extravagant for these times say so. Of course I'm not up in these things. I don't want to waste money on frivolity, if you think it so.

I was talking about holidays last night. When the war is over have you any 'particular fancy' as to the seaside resort? My pen is running dry and I want to write home and so I must say goodbye once again, now nearly 'lights out' and I want to post this in the morning.

Wednesday 2nd May 1917
Dearest,
Today is the second of May and is really a splendid day, makes me wish I could go for a stroll with you, some hopes. When will that

---

[142] *http://www.1914-1918.net/renumbering.htm* is a useful website explaining the 1917 renumbering of the Territorial Forces.

be – this summer I hope. I suppose by now though you are quite used to being without me – don't miss me much, eh? Won't it be ripping when we can renew our old strolls. How about a few days at the Hope Hotel or some other hotel at a much nicer place. It is now practically a year since I saw you. Pity I had only just come out of hospital, I had lost half my energy. However, we had a nice time didn't we. I still think the war will be over before I get another leave.

Johnnie Blair has just 'slicked' a nice little job, cook to our A.D.M.S. (officer in charge of medical work in our Division). Hearn had it before, but he has been evacuated sick.

I have just made a bed. Two boxes and a trench board. I am going to sleep tonight in my little shanty where I keep my cooking utensils and coal. A little shed with three sides, the 4th side is open to fresh air ad lib so I shall be able to gaze into the heavens when I turn in. Does it sound inviting? When I come home I am going to live like this and save money. A good idea, eh?

Thursday 3rd May

I didn't sleep in my new bed last night, the Germans sent over gas and so we had to sleep with our helmets by us and I retreated to the hut which is canvas lined. However, tonight I'm sleeping in the open air.

I expect I shall send home a registered envelope in a day or so with a £1 or so in it. <u>By the way how are you keeping our wealth</u>? In notes, silver or gold. I hope you haven't got a collection of postal orders because they run out you know, after a time, become void. We should be close on £80. By Aug I hope to have £100. I shall gradually draw out some of my Army credit.

The fellow who helps me in the Mess (a very ignorant chap) has, owing to my influence, got a mania for sending his money home too and together with his wife's aid (he was married about 18 months ago) has saved nearly £50. Jolly good isn't it? He daily yearns for the time to come when he can leave the army and buy his little home. Just a few yards from my 'engine'[143] is a tree in which some sparrows

---

[143] The mobile cooker in the field kitchen.

are building a nest, it's quite interesting to watch the little home grow. Everybody's doing **it** now.

I am anxiously awaiting your expert criticism of my 'poem'? I hope you haven't forgotten it. Excuse my saying so, but I don't think you write me as frequently as you used to, Why? I may be wrong but I think you could write more often. If you tried you could write longer letters too. Girls write much longer letters than fellows as a rule. You write oftener than I do to you, I know. But as I have frequently said before, I am lucky to have a green envelope once a week. In the very near future I expect I shall only be able to send an occasional Field PC. One letter or note in 4 or 5 days is not much, is it. You only have me to write to, I believe. I write occasionally to Alex, Harry, Ada, Mother and Dada, very occasionally W&S and WM and RWB, and my facilities for writing are not like yours you know. I know a fellow who has had a letter every day from his fiancée since he has been in France. And I know one that hasn't. If I were home could you and would you, spare time to see me every night or every other night for a few moments. If you could, why not spend those few moments writing now that I'm away. Comprenez? That's got you, hasn't it.

Friday 4th May 1917

Have just returned from the baths feeling fit and fresh and am sitting under a tree in the evening enjoying the cool air; have just poshed my hair up which only takes a second or two now as I have no parting and no glass is required (though of course I have one). I shall adopt this style after the war. Aren't I getting vain? I am sure you'll like it better than the other style. I think somehow you'll notice a difference in me when I come home this time. I think I am broader and look a bit older (still mischievous though).

Excuse writing won't you, I'm trying to scrawl on my knee. What do you think is the general opinion as to the length of the war in England. Out here we reckon after the summer.

Thursday
My dearest,

First of all I hope you will excuse my not writing. I trust you understand my position. I have only just received a 'g e', the enclosed letter I wrote a week ago. I received your nice long and somewhat sarcastic letter yesterday. Thanks very much and in haste, standing up, I'll try and answer it. So you are getting your summer dress ready. Really I wish I could just come across and see you in your new garb. You have solved the mystery of the 8 letters. I like the way you have evaded my question re age you hope to get married. I know <u>you</u> have not fixed a day or year, but you would be singular fiancée if you had not <u>some idea</u> of the year. I remember how you used to evade my questions in days gone by. If I were home I should make you answer me properly. You say my ideal age is 30 yours 45 and then you add 'only 15 years difference'. Some 'only'. Now as to your particular fancies. Diamond ring. To wear. Go Hon! Another bracelet. To wear. Really! and *'to one of your intellect I thought it needless to say what I wanted them for'.* Thanks. I should never have expected that from you. Re the wedding ring at 1s/6d and the offer of finding me the bride to match. I don't think you would have any trouble – they'd flock in. Any rate, I'll give you 5% on the price of a ring in the event of your being successful. Is that agreed?

Re the limited time to write. As I have said before if I was to come home and ask you to come out for a walk would you say 'my time is limited?' <u>I'm surprised at the wording of this part of your letter</u>. Re the poem and The Trench Echo. Ask Harry. He is a better judge. If passable, no, if he should say 'very good' yes. Nom de plume 'WS' France.

Re the Belgian lace, it is 4 frs a metre about 2 inches (I believe) wide or thereabouts. Re the lace for your bottom drawers, sorry! drawer. If you really would like some say so. Wedding Veil. If you want a square what size? Re my passion for lace. I don't know a fellow that hasn't. It's effeminate that's why. A man loves a very effeminate woman. You say you would like to know some of the things I think about you during the day. You say you know one, 're letters'. Correct. And it's about the only one that brings a frown.

Re Ilfracombe. A good idea. I should think it a very expensive place though. Your new song is very nicely worded I like it immensely. Re your last sentence. The nicest part of your letter. Will have heaps of kisses. Thanks. I reciprocate it doubled.

Tuesday 22nd May 1917
Dear Daisy,

Thanks very much for your letter. Have just returned from a job up the line dugout building about ¼ mile from front line; we had a rather exciting time – too exciting for my liking. Tomorrow I'm on a tree planting scrounge. It's wonderful really what an elastic term 'Field Ambulance' is. At the moment of writing I'm in the cellar of a once very fine chateau. It must have been lovely here before the war, but now a veritable hell at times. It will be a grand day when national prejudice or so-called 'patriotism' becomes a folly of the past and the arbitrament of the sword is wrested of its usurpation and granted to arbitrament of reason. However I think this war will teach us a lesson. I really believe that when peace comes it will be lasting.

24th May 1917
Dear Daisy,

Have just returned from a sand-bagging job and at 3 o'clock am. I'm on dugout making in the support trenches. I received your letter this morning. So you had a good time at the Albert Hall on Saturday. I should very much have liked to have been there. I suppose Twynholm was well represented.

A few days ago I received a copy of The Watchword and I've mislaid it somewhere. Could you get another copy for me, as there is a little piece I want to cut out. Will you please get me a copy of Bacon's Essays. The Wayfarers Library publish a cheap edition. And would you also get me a small and compact encyclopaedia (something after the style of the dictionary you sent me some time ago). Some job! Hope you don't mind.

I am keeping quite well and am in fair spirits, except for a severe attack of homesickness. Could do with a dose of leave, you know: that would no doubt cure me (for a short time). Unfortunately, others are suffering from the same malady, ADMs, officers and parsons especially, and as the remedy is scarce we poor privates suffer on.

> **ALBERT HALL MEETING** *Resolutions to be moved this Saturday 19th*. *"That, in order to avert the danger of famine, this meeting calls upon the Government to prohibit the manufacture and sale of alcohol during the war and the period of demobilization, and thus save the food of millions of persons, now being destroyed by the brewers and distillers."*
> **The Spectator newspaper of 18th May 1917 (abridged).**

27th May 1917
My Peach,

Some start! I have just read a book which suggests that it is not good enough to commence a letter to the girl fiancée with 'Dearest', not romantic enough – too cold. Terms such as the above or 'My Apple Blossom' are more appreciated especially if she loves fruit. If she loves astronomy 'My Guiding Star' is better or such like. Is that so? If that is so let me know and I shall be wiser in future.

I am still up the line. I have three jobs up here, one in the trenches proper and the other two in the artillery zone. This morning I was a few yards from the front line, the sun was shining and the birds were singing. A thrush perched on a tree just near where we were building our aid post and sang so beautifully and yet the shells were flying about and any second might mean death; it seemed so wicked to fight. We have not long been on the aid post and already three martins nests are in course of erection inside it.

I expect I shall be 'up the line' for another fortnight. We get a fair amount of time off up here. As it is not exactly safe to walk about we spend most of our time in our billets, a cellar in a large chateau. I say a chateau, it was once, but now only a brick wall and debris remains. The cellar has been rebuilt and would want a lot of knocking down:- bunks are fixed up inside and it is really very comfortable. We have a fair amount of books down here and a gramophone and so you see we make the best of a bad job. I am reading a lovely book on poetry. I came across this today:-

> *Bluebells fragrant blue as the sea*
> *Ring out your secrets softly to me*
> *Tell me of far away over the sea*
> *Someone is loving and fighting for me*
> *Bluebells faded gray as the sky*
> *Whispered the message brought the reply*
> *Tell her I think of her, kiss her goodbye*
> *Spring comes again love cannot die* [144]

I asked you in a note yesterday to send me The Watchword. Why I want it is for a piece of poetry 'If' (for girls). Please read it – it's great – make a copy of it and keep it. Some parts especially note. When I get time I'm going to write a piece of poetry especially for you. But in the meantime I want you to write one for me alone. I expect you'll be done first. Agreed, dearest?

Bought any more tea cosies yet or anything else in that line? If I asked you to tell me all you have in your bottom drawer would you tell me? Yes? Let me have a list. Or is it too secret. I am rather anxious to know, you know. Well, I cannot write any more tonight. When I come home again I'll have lots and lots to tell you. After I had written you the letter I turned in and wrote my poem so I'm first. Written in bed at 11pm up the line:

<u>My Beloved</u>

Two long years have I spent from thee
My Beloved, mine own Beloved
And so lonely has it been to me

---

[144] I have been unable to conclusively identify the author of this poem. It is similar to one which appears in *Henry Williamson and the First World War* by Anne Williamson. However, it was written in his, Henry Williamson's, army notebook in pencil in late April 1917. Will is apparently quoting from a published work, so it is unclear if Henry Williamson wrote the poem or was himself quoting it from somewhere else – Ed.

My Beloved, mine own Beloved
That absence makes the heart more fonder grow
And that my love for thee is still aglow
I'll Daisy to thee one day show
My Beloved, mine own Beloved

T'was not my wish that we should thus be parted
My Beloved, mine own Beloved
Ofttimes I'm sad and broken hearted
for you Beloved, mine own Beloved
For what is life to me without thee dear
But dismal days and long nights drear
And many a time a silent tear
for you Beloved, mine own Beloved

Thou knowest Daisy why I left thee
My Beloved, mine own Beloved
T'was to try and do my duty
My Beloved, mine own Beloved
And to do the best I can
To prove to you that I'm a man
Worthy of your gentle hand
My Beloved, mine own Beloved

And soon to thee I'm coming home
My Beloved, mine own Beloved
Never again from thee to roam
My Beloved, mine own Beloved
Peace shall reign instead of strife
Thou art the sunshine of my life
And thou shall be my loving wife
My Beloved, mine own Beloved

31st May 1917
Dear Daisy,

Thank you very much for your letters. I am still up the line in a hot quarter,[145] keeping fairly fit and contented (sometimes). Sorry to hear you are not enjoying the best of health. I think you are trying to do too much. I suggest your knocking off a few of these honorary positions pro tem. Regarding the lace, when I get a chance I'll get it for you.

14th June 1917
Dear Daisy,

I am now out of the line, I expect during the next few days we shall be 'resting' – in other words trekking in the boiling sun, full pack. What a life! And the papers tell us we are beginning to beat Germans. What hopes!

15th June 1917
Dearest,

As I have a green envelope here goes for a letter. At the moment of writing I am about 8 miles behind the line in a field flopped down under a tree. Needless to tell you I was in the Push at Ypres, I expect you guessed that. I was in the line 3 weeks before and it was a rough time. I can't tell you all my experiences but suffice it to say not a day passed without some narrow escape. To be perfectly frank it was hotter than the Somme without a doubt and since we've been there we've had

---

[145] They were working with the 4th and 6th (London) Field Ambulances during the action at Messines. The War Diary of late May 1917 contains a lot of memos regarding distribution of officers and bearers around the various collecting stations and aid posts. On 29th May, Will's bearer section was detailed to clear casualties from the Spoil Bank regimental aid post. The War Diary contains several requests for more men, including a handwritten note sent at 11.10 a.m. on 7th June, from the officer in charge at Burridge Post Advanced Dressing Station: 'please send up as soon as possible remaining men. . . . 4th FA bearer division. . . . also any men from Woodcote Farm ADS who had been sent down with cases and remain there. . . . please send the bearer subdivision of the 5th LFA that are resting. . . .' The War Diary itself simply records 'June 1st–11th Active operations against Witschaete and Messines positions.'

8 killed[146] and about 20 wounded; I marvel there were not more. God alone knows why I came though all right. Many a night when you were in bed and asleep have I been in the line in a hell of shelling and many a time have I thought to myself, "Daisy little knows I'm here crouched in the darkness wondering if this night's going to be my last." It's an awful experience, words can't describe it. If the people of England could see what it's like out here Peace would be proclaimed right now.

You ought to have seen my billet. It was at a farm shelled night and day: we had about 50 casualties the moment I was there. The Dressing Station was built inside with iron cupolas and a few tons of concrete and sandbags outside, it was fairly safe. The billets were likewise and under one was a cellar with at least a foot of foul stagnant water: walls were green and raised up a few feet from the ground was a rough bedstead on which I slept. Stinking and vile yes, but how lovely it was to light up a bit of a candle and have a few moments to read feeling a sense of security after a day or night of anxiety. It was a little Heaven to me to come back there. I expect a month or two would have given me galloping consumption but what did that matter, it was my only resting place for the last fortnight and that's all I cared. If I had caught a fever down there I should have been as happy as a schoolboy (anything to get home).

I read in the papers the other day that the British Tommies at Ypres didn't want relief and asked to carry on when a new division arrived. I won't tell you what the boys said when they read it, "- - liars". To be perfectly frank as far as I knew the troops out here and surely I'm in a position to judge, there's hardly a man but what would give every penny he has and sell every mortal thing he has got to get out of it. Excuse such a gloomy letter but I'm not feeling very fit, absolutely bored and fed up.

PS. . . . Let Home know news, just off on trek.[147]

---

[146] Including his friend Ernie Austing who was killed in action on 5th June 1917. He is buried at Poperinge New Military Cemetery.

[147] On 15th they marched from Westoutre near Poperinge in Belgium to Caestre in France, a distance of about 15 miles. The packs were taken by baggage wagon. On 17th they continued to Blaringhem, another 15 miles. Frank Orchard, who had joined the 5th LFA at the beginning of March, wrote to his mother that they had arrived at 11.30 p.m. and then had a cold bath in a nearby stream.

27th June 1917
My dear Daisy,

Received spikes today, thank you very much. However I am afraid they have arrived too late. There were no Div Sports (running) instead we had a Gala in the canal.[148] I took part in the Div Team Race; the three London Ambulances were allowed one team of 8. We came second. I swam 4th leading by ½ a length, and our 7th man let us right down: we ought to have had a decisive win.

We had our usual Ambulance Sports and some new men made things very hot. Owing to sectional jealousy I decided not to win in the 100 and 220.[149] After persuasion I ran in the 220, won my heat and fell over just on the tape in the final and came second. The mile, after a most exciting race, I just won, 440 I got home easily and ran in the team. The enclosed photo was just before I reached the tape in the team. I ran last, a ¼ mile, had 20 yards to catch up on a good man and to the delight of my section I caught him up and passed him. It was a fine race I didn't expect to get home, but I was disqualified most unfairly. However, although the others got the prize there was no doubt who were the real victors. I won 40 francs. 10 I didn't take in 220, I gave it to the 3rd man as I did so well last year and 20 frs I'm putting towards a 'bust-up' in the near future in my section: so I have 10 left which will about pay for the spikes etc. Considering I had a lot of swimming to do in the way of practice and was very stiff on our sports day I was quite pleased with

---

[148] In a letter of 28th June 1917 Frank Orchard also mentions this gala, with such games as pillow fights on wagon poles over water-filled tarpaulins, obstacle and sack races as well as the swimming events. The War Diary of the 6th LFA for 26th June 1917 recorded 'Divisional water carnival and sports held in the canal at Blaringhem'. Maude records that locals came from all the villages around to watch.

[149] Will had a justified reputation as a sprinter. One evening as he was cooking the evening meal at a dressing station a little behind the lines, Will saw a runaway horse with an injured man, his feet caught in the stirrups. He took off on a diagonal course and intercepted the horse, managing to catch its bridle and stop it. A group rushed over, a sergeant took the horse and thanked him, 'well done', while the others cared for the wounded man. Will then rushed back to his kitchen fires, which were unattended.

my running. The spikes I may send home later on but the vest and knickers will come in handy. (Unless you would like me to return the knickers with some Belgian lace – Hem!)

I haven't had many nice long letters from you lately. I hope to send you home some more money soon. I've got nearly 100frs lent in the corps which I hope to receive in the next fortnight. That is why I have not sent home much recently. I have been awfully busy lately arranging sports etc, and have had no time to write but will do so soon. I was on the Div Committee (about 8 of us, all officers except myself) proper swagger committee.

Now as regards your 'especial longing' I am sure I know. Do you doubt me? Shall I tell you – To be Mrs William Stocker <u>very soon</u>. Am I right? No? To be the proud mother of a blue eyed curly headed little boy. No? To make use of your silk night dress. No? Well! All three. That's right, isn't it? Please don't blush, your aunt will want to know what you are reading. By the way, have you allowed anyone to see the 'poem' I sent you, if so, who?

You will be interested to hear that leave is going fairly strong now. We are still on trek and soon we shall return to near our recent front and man a Div Rest Station and possibly assist the 6th London F.A. in running an Advanced Dressing Station. I am now a plain bearer, but hope to soon get a 'special duty job'.

I am writing this letter under a tree, it is raining hard. When it 'packs up' I'm off to my barn. I am now about 30 miles away from the line and can hear the guns very distinctly: so perhaps you may try to imagine what it is like among them. Do you know, Daisy, I more and more day by day yearn and yearn for you. I get awfully discontented out here now, sometimes especially so. I reckon we ought to have an armistice and see if we can come to terms. I wish the people of England would realize it. I don't know what it is like at home, but out here except for a very few short spells life is a constant Hell.

However, I must not strike mournful notes, it gets one down more. Let's look forward to the day when we can sit on our own sofa and read the 'War Budget' of happenings and experiences of the past.

30th June 1917
Dear Daisy,

Have just returned from the trek. As I informed you in my last letter, we had a very good time. Exactly what we shall do here in this village about 10 miles from the line, I do not know, rumour hath it that we shall run a Div Rest Station. I am quite well and in fair spirits.[150]

Sunday 8th July 1917
My dearest,

Now regarding the lace, I might tell I have some on order now and the lady doing same said it would be a nice present for my fiancée (for her pantaloons) hence I suggested returning some (pantaloons). Are you clear upon the subject? I'm afraid I've gone too far!

So I guessed your especial longing. I shall be a happy man when it is realized. Referring to the poem. I don't quite understand you. Of course it's for you. 'THOU' is singular, surely. You say you are disappointed. Don't talk like that, please. However, I'll try and write you another verse when I have finished the letter. Still disappointed? As to leave. I believe I am about 70th on the list and at the moment 'leavites' are going about 10 or more per week, so if I am lucky I'll get home during your holidays. Wouldn't it be ripping? My Word!

I have just received another letter from you. Thank you very much. You say you feel very lonely and lovesick. So do I. Another friend of mine got married when he went home and everybody going on leave is asked the same question: 'getting married?' I saw J. Blair last night and he asked me the same question; he said if he could get another leave he would, right away. He says he would if he were I. Have you noticed how other people can judge your own private matters better than you can yourself. Can you guess my answer to the many enquiries? Here it is. I might and I might not. If I did, I should have no ceremony in the way of feast, it would be very very quiet. I should buy nothing, or very little, return to France after leave with no home only a wife and she would carry on 'as before' until after the war. And my leave would be my honeymoon. Some scheme.

---

[150] 'Field Ambulance marched to Thieushouck via Hazebrouck.' War Diary 30th June 1917.

I believe I told you we are running a Div Rest Station as well as a large hospital.[151] We have a party of 6 or 7 up the line. I am a dresser and orderly at the DRS, so I have a special duty job, not a bad one either.

I see by the papers you have had some more bomb raids on London, hope they keep well away from you. We often get raided out here when we are miles behind the line – night raids. Did I tell you that after our Gala we had an open air concert illuminated by Chinese lamps and the German airplanes (who seemed to have followed our division out of the line, no doubt well informed by Belgian spies) bombed the place just after the finish. How they got to know we were there I cannot understand, unless an odd one or two Taubes making for a Belgian or French town spotted the lanterns and guessed it was a fête. We often get a nocturnal visitor out here, you know, when we think we are well away from shell fire. They get reprisals out here though.

You might be interested to know some more of our boys are going home on leave tomorrow. Remember Sturt, he's one of them. One of the boys (who was frying bacon the night we left St Albans remember) wishes to be remembered to you. I might add he has just been honoured with a Military Medal, a Private Millson.[152] The gendarme in that photo I sent you a year or more ago. Oh! I do wish I could go home. You can't imagine what a life this is out here 28 months of it. How are you going on by now? Awfully 'fed up'? Never mind, cheeroh! I still believe the nations will come to terms very soon.

Well, goodbye for now dearest, I'm sure the future will more than repay the horrors of the past and present.

23rd July 1917

Dearest,

Thanks very much for your letter. You say you hope I haven't got the 'blues' like the card I sent you. Well! I must own I have and shall have, now until the end of the war, more or less. I am glad you have received the snapshot I sent, that was the photo I referred to. I have no other. As a matter of fact, where we at present are stationed there is a photographer's and a lot of the boys are having their photos done.

---

[151] At Westoutre.
[152] Sydney Thomas Millson.

They are not very good photos, but they do a good trade. I think the reason is that the boys coming out of the line get up to anything to break the monotony of life and so go off in groups and have their photos done in all sorts of gear. I was thinking (now don't laugh) of having mine done in a gaudy costume which I had presented to me for swimming in the London RAMC team. Hem! Swank!

Now regarding the lace. Very sorry I ruffled your dignity! You ruffled my hair once and I was cross – remember? I have ruffled your dignity, you have resented, but not cross, so you are the better tempered of the two. (What do you say? You are quite aware of that?) So am I. However, when I come home, I shall ruffle something else and I don't think you will resent or be cross. You know what I mean, don't you, no? Yes you do. 'There's many a girl gets her hair out of curl in the twi-twilight.' Now you know. Will you resent? Just let me know, will you.

I am longing very much to see you again. I haven't got the spirit of say a year ago. I had then a sort of acquired cheerfulness, but now merely a kind of 'hanging on'. Thirty months out here will knock the spirit out of any man, who really does see the line at all. It's time us 'veterans' went home. There's not more than a handful, so to speak, of men who have been in sound of the guns for that length of time. I wonder why more of the boys don't go off their heads. People at home can never realize what it is like out here in the line. It's not to be wondered that there is hardly a man in the British Army that does not give way frequently to drink and other vices. I'm writing very gloomily but there you are, it's the truth, absolutely. However, we'll pass on.

Now for something more cheerful. Some more of the boys are going home on leave tomorrow and of course my turn is gradually coming round, but I'm afraid it will be after August 27th unless peace is proclaimed beforehand. However, if we miss the nice country summer walks we shall have the bewitching fireside when the lights are low. Hope I'm not 'ruffling your dignity'. Am I? xx.

I'm glad you like my scheme for a 'War Marriage'. I personally am enraptured with it, but I hesitate. If I had carried out my scheme at the <u>beginning</u> of the war I should have been nearly £80 in pocket. Now – (don't blush), if I asked your consent to our further unity when I go home on leave would you give it? (Question 1) Now you know my entire position financially. My credit at home and my army credit (about 1/10th of my home credit). What do you think really? Don't ask anybody's opinion. (Question 2) Please let me know your thoughts exactly.

9th August 1917
Dearest,

I have been seriously considering your 'consent'. Now, in the event of our marriage what arrangements would you like? Do you suggest Twynholm? As a matter of fact I'd rather not. I'd sooner have a country chapel, spend a few days at the place and the rest at my home together. You know more about this sort of thing than I do. What do you suggest. I don't wish to hurt anybody's feelings but I should like something quiet without big parties etc, and yet at the same time I do not want you to miss any of the paraphernalia (if I may so term it) which is so looked forward to by intending brides. Now what have you to say?!

13th August 1917
Dearest,

Have received your letter. Needless to say I was sorry to hear of our misfortune.[153] It was not a small sum, on the contrary it's a heavy blow to our financial position. It's no use crying over spilt milk, but at the same time I make bold to say that the Devil himself would not have robbed me of that amount if I were taking it to a bank. If you had taken proper care of it no power on earth could have robbed you. Not because you had your bag opened, that's quite excusable, but knowing you had such an amount in it you should have paid every attention to it. I might add Daisy, that only unusual thrift and economy has enabled me to accumulate what I have. Apart from home expenditure I spend nothing. I do not wish to be harsh, that is not my intention (if you think so tear this letter up) but I fully realize the adverse circumstances which will follow the war, and I'm doing my best to cater for it. I'm afraid the present time fiancée fails miserably to see this, if they did they would make better efforts to help.

---

[153] Daisy had had her handbag 'picked' while travelling on the London Underground.

Please don't misunderstand me; when talking confidentially to you I always tell you what I think. The endeavour that you are going to make is good, but it seems to me like taking it from the left pocket and putting it in the right. If it has taken the loss of £13 to discover you can save £13 you must have been slack somehow. This is the Golden Age for women financially, for those who have brains and foresight. I hoped to have over £100 (apart from debts) by July, it's now August and I'm long way off it and I'm dissatisfied, very. I hope you won't upset yourself over the misfortune or my letter. If you do you'll be very silly. I do not feel a bit cross but frankly I <u>do</u> feel disappointed (I trust you appreciate the difference).

I note that you are feeling better. I don't like to hear that you are not well, although of course, I like you to tell me. Look after yourself for my sake. You ought not to be ill as much as you are. You shouldn't require the amount of medicine you take. Try a little more walking, strive to live more naturally, get more open air, methodize your life. Then if you are unwell you must be incurable.

Sunday 19th August 1917
Dearest,

At the moment of writing I'm quite 40 miles behind the line,[154] resting my back against some sheaves of corn basking in a beautiful sunshine. I've left my hat behind and I'm smoking. I came here for the purposes of writing you a letter. My previous correspondence is in my mind and also your last letter. First of all, you say you want forgiveness. It is granted. I think quite as much of you as ever. Are you satisfied that you are forgiven? Your misfortune (can't call it a failure or mistake) is now past history. xx. I am more than glad to hear you are quite well. Some of your latest correspondence gave me the impression you were most unwell.

As I am sitting here, in the foreground (about a mile off) is a large French town. I haven't visited it yet, but on passing through it I noticed quite a lot of English girls with WAAC[155] or something on their collars, typists and cooks I understand. All the boys make

---

[154] At the Manoir de Scadembourg, St Martin-au-Laërt.
[155] Women's Army Auxiliary Corps.

for the towns, it's such a change after the line, but unfortunately they spend their money in questionable houses and drink shops. However, one can't judge them too harshly, I know their hardships and also human nature. But at the same time it's a disgrace how some of them carry on unknowingly to their wives and fiancées.

I don't know whether I told you that I scalded my foot with a boiling dixie of tea about a fortnight ago. I am not allowed to walk about much and must not wear a boot or puttee. It's also affected my knee and ankle and so I have to sort of hop about. It's a nuisance, there's a fine stream near here and I can't go for swim. Hard luck, isn't it?

Leave is going along very slowly. I still think that it's just as likely that the war will end before my turn comes for leave. I often wonder exactly how the war will end. Wouldn't it be fine if Peace was declared so soon that my coming birthday might be spent at home with you. Well, I must now bid you goodbye it is just dark (how I wish you were with me now) and I must get back.

PS. . . . The knife fork and spoon combination I do not need now.

1st September 1917

Dear Daisy,

Thanks for your letters. I have not written before as I have been hoping to receive a green envelope. Your various questions I'll answer later on. I'm glad to hear you are enjoying your holidays.

I heard about Esme Howard from my father.[156] It's heart-breaking to hear of all the boys 'going west' one after the other. I can't seem

---

[156] 'Esme Howard was killed in action on August 5th. The news has affected the Church with profound sorrow. Nothing could have brought the War home with greater intensity than the death of one who loved his church and was loved by all its members in return. He will be missed for his happy disposition. The death of one whose life was full of promise is a sad blow. A memorial service was held at Twynholm on 26th August. The earnest sympathy of all is extended to his young wife who is expecting her first child.' **Joyful Tidings, September 1917 (abridged)**. Private Esme Howard is buried in Artillery Wood Cemetery, Belgium.

to realise that Don has gone.[157] I met him first in an 11 yds race for boys under 11, and dozens of times did we run and swim together since. Dada seems quite upset, for as you know, he almost lived at our home. However, I suppose we must expect such news in these mad times. I often doubt whether the objects for which we are fighting are worth the wholesale sacrifice of millions of human lives.

Detail from the West London Band of Hope Challenge Cup, 440 yards
The winners in 1908 and 1909 were Don Munro and Will Stocker.

9th September 1917
Dearest,

Thank you very much for your letters. First of all I wish you to excuse my not writing before. I have had no green envelope, they have been temporarily stopped. This one I had given me by a friend. Therefore I could not answer your many questions as I'm not fond of Officers Messes knowing all my private affairs which would be the case if I wrote an ordinary letter. If I had a green envelope

---

[157] 'It is with deep regret that all will hear of the death of our brother Lieut J. Donald Munro, AIF, RFC who was killed on Tuesday 17th whilst flying at Upavon, Wiltshire. Some five years ago he left for Australia but not before he had endeared himself to us all. As a schoolboy all London knew of his prowess as a sportsman and athlete.' **Joyful Tidings, August 1917 (abridged)**. Will's brother Harry had been best man at Don's wedding and now found himself helping with the funeral arrangements. 2nd Lt J. Donald S. Munro RFC is buried in North Sheen Cemetery in the London borough of Richmond.

issued to me every day you would get a letter every day. You seem to think I abhor letter writing, I do detest writing some people, I love corresponding with a select few – my people and my future – x. Do you understand me? Yes? Righto! I'm forgiven.

You made enquiries about my foot. It is now quite well. Apparently you were under the impression I had to go away with it. Such is not the case. Our division moved right out of action for a few days and I accompanied them. We are now back again on the same front running a hospital[158] a half dozen miles or more behind the line and supplying a few bearers for the line to help the other London Ambulances who are (for a change) running the line. We get heavily bombed here during the night. I suppose you have heard that the Germans are making a mark of hospitals.

I have not heard from Curtis yet. When you return you might phone and ask if he got my letter. I hope he hasn't misconstrued my remark about 'Fleet Street'. It didn't strike me as a knock until you mentioned it. Now I fail to see how it caps him. You might see what you can do for me. You also said that you would report upon Harry's criticisms and also my people's. I take great interest how the firm and a person like Harry take my infrequent 'summaries'. I'd like you to let me know <u>more precisely</u> my people's remarks. I'm only anxiously awaiting Curtis' reply because of what the firm thinks. I should also like to know if you have heard from the firm with my remittance.

Now for the answers to the questions you have been patiently awaiting. First of all my leave is a long way off, unless the authorities are more generous with 'Permissions'. I'm well over 50 on the list and recently only 2 or 3 a week have been granted. Of course we <u>may</u> make a sudden onslaught like last leave and go 20 a week. <u>**2**</u> I don't think special leave is now granted for marriage. Of course I could try when I have thoroughly made up my mind. <u>**3**</u> Your Hatfield scheme. I thought of it, but I hardly like the two witness idea. Why not an early morning ceremony say at 7 o'clock, my people come and there would not be a lot of unnecessary fuss and publicity. <u>**4**</u> I think white is the colour you'd better wear, any other colour seems

---

[158] Casualty Clearing Station at Remy Siding near Lijssenthoeck.

inappropriate. Don't you think so? **5** I'm not out for too cold and Puritan plain a ceremony. **6** If the matter goes farther I of course will, or you can (hem!) acquaint my people of my intentions.

Now what about the following, shall I say, encumbrances. **1** What about the firm. I wonder how they'll take it. **2** <u>Exactly</u> how to arrange matters after the War. **3** Is it wise to proceed during the war, or would it be better policy to wait and see what W&S are going to do after the war. I'm not clear exactly what course I shall adopt after the war. Perhaps you will let me know what you think upon these things. We have nothing to lose during the war, it's directly after. I wish I could talk to you personally and perhaps you would see more clearly what I mean. However as that is not possible you will have to endeavour to elucidate my ambiguous correspondence.

12th September 1917
My Dearest,

I have received a green envelope and so here goes for a real letter. I suppose you have received my letter answering your interesting questions and I await your reply keenly. Little did I think nine years ago when I wrote my first love letter to you that nine years after we should be contemplating – well! What shall I call it – yes! I'll be frank 'Marriage'. I don't suppose our people ever thought then that the little seed of companionship then sown would one day blossom to such great friendship.

> *When I was a boy at school*
> *I fell in love with a sweet young thing*
> *I gave her a brass engagement ring*
> *We swore to each other that we'd be true*
> *When I was a boy at school*
> *I loved that thing for a month or two*
> *Then I regretted it, as most fellows do*
> *But that didn't matter she fell off too*
> *When I was a boy at school*[159]

---

[159] *When I was a Boy at School* by H. E. Brenton and Mel B. Spurr, 1895.

I've often thought that our people expected the above to be our career. But they made a profound blunder, didn't they? Sometimes when I turn in at night my thoughts travel back right to the very first time I spoke to you and all that has since happened. I think of walks at Forest Gate, Bow Road Station. When I kept my appointments so well, I was always so punctual, wasn't I? I can picture you now with your long flowing hair and a light grey overcoat. My first visit to your aunt (when I was shy) Remember? When I met you at Mansion House Station once coming home from school. Do you remember the following Christmas when you first came to my house. And I'll never forget my parents' words, remarks, after the party. After referring to one or two guests and passing pleasantries, they came to you and said, they were my Mother's words 'I think Daisy is a very nice girl indeed.' I felt much flattered, I know. And I well remember the first time I sat with you in chapel (I don't mean the occasional visits during a certain lantern service) on the left of the hall not far from the clock, remember? I refer to the Sunday morning when your grandmother called me down, or rather beckoned me.

And can you recall the particular evening when I tore up some of your 'classics' outside Whiteleys and you were cross. Remember? I do. And (don't smile) do you ever remember making an appointment for 6 o'clock one morning to meet me outside your house. It must have been in the winter months for it was pitch dark. Do you recall my return at 8 o'clock when you 'didn't like coming down to open the door'. You say you don't remember it – I do! Can you recall the first time I held your arm, I believe it was Whitsun Monday, and the first time I put my arm around your waist (it was to save your getting wet I think) – it was really the fault of the umbrella I think – it was too small. Do you remember the first time you asked me to kiss you – No – nor do I, but can you recall the first kiss I gave you – I guess you haven't forgotten that. And so on and on. I often revel in the happy past and my heart throbs with excitement when I endeavour to imagine the happy future.

I had a dream last night – such a nice dream, I dreamed of you. I do nearly every night but last night was really great. I was with you and was trying (don't blush) to kiss you and just at the critical moment I woke almost, and I felt so disappointed and so I fell asleep and dreamed again exactly the same thing and you were trying to frustrate my endeavours and I felt myself awaking up and just as I was coming to I made another brave attempt and succeeded beautifully and as I lay half awake and half asleep I felt so happy for it seemed so very – like a vision.

Although I sometimes think you think otherwise, I think about you all day and whenever I lay down to sleep, among other things I pray for our reunion and future. I ofttimes think that our coming together was a Divinely arranged plan, for our early meeting and long unbroken friendship is not common in these days, is it? I received a letter from you today – I was expecting a bunch as it was my birthday yesterday and I had none then, better luck tomorrow perhaps – and in your letter you ask about leave. Well! Before the alphabet starts about 2/3rds of the Ambulance are to go – it was only the last unlucky ones who had no excuse for their first leave who went alphabetically and two more only have to go now before we commence alphabetically. As I'm an 'S' I'm one of the last to go, but I expect I shall be home about November perhaps Xmas unless we come to an agreement beforehand with Germany.

Sunday

I have a letter of yours I received today in answer to my long letter. Thanks for the letter. It was intended for a quiet 'ticking off', wasn't it? First of all the Field Card request. I don't like field cards, they don't convey anything much and when I sent one once before it gave you all an impression I was in the trenches when I was not. However I'll do my best to write more open letters.

Now for the answer, what <u>s u r p r i s e d</u> you so? I refer to what I said about witnesses. When I said I did not like the two witness idea I thought you meant a ceremony with only two witnesses without <u>our</u> people, a sort of elopement wedding. Our people I should certainly have said when I referred to an early morning turn-out. By 'publicity' I meant spectators.

The piece enclosed you can have back. I don't think you have any reason to talk about my being 'unfair' and 'one sided'. You (above all people) ought to know I always strive in all things to be fair. I don't like these insinuations of selfishness. If in error I should be selfish I should thank you if you kindly told me, but there is no need to be 'nasty' over it. I know it's a feminine failing to constantly hint and insinuate how badly they are done by. But you've no need to develop that spirit. You know what I mean.

The objections you answer quite well. But before we make our minds up definitely I should like you to tell me exactly how you suggest proceeding directly after the war when I'm dismissed. Where do you suggest living during the time we are fixing up a home?

PS. . . . One 'objection' (excuse term). You see after the war I can't fancy myself staying long at W&S. I can't see clearly what I'm going to do. That I shall get on well whatever I do I'm convinced, but I cannot quite define my course.

22nd September 1917

Dearest,

At the moment of writing I am sitting on a fallen tree. It is evening and a beautiful autumnal sunset gives me ample light to commence a letter to you. A few yards off is the little village at which we are staying for a day or two before further continuing our trek. I have been working all day cooking for the sergeants and I have selected this little quiet spot in order that I may write in comfort and solitude during the respite before supper.

First of all I am going to talk about the subject which I know you're thinking about now day and night. 'Our Partnership'. (Some way of putting it). I am still considering the matter, and one arrangement connected therewith until now I have forgotten. Perhaps you have thought of it and have not cared to broach the matter. In the event of the 'union' coming off, what do you suggest as regards my Mother's allowance?[160]

1. Carry on as before
2. A slight deduction.

When we have finally settled everything I shall write her, but I should like to know your thoughts. It is not a delicate subject like it

---

[160] Western & Son paid Will £1 a week throughout the war; he gave half to his mother.

might be in some homes. For Mother knows I would be the last to do her any injustice and vice versa. But of course whatever I do the question arises. Comprenez? It's not a difficult matter, but of course it must crop up.

Another question I should like to ask is how much is the whole affair going to cost counting everything (combined expenses). Could you give me a list of expenses? You are more learned in these matters than I. Be perfectly frank. Have you hinted to anyone at my home or yours yet? I do not mind, but I'm curious. I had a letter from Ivy and she subscribed her letter thus:- 'Your future sister in law'.

What about invitations?

28th September 1917
Dearest,

I am now I suppose 100 miles from the Ypres front, I am glad to say.[161] I expect you have read or are reading about the systematic pushes which take place up there just like the Somme a year ago. This front is now very quiet comparatively, but as a rule the 47th soon cause trouble. I am living in a village about half a dozen miles from the line which only a few months ago was in German hands so you can guess it's in a fine condition, it's seen a few thousands of shells.

You will be pleased to hear leave is continuing and going very strong and if it keeps on at the present rate I shall be home in 5 weeks time. Leave, I understand, is going to proceed quickly, about 15 a fortnight; I think it's official, at any rate seven go tomorrow. So we shall have to buck up if we are going to unite. I should say I shall have to be quick. There is one thing which troubles me. Although we shall have a fair amount by us when Peace comes I don't exactly fancy going back on my old screw[162] as a married man. Of course W&S may increase it, but they may not and if they shouldn't what then? I don't like the idea of being married on my original salary (I

---

[161] 'Anzin. Will came home from here to get married. Swam in nearby La Scarpe River in November.' – Daisy's notebook.
[162] Salary.

should want a **Big** increase). What have you to say? That is about the only reason which prevents my absolute willingness.

PS. . . . I am sorry I cannot yet give you a definite answer regarding marriage, but when I have your replies I shall be in a position to decide.

10th October 1917

My dear Daisy,

Today I was speaking to a friend of mine who was married while on leave and I asked him about the licence. He said his wife obtained one from an address in Ludgate Hill and paid 12/6. He ridiculed the idea of paying £2.10.0, he is writing home and will let me know the address.

<u>I have now decided to marry you when on leave, so you can make the necessary preparations. (Don't blush)</u>.

Now listen to my suggestions. First of all I hope to be home in five weeks perhaps four and I want the ceremony the day after, if possible, I shall inform my people by this post. I suppose I haven't to ask your people's sanction, have I? I should much prefer the slender repast at my Home unless you are particularly keen on having it at yours. The ceremony I suggest early as possible in the morning. I suggest a taxi for conveyance. Was this your idea?

In your list of expenses you suggest a hat – I prefer a veil much, unless you have some objection. I don't want anything slipshod. I want things not gaudy but really nice. I do not suggest going away unless you have some scheme. Could we not live at my home in the present Drawing Room while I am on leave. We could have a nice fire in the evening and make ourselves homely and yet at the same time my people could have me too while on Honeymoon (hem!).

Of course you will have the time off from business while on leave. You say no bridesmaids and no reception. I presume you mean no wedding breakfast by Reception. I do not know what your scheme is, but if you decide on Wedding Breakfast (and I do not see why not) it means presents you know. If you do suggest bridesmaids I propose Elsie and my cousin Ethel. If we have a Breakfast it does not imply that every one of our multitudinous relatives will appear. I presume only a small select assembly. Now please carry on as you think best and I suppose it would not be out of place to (if you think fit) have Mother's opinion on some things.

With regard to WM's remarks you are so anxious to hear. He said that he was well informed of my doings out here 'by a very close friend of mine who by her <u>quiet and conscientious work at Twynholm was winning many friends</u>.

PS. . . . The enclosed letter you had better post. (Go Hon Really). I shall be glad to hear how your people take the NEWS and how you fare at my house the first appearance you make there after they receive the letter.

> *A bright letter from Bert Coward who has had the pleasure of seeing Will Stocker, who, by the way, is expecting to get leave shortly – a very important leave too, if rumour is reliable!*
>
> *We regret to state that Ernest Owens has again been seriously wounded and is at present lying in hospital at Newton Abbot, Devon. His right arm has been amputated at the elbow and one foot and his side are also badly injured. The latest reports from him tell of good progress which will doubtless be hastened by the presence of his wife and little boy, who have gone to be by his side.*
> **Joyful Tidings, October 1917**

October 1917

Dearest,

Thanks for your letters. You are making me quite excited. I am very sorry to hear about Ernest[163] and the scheme you thought of struck me as excellent and so carry on.

Re Bridesmaids. Perhaps your idea is best. **1** You say 'cousins', who do you refer to? Dorie and who else besides Irene. Don't have a Sunday School Treat. **2** They will require explicit instructions as to what to do.

---

[163] Will's brother-in-law.

As to Uncles Henry and Bob. Why query them, has Mother some slight objection? If so, don't invite them. If not please yourself. The offer of Mother is fine and I am writing her in this envelope. I am glad your people are taking such an interest in the Breakfast. <u>1)</u> Which room will it be held in? <u>2)</u> Needless to say there will be no intoxicants whatever. I mean perhaps some of your Father's people may expect just a little. I'll write Harry for Best Man. Of course we shall have photographs. Just you and I. Did you mean a group. I'm glad you are having a veil.

You talk of something	Old
..	New
..	Borrowed
..	Blue

May I ask what is the 'something blue'?

Well it is now quite late and I have had a lot of writing to do tonight. I believe I have answered your questions.

Sunday
Dear Daisy,

Thank you for your letters. I suppose you are fairly busy just now. I hope to go on leave about three weeks or a month from now, so you have a fair amount of time in front of you still. I have not written Harry yet, but will do so when I get a green envelope. I had a letter from Home today and was glad to hear Ernest is progressing. I'm very much looking forward to seeing him when I come Home.

I suppose you handed Kershaw my letter. I think some of my remarks will stagger him. I'm anticipating a voluminous exhortation to cheerfulness in his next epistle. Did I tell you I had a letter from Curtis in which he informed me that Maddison has been badly gassed at Vimy and may lose his sight.

Monday November 1917
Dearest,

I have just received a green envelope and so here goes for a nice long <u>personal</u> letter. I always consider that a censored envelope cannot contain a real personal letter. It certainly can't be a 'love letter' inside it. Since you received my last green envelope you have asked me many questions some of which I may have forgotten, and so if I miss anything please ask again. First of all I was waiting for a green envelope in order to write Harry. I hardly liked writing him in an open letter. However, I do not think the delay matters. My Mother's idea of a party is a very good one and I propose adopting it, and below suggest a few guests. Please add or query, or cross out any you wish.

> Harry
> Ivy (and your sister or sisters if you like)
> Your Aunt Ada (if you like)
> Clara (and her sisters if you think fit)[164]
> Charlie Perry and wife (if you like)
> Harry's girl favourite (whoever she may be)
> I think my cousins Eva and Steven should come (don't you?)
> And what about Uncle Harry's boys (Ask Mother)
> Perhaps you have a girl friend you would like to come
> Uncle Henry's daughters should be represented

These are merely suggestions which please alter according to wish. But if possible try to get a representative of relations in every case besides friends. We don't want to hurt any particular family's feelings. Comprenez? I should like a list of those Mother and yourself propose. Before I go any farther I better tell you when to expect me home. All being well Monday or Tuesday week. I am 15th on the list – 12 go every Sunday. About 10 days from the time of receiving this letter. Isn't it great. I suppose you know I'm getting 14 days not 10. I'm beginning to feel very excited. I shall want to keep hugging and kissing you I know (don't blush). I am so looking forward to the time we shall have together Day and <u>Night</u> (Hush!). You say you hope the castles you are building in your imagination will be realised. I think they'll be much finer actually than you

---

[164] Clara, Agnes and Mary, daughters of Gavin Melville, treasurer at Twynholm Church. Clara was married to William Munro, Don's brother.

can imagine. I'm sure of it. Fancy being together all the time and married. My Word! Surely a foretaste of Heaven. You, no longer Miss Palmer but Mrs W Stocker, my wife. Great! All in ten days time. How Lovely! xxx.

Now for business (as you call it). I believe I have to buy presents for the bridesmaids. If that is so, how would a souvenir brooch something after the style I bought Mother for her birthday. Would that be good enough? It would certainly be appropriate. And I believe I have to buy you something too. What would you like? I suppose I'm allowed to ask you. Please tell me what I have to buy. A ring, 3¾d. By the way I shall have to buy one or two articles of clothing. I hope to get fixed up before I come away with top clothing: articles I don't get I shall have to buy. So far I must buy gloves, pyjama suits, handkerchiefs, slippers. Have we got a weekend case for Devon? I'm still wondering what the something blue is. Is it a waistband? Oh no, that would look out of place on a wedding dress. That's puzzling me you know.

You asked me in one of your letters whether I should have one or many if I had my time over again. I think I can honestly say one. For although (being natural) I adore the opposite sex, while I, Wm Stocker, shall always possess a certain amount of stability which would centre my affections on one and not many, providing the right one came along. But as the right one has come along <u>without a doubt</u> all my love is on that one bestowed. Comprenez? Well I must now bid you goodbye. Keep yourself fit and well so that when I come home you'll be in the peak of condition.

PS. . . . I should be home about the 19th of the month.[165]

---

[165] When Will was home on leave to get married, one of his uncles, understandably bitter after the loss of his own son on the Somme in 1916, told Will that it was alright for <u>him</u> just being a stretcher bearer, a nice safe occupation. Will was furious. How come there were places where only the stretcher bearers would go, at times walking up to their knees, hips, or waists in mud, trying to carry back what was left of the living? How come when the Germans made a push on two sides, Will and his comrades had been caught in a v-shaped wedge but were still going out with the stretchers? How come very often entire stretcher parties did not come back? Will eventually forgave, but never forgot, the remark.

Will and Daisy on their wedding day 22nd November 1917

Twynholm Hall Wedding Miss D E Palmer & Private W Stocker

On Thursday last week, 22nd November, at Twynholm Hall Fulham Cross (Church of Christ), the marriage took place of Private W Stocker RAMC, on leave from the Front, to Miss Daisy Edith Palmer. Private Stocker is the second son of Mr & Mrs Stocker, well known workers of the church, and the bride is the eldest daughter of Mr & Mrs Arthur Palmer also of Fulham, and the grand-daughter of the late Mr & Mrs James Maisey who were well-known residents of Walham. The bridegroom joined the RAMC 5th (London) Field Ambulance three years ago and has spent nearly all that period in France. Before then he was an active worker at Twynholm and rendered excellent service as secretary of the Sunday School and other branches of the Church's operations. The bride has endeared herself by her devoted life and labours.

The bride wore a white silk crepe dress trimmed with real Brussels lace (the gift of the bridegroom) while the beautiful veil was kindly lent by friends of her mother. She carried a shower bouquet, and was given away by her father, Mr Arthur Palmer. The little bridesmaids were Miss Doreen Malivoire and Miss Dorothy Williams (cousins of the bride) and Miss Irene Stocker (sister of the bridegroom). Their dresses of pink crepe with white silk trimming were very pretty, and each wore a silver brooch, the gift of the bridegroom, who brought them from France. The best man was Mr Stephen Holgate (cousin of the bridegroom) who performed his duty admirably. Mr R Wilson Black JP performed the ceremony, assisted by Mr W Mander BA.

Both the young couple are extremely popular, and in spite of the fact that no public announcement was made the Sunday previous owing to uncertainty as to date, Private Stocker being then in France, a large company assembled, including Mr H Lamb, choir leader. A guard of honour was furnished by the 16th Fulham Troop of Baden-Powell Scouts, of which the bridegroom's brother, Mr Harry Stocker, is the scoutmaster. He is on active service and so could not be present, but Mr W Mander BA acted as deputy. A reception was held at the residence of the bride's parents. The honeymoon is being spent at Torquay.

The Fulham Chronicle, Friday November 30th 1917 (abridged)

Folkestone
30th November 1917
Dearest,

Have arrived at the above and met all the boys. In fair spirits, don't know why, but I am. Keep your spirits up and the next time I meet you we shan't again separate. Something seems to tell me I shall see you again early in the New Year. Now don't forget: Keep Smiling and 'pray for me before the Great White Throne till I come back to Thee'.

Somewhere in France
1st December 1917
My Dear Wife,

Just a short note this time, I am quite well. The ambulance have had a rough time and we've had heavy casualties, by far the worst time we've had and that's saying something; just behind the line at the moment. Although it may be awkward to write you during the present time often, Please write me long and lengthy. I'll write you explicitly later. Cheeroh.
PS. . . . If you have news of Harry I shall be very pleased to hear.

> *Throughout November 30th and the following days our field ambulances carried out the evacuation of the wounded under great difficulties, but with unwearying gallantry and marked success . . . In the first twenty-four hours of the battle 4700 casualties passed through the dressing stations . . . the wounded had to be evacuated through an area heavily shelled with both high explosive and gas shells . . . three of the ambulance drivers were killed[166] and the RAMC suffered 70 casualties. Rarely have the medical services of the Division been called to face more sudden, difficult, and perilous tasks.*
> **History of the 47th (London) Division**

---

[166] Alfred Grice, John Griffin and Leonard Standring.

Sunday 2nd December 1917
My dear Wife,

Thanks for your letter received yesterday. I was very glad to hear about Harry, I've been anxiously waiting for news.[167] Please write and congratulate him on my behalf and tell him I shall be pleased to have a letter from him. Send me when convenient, a decent torch lamp, small but good one which lends itself to refilling. I don't think it would be a bad idea if in the parcel containing lamp etc you sent me a small piece of Wedding Cake. I have only had one small piece you know. Can I?

France
10th December 1917
Dearest,

I have a green envelope and so here goes for a letter. I am back with the Ambulance just behind the hottest front out here and My Word it was 'some' return. It took us about four days tramping, and hanging about railway platforms for hours at stretch in the cold frosty nights, sleeping anywhere, perished to the bone, existing on coffee and biscuits feeling about as miserable as Lucifer when he was thrust from Heaven to Hell. However, I was lucky getting leave when I did, I just missed our worst stunt. Our boys had an awful time and the ambulance alone had 40 casualties. I had my suspicions of the 'Bells of Rejoicing' rung whilst I was in England.[168] What a Hellish hypocrisy! The Boys are extremely dejected. And the papers say they 'have a quiet calm smile of confidence and satisfaction'.

Before I go any further please send me a fair sized bottle of camphorated oil for my feet.

Tuesday

---

[167] Will's elder brother Harry had finally been permitted to enlist in a non-combatant role. He joined the Non Combat Corps on 15th November 1917.

[168] On 23rd November 1917, for the first time since the war started, church bells had rung out across the country at the early news of a spectacular British Victory at the Battle of Cambrai. But the optimism was short-lived as the Germans forced the Allies back.

You might also in the parcel with the electric lamp and oil send me some mixed spice. I was sorry to hear about the watch. However, sans ne faire rien. Perhaps you might try somewhere else. I herewith enclose your Marriage Certificate. I have seen about the forms and am paying 6d a day. Under the new scheme the army pays the usual 6d deducted, so you should receive 2/6 extra allowance per week making 19/6, I believe. Comprenez? I expect you will be notified from the War Office in due course. I made the allowance payable at Fulham Cross Post Office. I hope that office is convenient, if not I suppose you could have it transferred to Hammersmith.

Although I may find it awkward to write to you every day I'll do my best to write often and please write to me very often, every day if you can, it's my only ray of sunshine in this God-forsaken hole. I expect you found it hard to pack up our room. I experienced great difficulty in keeping my spirits up and ofttimes a peculiar feeling enveloped me as if I were about to break down. But we mustn't pine, you know, but ever keep before us the happy day that's coming when our cruel separation comes to an end.

18th December 1917
My dear Wife,

Thanks for your letters; am writing you in a green envelope tonight. I'm in a snow-bound camp miles away from anywhere[169] – most inconvenient show we've ever struck – perishing cold.

Wednesday 19th December 1917
Dearest,

At the moment of writing I am some 20 odd miles behind the line just to the rear of territory won nearly 12 months ago. The last time I was here, or rather on the territory just in front, we were up to our waists in mud and in getting here I came on a motor lorry and it was very instructive to see the country and the very spot where we used to dread going now so quiet and funereal. I'm writing an article on the 'Old Somme Battlefield' which I'll do when I have time.

---

[169] Bouzincourt.

Well, Christmas is here once again and I am still separated from you. God grant that I be with you next! But although separated from you I have some consolation in knowing that we are now ONE. Our first Christmas together we were just boy and girl 16 and 15 respectively and now husband and wife. What a change ten years have made! What a lot has happened! I wonder what another ten years will bring forth! I anticipate great things AND little ones too. Don't you? I anticipate such a happy future you know. What a Heaven after this! One day I'll tell you all about everything and you'll be surprised to hear what the boys go through, I am sure the people can't know how things really are. Well, I must now bid you goodnight.

Thursday 20th December 1917

It is evening again and in the short respite before supper I'll write a little more. Still very cold here. When I wake in the morning my boots are stiff and frozen and my socks are frozen too as the snow wets my feet during the day.[170] My towel is also frozen, as a matter of fact my boots stick to the floor. I have never felt the cold so much before. Fuel is very scarce too and so our fires are not great. Well! I mustn't burden you with our trials.

This morning when I got up at 6 our 'great pianist' was playing on a portable organ some Christmas carols and a peculiar feeling came over me, that sensation I felt when going home on leave and also after I left you, a feeling of emotion which a woman may give vent to, but not a man. Ofttimes, you know, when I lay and think of all the times I've had and the horrors I've seen I could break down. I hoped that last Christmas would be my last on foreign service. I think this will be. Peace must come next year.

Just recently I've been humming and thinking of a favourite carol of mine which we had on the Saturday at your home.

But with the woes and sin and strife

---

[170] John Blair's son Jim recalls that his father told them that he drew his tot of rum, but rather than drink it (he was a teetotaller), he poured it into his boots. He told them it prevented trench foot, which was so prevalent in the soggy rain-soaked muck of the trenches.

> *The world has suffered long*
> *Beneath the angel strain have rolled*
> *Two thousand years of wrong*
> *And man, at war with man, hears not*
> *The love song which they bring*
> <u>*Oh! Hush the noise, ye men of strife*</u>
> <u>*And hear the angels sing*</u>[171]

I wish they would.

But I keep ever before me our future. I can imagine such blissful times after the war, no tiffs, no quarrels, one long life of harmony, not even a difference of opinion. Quite possible with us isn't it, nay, highly probable. My Word! I shall appreciate it after this lot.

You ask me whether the boys received the cake. Yes they did and appreciated it too. Johnnie Blair has put up the banns and is hoping to go home on his third leave in a few weeks. He said he didn't think I would be first. By the way the boys somehow got hold of the account of the wedding in the local paper and they don't forget to remind me either and they keep on asking: 'How is Mrs Stocker getting on?' and when they see me black with smoke, which is very frequent in this camp as I'm smoked out in my cookhouse, they say 'I don't think SHE would like to see you now', to which I reply, 'I know SHE would like to have the chance'. That's right isn't it? Well, I must now see about supper. xxx.

PS. . . . Don't forget to send Alex a piece of cake and a photo.

27th December 1917

> As I saw The Somme while on a walking
> tour in France August 1914
> A golden sun and glist'ning corn
> Melodious song birds greet the morn
> The drone of bees in busy mood
> Echoes from all in gratitude
> The scent of coffee from the inn

---

[171] *It Came Upon a Midnight Clear*, Edmund Sears, 1849.

Romp the children in merry din
Melodious chimes from distant bells
Enhance all with magic spells
The peasant whistles at his toil
A lovely world and bounteous soil.

As I saw The Somme as a stretcher-bearer in Autumn 1916
The scene is dark there's endless rain
And men lie groaning racked with pain
The stench of corpses strewn around
And barbed wire ornaments the ground
The food is rough does not suffice
The men are filthy plagued with lice
Tired troops sink deep into the mire
And blasted craters screen the fire
A starshell rising overhead
Illuminates the hideous dead.

As I saw The Somme on Christmas Day 1917
when the armies had moved on.
The drama changes there is no sound
Deep snow has fallen on the ground
Black crows fly round in funereal flight
There's not a soldier left in sight
A mystic peace now covers all
As fluttering snowflakes gently fall
Ten thousand crosses meet the eye
Row after row till earth meets sky
Sons, brothers, lovers, friend and foe
Lie altogether beneath the snow
The warrior sleeps, war has passed
Deep silence reigns supreme at last.

William Stocker

1918

1st January
Dearest,

Thanks for your voluminous correspondence. You say you hope I do not think it slackness on your part keeping me without a letter. I think I'm the slacker, but I do my best I can assure you. I am so glad to hear you are getting on so well with Church work, it quite buoys me up – stimulates my original desire after the war. If Harry went in wholly for Church work he would be a great help to me. I had a nice letter from Harry and he mentioned the parcel. I am pleased you sent it.

The little paragraph about the socks I liked. I realised that evening you liked the job. It was a very homely night wasn't it. I couldn't help smiling about the letters you referred to breaking Saturday night appointments for chess matches.[172] However, you've forgiven me, I know. With all my funny ways I've always loved you much. I'm sorry now I spoke so nastily to you on that Sunday about your music. It's the worst of being too enthusiastic isn't it. But you'll forgive me, won't you, dear? When I come Home I do not see the slightest reason why we should ever make discords. Do you? I'm certain it's quite possible to live without discordant notes. It may not be for some folk but for us I'm certain it is, for 'our ideas just seem to harmonize' in all things don't they.

Rather good that friend of yours passing a remark about the locket. I'm glad you liked the poem. My Word! What a splendid time is in store for us. Some of the boys out here who are newly married have very poor ideas of marriage – so low and selfish. They have a wife as one would buy a motor bicycle for pleasure and sensation – nothing deep at all. I'm afraid some of these war unions

---

[172] Will loved chess all his life. Frank Orchard writing to his mother in a letter of 30th Sept 1917 says that *'one of our chaps has a pocket chess set, and I have got quite enthusiastic over it'*. It may have been Will as the family still has a tiny, battered, wooden 'peg' chess set which belonged to him.

will be very unhappy ones eventually. By the way before I forget, how about Steve's Best Man present. I am too far away from towns to get anything so you had better get something and explain the delay. What about a good book, say a theological one? He belongs to a Bible Class.

PS. . . . The Guards drank the health of the 47th on Christmas Day out of respect for the way in which we stood our ground by them at Cambrai when others retreated. And Haig has sent us a special message of highest praise.

Somewhere in Hell
8th January 1918
Dearest,

Since last I wrote you we have moved back to the place where I met the Ambulance after leave a few miles from the line.[173] We were bombed the first night! Just finished supper, been mucking about with damp twigs to boil up some coffee, succeeded after a struggle – army are hard up for fuel. Well! How are you getting on, dear? I hope you haven't been as fed up as I have been lately. Life recently has been 'blooming awful' (excuse the expression – it's as strong as I can put it). If I hadn't got such good times to look forward to I'd stick it no longer – life's a misery absolutely. I can't write any more now I'm turning in – might feel a little less downhearted tomorrow.

Feel a little more cheerful today. We had a few bombs dropped around us during the night. As we sleep in huts if one came too near we'd have 'some hopes'. Had a snow storm today, snow is very deep in places, in fact I believe one could be enveloped in it and disappear.

---

[173] Léchelle.

Will and Daisy with their bridesmaids
Irene Stocker (far left), Doreen Malivoire and Dorothy Williams

Received your photos. I certainly like them now. One individual remarked after seeing the proof: 'Wait till you have family like that.' I simply replied 'wait!' But we want <u>some</u> boys don't we? (Don't blush!). One of the photographs I'm going to give to Shrosberry[174] – so I think you had better get a few more.

By the way I have been very lucky with green envelopes and so I hope to write you more frequently. I've had still more 'red tape' enquiries about the allowance and so as to expedite matters I've knocked off the extra allotment. I've also made enquiries and been informed that I can transmit my credit to your account which I'll do. Well I must now see about supper. I have finished for tonight 9.30 – up again at 6.30. We are having some terrific weather – arctic absolutely. I must now bid you goodbye, dearest. Wish I could come home just for a night. However, next best thing I hope to dream of you.

---

[174] Harold William Shrosbree, nicknamed 'Shoes'.

11th January 1918

Dearest,

I'm glad to hear you are practising on Aunt Ada in the cooking line – is she insured? (I mustn't try and be funny otherwise I might fall in it). By the way, dear, the suggestion of yours for 'après la guerre' is a good one and may be put into practise when I come home. I was glad to hear Western's want me back. I think the epistles I've sent them have done some good, don't you? Before I forget, please send me another dictionary and if you can get it a pocket encyclopaedia and also by the same post a book on 'Doctrine of the Bible' or some such title; a small book which we had in the Speakers Training Class a few years ago. I think it's by Power. We used to have two of them in our bookcase.

You say that thoughts of such a sublime future make you nearly mad with the present, so also it does me and perhaps more so as the extremes are greater than yours. Please again excuse such a short letter in a green envelope. I've been writing a long time and must now pack up.

More or less 17th January 1918

Dearest,

First of all business – Hem! Regarding your allowance: I am not making any extra allotment as I originally arranged, and so the army authorities are correct. My fault. I thought I had acquainted you of my latest intentions. I altered my mind to save intricacy which would delay payment. I have today however, got our accountant, Charlie Wreford,[175] to make out a form remitting to you the credit in my book £5 (five pounds). And when I accumulate some more I'll remit again. It amounts to the same, doesn't it? I shall be interested to have the balance sheet. We ought to soon be getting along again.

Regarding Steve. Your suggestion is a good one. POWER I suggest. Please proceed. Get a nice covered one, if possible so as to look presentable.

---

[175] Barton St John Wreford, known as 'Charlie'.

other words postcard size). I want one to carry about out here and of course you'll send Alex one and it would be inconvenient if he had one as big as a poster to cart about. So you have distributed some of the prints. You say my sister Ada is jealous. I don't quite 'comprener'. Do you mean that she has been given one and said nothing? Or do you mean that she has not had one yet and is jealous because she has had to wait? You also say 'I know she does not like me in the least. I do not mind in the least <u>it's mutual</u>.' I don't like to hear that. I hope you are mistaken. What makes you think so. Why 'jealous?' Over what? However, I know full well that she is a peculiar tempered girl, but I do not like to hear you say the dislike is mutual. 'There's too much animosity in the world already, God knows, without harbouring petty dislikes. Love thine enemies and cherish the hearts that hate thee'. If you like I'll write her. There must be some big difference of opinion between you and I for I LOVE them all very much. And you most of all. How do you account for that? You're a STOCKER now, you know, so be careful xx.

Well! I feel much happier today, although yesterday there was a gloom over the Ambulance as we had some killed and wounded up the line.[176] Nearly all of them very recent additions and so of course it did not affect the boys as much as it would have done if they had been 'old boys'. Your letter was a good tonic you know, made me feel happier after I had read it. Telling me about all the nice things which await me, makes me feel very dissatisfied when I turn in on the floor at night. My Word! Fancy sleeping in a nice warm bed after the war every night with a lovely wife delicately clad cuddling and nestling close beside me. How I yearn for Peace! What a thrilling anticipation? Some lovely times are before us, aren't there? I want to ask you a question. What three things do you look forward to most after the war? Tell me frankly now and then <u>perhaps</u> I'll tell you mine.

Have you shown anybody at your firm our photos. I expect you have and what did they say. What does your friend Hestia think of them? Do you know I sometimes think that on leave I <u>at times</u>

---

[176] Maurice Cornwell and Sidney Foxon, killed in action 18th January 1918. They are buried in Rocquiny-Equancourt British Cemetery, France.

As to your exam. I presume it's theory. And you know best what to go in for. I said I would not touch on that subject again. However, as you have asked my opinion, I give it. Your music bill is a big one apparently, apart from money previously spent. That is so, isn't it? Are you deriving adequate benefit from all your expense and time. You told me whilst on leave, it might be remunerative in days to come. I doubt it – it <u>might</u> – and thus your expense and time will be compensated financially. Nevertheless, if not repaid financially for all your labour and expense knowledge is always worth acquiring PROVIDING the <u>time</u> and <u>money</u> spent on accumulating such knowledge could not have been put to better use. Seeing that I asked you to specialise in music not for mercenary ends, but primarily for <u>our</u> mutual recreation in days to come I think all the time and money you are spending on theory is <u>sadly lacking in its main object</u>.

I hope you do not misunderstand me. I've tried to be straight, frank and explicit. I might add – that if you have fully satisfied yourself that you cannot learn PRACTICAL music – righto carry on with the THEORY in the hope of teaching me something which will facilitate our <u>mutual recreation when I come home</u> (the primary object). But if you think you can get on with the practical go right out for it and only spend time and money on the necessary theory that will aid you in accomplishing that end. I hope, dearest, I haven't written too strongly on the matter. If it savours of harshness, I know you will excuse me; put it down to my awkwardness in expressing my thoughts. xx. So much for music.

You say I 'must be in love' because I put 1 Dec 1918, so I am. Referring to Bert's remark you ask me if I have 'a happy smile'. I'll ask you – Have I? My pencil has nearly gone west so excuse such awful scribble. Pouring in torrents tonight. My Word! We are having some weather! The cutting I'll answer in 'my next'.

Sunday 20th January 1918
Dearest,
Thanks very much for your letter. Referring to the photographs, I thought it would be much better if Alex's and my active service photo was mounted on a smaller card so as to fit a letter case (in

appeared, shall I say, a little cold towards you. I think you thought so at times. If you did, wait till I come home and I'll dispel that. As a matter of fact I felt at times overtired. I expect (if my imagination is correct) it was that my weary war worn frame was overpowered by sudden felicity. 'Compris'. As soon as we got into bed I wanted to go to sleep instead of having a nice spoon and talk. I tell you this in case you misjudged me.

Well, dearest, I must now say goodbye. With LOVE and its usual and inseparable accompaniments.

Sunday 27th January 1918
Dearest,

I haven't heard from you for a long time. I'm told they are censoring letters from Home now. I suppose they don't want the boys to know the truth as to the state of things at Home. However, write as openly as usual. By the way dear, I hope you did not object to my remarks on music. I trust you took it in the spirit in which it was given.

I'm anxiously awaiting these photographs, or one of them rather, of yourself in your wedding garb. I hope they do you justice. Comprenez!

Monday
I'm sorry to hear that you have difficulty in obtaining necessary food. What's the matter with rice and oatmeal? Not a luxurious dish I know, but nourishing and sustaining, pearl barley, barley, beans etc. If I were in your position I think I should go in for stuff which, although not extremely inviting, I know would do me most good. I had a ripping dream the other night. I dreamt I was back with you – it seemed so real too, it was like returning from leave when I woke up. However, there's a good time coming.

5th February 1918
My dearest,

Have just received your letter as you will see by the paper. I shall be very glad when I get a pad as where we are now is barren territory miles from civilisation.[177] We have a few canteens but they sell only

---

[177] Léchelle.

tin stuff etc, and cannot get pads. The only villages about here are ruins, only a few bricks standing, so you see we are in a very desolate show.

So you've had some nasty raids, and so have we, every fine night. The other night they dropped three very close only a few yards from our camp. It's jolly rotten lying under a tin roof and hearing the show going west around you. Imagine yourself laying in bed at 65 Crabtree Lane and Petley Road and Niton Street[178] being blown 'sky high' and all we can do is lay and wait and they keep coming and going. However it's nothing to the line in a stunt. And of course out here you are not your own boss, you can't do what you like.

John Blair and Grace Hanley, Liverpool 23rd January 1918 (photo courtesy of Dave Blair)

Well! Now for something a little more cheerful. Johnnie Blair came back today and had a fine time. He is sitting just in front of me writing: he has just been made a sergeant, being senior corporal: so I cook for him – rather singular isn't it – with an ace of luck I would

---

[178] About 120 metres away.

have now been in his position. I spoilt my chances of promotion when I went into the officer's mess for two years. However, I've got (as jobs go) a good job. I've got my own little cookhouse and am independent, my own boss as sergeant's cook, I am well treated. I only see the line in 'stunts'. I've always got plenty to do which makes time pass; it's a set job and suits me well till the end of the war. So to be perfectly frank it suits me better than promotion.

You ask me what three things to do I look forward to most. First of all PEACE, but that being granted.

1 Our first baby
2 When we get our home arranged, a haven of Peace, Happiness and Rest
3 Excuse my saying this. To bestow upon you the fullness of Love and Passion and its accompaniments. Do you comprenez. I yearn to have you in my arms again. If you could come to me right now I would squeeze and hug you and kiss you. However, I must not 'run away with myself' but after 3 years of this life one's emotions and passions grow very strong, and isolated from all good influences and mixed up with men at their worst, one has difficulty in exercising self government.

I was pleased to hear about the wedding present. My Word! We are getting on aren't we? I'm glad to hear that you are preparing for my return in the way of night apparel. I am very fond of fancy underwear (I ought not to say so but I am) extremely so – one of my weaknesses. Now you know what to do. By the way did you know or rather had you already discovered my weakness about mentioned? I should like to know.

So you have bought a piano stool. That's right. If you see anything <u>very</u> useful and <u>very</u> good and <u>very</u> cheap get it.

You asked me about the wedding ring. Do I consider it is looked upon by bridegrooms as feminine vanity? Yes – more or less. I've heard all sorts of theories attributed to it. Something about being a circle and having no end as symbolic of the love which exists between giver and receiver. I can't think of other ideas I've heard relating to it. Tell me. X

Sunday 10th February 1918
My dear Wife,

Thank you very much for the parcel containing books and wedding cake, pad and pencil. You remark upon the girl on the frontispiece. Well, I must admit she looks rather nice, especially considering that I have not seen a girl since I came back from leave. Where we are, we are miles from civilisation. I wish you had sent a big, I mean thick, pad. I admire your business instinct in buying a second hand copy of Bacon's Essays.

As regards <u>our</u> Wedding Cake, I received the other quite safely. I am still anxiously awaiting the arrival of this special photograph of yours. By the way you have still to send a wedding photo for Johnnie Blair. I presume you have given Uncle Henry and Arthur a print – you haven't told me yet if you have distributed all the photographs.

Edie's remark about your night attire made me smile – a good job I wasn't there when she said it or I would have blushed – have you ever seen me blush? I don't think I do blush now I come to consider it. May I be so inquisitive as to ask why the apparel in question should be so thin? Please suffice my curiosity. I know how you are going to evade my question by saying "to please you (me) when you come home". But don't you like it too – why? And is this said garb thinner than the one you had on our honeymoon?

I have just been looking through my pocket case at my collection of photos and I feel after looking at yours like the little boy gazing in a shop window at some fancy tarts – so near and yet so far sort of feeling – it arouses my appetite not to eat but to <u>spoon</u> – fancy spooning with one's wife – rather unusual – but we are unusual people.

You might be interested to know that leave is going along very rapidly and 'last July' men are going again now. A more generous grant of leave is given now and I think, unless the war ends before and without being too optimistic, I should be home again in June. I am about 90th on the list owing to the number who left us during the Cambrai 'stunt'. I was this on the list last August so you see I am not so very far off. I was told today I should go in three months.

I see by the papers that Ukraine, southern Russia, has signed Peace – it's a move in the right direction. I'm anxiously watching events this month as PEACE seems to me only hanging in the balance. I wish the people of England would make greater efforts, <u>hang</u> Alsace Lorraine, which seems the chief barrier.

Tuesday

I heard from Mother today and she informs me that Ernest is home – jolly good isn't it.[179] I expect you'll be round to see him and don't forget to remember me to him. I have been extremely home & lovesick the last few days. I'm always so more or less, but particularly recently. Tomorrow is the 13th. My prognostication is nearly due. I wonder. However, we must trust in Providence. Surely the war must soon end now. This letter is too frivolous to start now writing about deeper things, but before I close might I remind you of my request regarding prayer 'till I come back to Thee'.

13th February 1918

I see by today's paper that the whole of Russia has 'packed up'. I personally am glad to see it as I think it's the forerunner of a General Peace. Rumania will be next and then Austria, I think.

Saturday 23rd February 1918

My Dearest,

Thanks ~~awfully~~ – sorry, mustn't say that may I – for the letter photograph etc. Everything will suit A1 – thanks. I'm sorry to hear about your own photograph – I was so looking forward to it.

Re the 'flimsy question'. You're an artful bounder, you know the way you have evaded my question, however, I think I comprenez. You don't like saying "Yes". Isn't that so, now? By the way, in reply to one of your recent letters regarding my indifference to 'pretty things' when on leave. I'm sorry you've got such an impression, but I can assure you, dearest, it's entirely wrong. Especially wearing apparel. And although I may not have mentioned it at the time, there was not much you wore that passed my eye not forgetting the something

---

[179] Ernest Owens is expecting to come to Roehampton House very shortly. He will be fitted with an artificial arm and will then, presumably, be discharged. Ernest will face life with a severe handicap, but the splendid courage hitherto shown will help him to triumph and win success. **Joyful Tidings, February 1918.**

blue. It would be lovely to have another honeymoon in the glorious month of June. My word! What thoughts.

I'm glad to hear that you have been honoured to sing at Kentish Town. You know, that when I was home on leave I expected to have been deluged with songs and music from you, but you seemed not to have the desire and to be perfectly frank I missed having a good sing myself owing to Harry's absence and I even feel now that the last leave was lacking compared with the first in that particular direction. By the way a gramophone is playing in the mess now – it's great – a violin, harp and flute trio.

I love music passionately and I expect you'll be pleased for me to tell you that *Robin Adair* which you sang to my accompaniment, I liked very much indeed and I hum nearly every day thinking of you. But you never suggested your singing to me until I was on the last days of my leave. You asked me a little while ago what songs should you buy to practise for me to sing. *Absent* (you have), *Songs of Araby, Shipmates of Mine*. And if you can, learn to sing to your own accompaniment.

Re our account. Are you including in it your separation allowance? I think you should for what is yours is mine and what's mine is yours – your joys are my joys, your sorrows are mine and all that life has in store for us shall be shared and mutually met. I should very much like to see the BS. Well! I must now bid you goodbye with love and every good wish and kisses which will accumulate until I come back.

Sunday February 1918

My dearest,

First of all you say it is 'too great an offence to ask forgiveness'. If you have burnt both the letters, as I asked, the matter can be, nay, will be forgiven and forgotten, as far as mortal can forgive and forget. You also ask me to be harsh and cruel, not kind. I don't think I've ever been harsh to you, and I couldn't be cruel if I tried to, and as 'Love is Kind' I can't, therefore help being the last, although you forbid it. I think, if you'll permit me to say so, you sometimes query the depth of my affection. You know I like you but you occasionally doubt whether I LOVE you, I think it's due to my independent spirit.

The worst part is I can't disillusion your mind, you must do that yourself. I know too that you ofttimes attribute actions of mine to indifference, when it has not been the case. Might I ask you to please in future, not let others influence your ideas on such matters. I can guess whose remark it was contained in the PS about 'forgetting or worse still not recognising I had a wife': it was your aunt's. I wondered when I read the PS what you said in reply, whether you agreed. If such a thing is said again kindly but firmly rebuke her or anybody else.

I cannot say any more now but that I'm now going to let the matter drop and hope we shall be dearer to each other than ever before and not allow the harmony again be broken.

Monday
Dearest,

I expect by now you have received the much desired letter and so I hope you are happy again. If you've got your doubts look in the looking glass and see if you really look happy and don't leave it until you are sure.

Regarding Steve's book if you cannot get it – alright, but if you can think of any good substitute get it and I'll concoct a letter to make it good. I would also like you to get me a pipe, a nice once bent, a mount and a good one. Now see what you can do. I hope you don't mind, dear, it's an unusual article for a lady to buy.

This evening I've been to the Orderly Room to see about the remittance. After much ado about nothing I find I'm £9 in credit and I'm arranging to send to you about £5 possibly more. Every little helps towards our little home, doesn't it? My Word! There's a good time coming. How's the watch going on – keeping good time? Do you always wear it? And do you always wear the engagement ring, the little chap with the diamonds in it, or the chaste one? Do you remember some time ago I asked you to save your hair combings for a chain for me. Are you still doing it? I should very much like a hair chain made from your hair for civil life.

By the way when Willie II or Daisy II arrives which photo of your locket are you going to turn out? Ha! Ha!

Sunday March 1918

My Dearest,

It is Sunday evening and as I have an hour to spare and a green envelope. I notice in the paper today that you have had another raid in the SW. If you find, dear, that they worry you, you should move, if possible outside the London area.

Well! How's the trousseau getting on? I'm unusually interested in its growth. I wish I could slip home occasionally and stay the night, don't you. Ah! but think of the time when I shall stay with you always. My Word! What ecstasy! It makes me so impatient and rebellious though now. However, there's a good time coming so we must keep smiling.

Do you know I dream of you nearly every night now. I suppose it's because I think of you so much during the day. But there's always something funny about the dream, you seem so near and yet so far. I often imagine the future and I can only see felicity so I'm sure there's a good time coming, aren't you? I sometimes try to fathom the meaning of all this awful bloodshed and suffering, but it's beyond me. I wish all concerned would make greater efforts for Peace. Well, dear, I must now get supper ready and I'll continue afterwards.

Monday

I was too late to continue last night so I'll carry on now. I received your letter today and photograph. Merci bien. I am glad you sent one on to Alex. I'm looking forward to the nice letter as promised tomorrow and a pipe. By the way, you'll soon have to let me know what you want for your birthday: make a list of things. What about a fortnight with me or much better – now what could be better? My return home safe and sound for good? Unfortunately, I cannot give you these things – wish I could.

I was thinking a little while ago about a Sunday School excursion to Horsenden Hill when you were ~~flouncing~~ strolling about with your loose long hair flowing down your back. Lovely! I have still got some of it in my pocket case. Once upon a time you were going to write me a poem. I don't think I ever received it. Did I? Well! I must now prepare supper – busy man you see.

Tuesday 12th March 1918
Dearest,

Thanks very much for your letters. I was interested in the BS and what with a remittance of £8 and our allowances, we should reach a century in a few weeks.

I have not lost my luminous watch yet – I broke the glass a few days after my return, but I have a dust case over it and so it's quite all right. Oh! The main spring broke and a chum put in another spring from a broken watch and it's now 'in perfect order'.

My Word! It's dark, I can hardly see – must get a light. I was very glad to hear that I was wrong in my assumption as to who made that uncalled for remark. I thought it was your aunt as she spends most of the time with you and is at times inclined to be impetuous. However, I am glad I was wrong.

Rather funny your finding that £1 note in my pocket. I get some queer accumulations in my trouser pockets. I've just put my hand in my pocket and this is its contents:- a comb, a bachelor button, a piece of string, a halfpenny and a letter from you – some conglomeration – like a schoolkid.

I suppose by now you are getting quite used to your name. I expect you are still Miss Palmer at business. Don't your sisters ever tease you and call you Mrs Stocker instead of Daisy? I often lay awake at night quietly chatting to Johnnie Blair about our honeymoons. He is always very frank with me, we get on champion together no squabbles like the Hatfield days when 'two of a trade disagreed'. Did I tell you that Charlie Wreford had an accident and fell over in the dark and broke his glasses and has lost an eye owing to pieces of glass entering in it. Hard lines isn't it? Old 'Bully' known to you as Ernest Bull is very queer at the moment. There are constant rumours of moving and we are practising certain movements in the event of a German smash. We expect one soon, but I think if he tries it on the British front he'll 'catch a cold'.

Saturday March 1918
Dearest,

I don't know whether it's my imagination or no, but you seem to be very slack with your letters to me, I think within the last fortnight

I've two notes – if you've sent more I have not received them and I suppose one day you'll send me the pipe I asked for. Surely you pass sufficient tobacconists going to and from business to have sent one before. If you are really too busy to send the many things I ask, please say so and I'll get my Mother to send them. I should also be glad if you will send my spikes (running) out to me; they may be useful. Only please write more often – it's about my only ray of sunshine in this Hell upon Earth existence, that's as dismal as it is damnable.

Sunday 17th March 1918

I feel in a better mood today, but, I nevertheless think you should write oftener. I've been extremely busy the last few days with feasts celebrating our 3rd anniversary. We have not moved up the line yet and may not at present if the Germans abandon their offensive. Three years ago I sailed for France. I thought I was only going away for a few weeks or a month or two. My Word! If I could have seen all I've been though I should have gone mad. But I've a lot to be thankful for – we both have. I've been lead wonderfully – marvellously, although I must admit at times I feel very impatient and rebellious and get bad tempered (especially when letters are infrequent). Poor old Johnnie Sergeant Blair doesn't half get 'fed up' at times too. It's a trying and demoralising existence is this, it's not to be wondered few fellows keep straight.

I see by today's paper there is more Peace Talk – I do so wish it would fructify. I'd give every possession in the world of mine (except you, of course) for PEACE, shirt and all and start life again. I don't feel like writing any more tonight so I'll pack up.

Yours well fed up

18th March 1918

Dearest,

I'm going up the line tomorrow to a, once upon a time, village[180] – it's a pretty hot shop. There we shall establish an advanced Headquarters; so tomorrow I shall be in a dugout, I suppose, of some

---

[180] 'Metz-en-Couture near a little church by the cross roads.' – Daisy's notebook.

sort. I don't think it's for long. However, cheeroh, I've had much worse. I've just written you a few times. I've received the pipe, it's fine, very good indeed – thank you. I'll write you again tomorrow or the next day.
PS. . . . Shut your eyes and imagine xxxxx. WITH LOVE

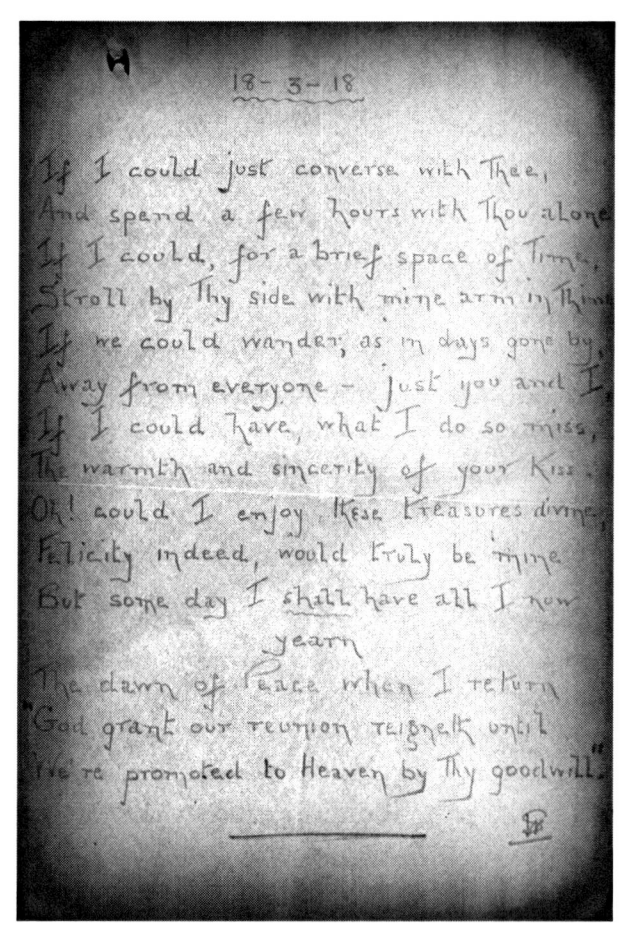

If I could just converse with Thee
And spend a few hours with Thee alone
If I could, for a brief space of time
Stroll by Thy side with mine arm in Thine
If we could wander as in days gone by
Away from everyone – just you and I
If I could have, what I do so miss
The warmth and sincerity of your kiss
Oh! could I enjoy these treasures divine

Felicity indeed, would truly be mine
But some day I <u>shall</u> have all I now yearn
The dawn of Peace when I return
God grant our reunion reigneth until
We're promoted to Heaven by Thy goodwill.

WS

'The night of March 20th–21st was quiet . . . The world, however, woke up at 4.15am on the 21st to excessive noise of shells and guns'
History of the 47th (London) Division

No 2 Canadian General Hospital
Friday 22nd March

Dearest, Excuse writing, written laying on my back. You can see by the above address, that I'm at a base hospital somewhere on the coast.[181] I'm hoping on going to England in a day or so. It was not long before I was wounded up the line.[182] We were having a rough time of it and had several casualties. I was just about to bring in some wounded in a murderous barrage and a shell fell among us. I had a lucky escape – I thought it was all up. Some of the boys caught it very badly.[183] I got blown down and had a part of my left heel and boot blown off. Had a rough time getting down out of the line. The train was shelled loading up and for many miles behind the line. I was on thorns, badly shaken up. But I'm very happy now. Sister thinks I shall go to Blighty. I'm nicely fixed up with a sort of cage round my foot and I don't suppose I shall be able to get up for many weeks: I had some sock and shrapnel taken out of my foot this morning. I'm lucky to get away so early in the 'stunt'. All the patients

---

[181] Le Tréport.

[182] March 21st Battle commenced, heavy shelling around advanced HQ, RAMC casualties – 2 officers and 5 other ranks. **War Diary.**

[183] Charles Double died of wounds on 24th March 1918; he is buried at Étaples Military Cemetery. Victor Saunders died of wounds in August 1918; he is buried in the Devizes Road Cemetery in Salisbury, England. Also injured were Pte Charles Riggall, Captain Charles Gozney, and Lt-Col John MacMillan.

reckon I've got a 'dead cert blighty' and my next door neighbour says he'd give £20 for my chance. I told you there was a good time coming – it's come.
PS. . . . Let Mother know.

> 'Among the first casualties of the new offensive we have just learned that Will Stocker has been admitted to the 2nd Canadian General Hospital in France. He writes cheerfully despite the fact that part of his foot has been blown away. We trust that we may see him in England before long.'
> **Joyful Tidings April 1918.**

<u>Not</u> Somewhere in France
Ward 18, Ontario Hospital, Orpington, Kent
3rd April 1918
Dearest,

Thanks very much for your letter and the box of matches. I'm looking forward to next Sunday already: it seems so near. I have just been X-rayed and they took me to the room on a wheeled chair – it was a bit awkward sitting with my foot but not so bad as I expected and so I reckon by next Sunday I shall be able to sit in it quite comfortably and you can take me out. It's just struck me – it will be great won't it if I am allowed up – what do you say? You can wheel me away from everybody to some sequestered spot and we ~ it will be fine, won't it.

You must let me know how you get on at your new berth. By the way don't forget my apples, will you dear. Thanks very much for the eggs. I had one today – it was really fine. You must let me know what you want for your birthday. You want something I know. Would you like a dress or hat or material. How about material for 'flimsy' wear? Shoes, silk stockings – What! Brooch, ring – hem, fur, gloves, boot laces, boot polish, boot brush, toothpaste, toothpick, comb, hair pins, hat pins, 'something blue'? Would you like something for our HOME, picture cord, tin tacks? Let me know what you want. By the way I found a piece of poetry in this pad – bit of your composition?

Thursday 4th April 1918
Dearest,

It's a fortnight ago today since I was wounded. My Word! Can't a lot happen in two weeks? Sometimes I go over the scene which brought me here in my mind, and I feel so grateful that I came through so well. I have been X-rayed and I think all is well. The orderly assisting the sister yesterday said 'I don't think he'll ever see France again' and she replied 'Oh no'. I should think whatever happens I will be given a job in a home hospital, owing to my long service in France.

Just had my foot dressed by that nice sister. It discharged more today, but it is getting on well. She has just said again: 'You'll have no fear of seeing France again.' This little diagram will show you better where I'm hit. The part shaded, all the muscles & nerves, tendons etc have gone: this part ## is therefore numbed comprener? I'm looking forward soon to some weekend passes. My Word! What times we shall have.

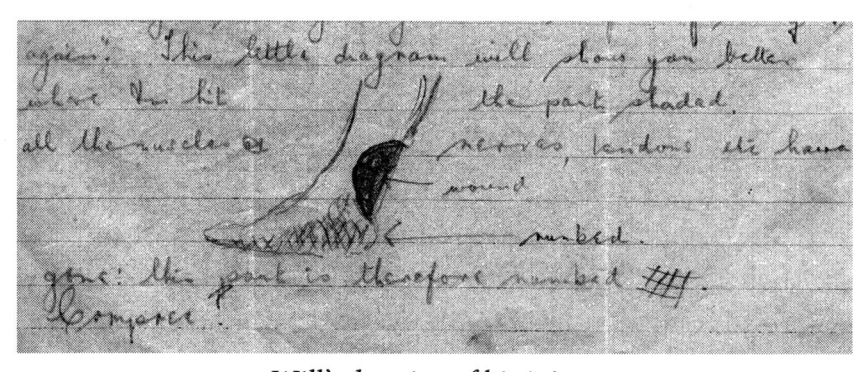

Will's drawing of his injury

Ward 15, Ontario Hospital, Orpington, Kent
Monday 8th April 1918
Dearest,

I have just written four letters, am I not industrious for a poor sick and feeble bed patient? I very much enjoyed your visit on Sunday and I am already looking forward to next Sunday and when you come I should like you to bring another book and you can take the two I have back. I am very much looking forward to the time when we can go out together for a nice walk. What about a nice stroll over Wimbledon Common over by Queensmere and the Bridle Path xx. LOVELY! Roehampton or Richmond Park, eh? However, it's nice to see each other every week and not every 18 months.

Well! You haven't told me yet what you would like for your birthday – you had better let me know soon. What about a toffee apple or sugar stick? Well, I must now bid you goodbye. What does the stamp signify? It won't stick on straight.

10th April 1918
Dearest,

I had a welcome surprise this afternoon. Try cousin Ethel Stocker and Mother visiting me. I have just written a letter to Ernest and Ada asking them to put the £10 I lent them some time ago to a post office account for Basil – opening it when he is 7 and putting by 3d or 4d a week till he is 21 and then he will have £10 as a 21st birthday present from Uncle Will. I will let you see the letter I wrote them on Sunday. I got your letter this morning. Thanks very much. My Word! There's an even better time coming. By the way I have asked Mother to let me have a looking glass – or I should say asked her to ask you to get me one for shaving.

> *London Association of Churches of Christ*
> *10th April 1918*
> *Dear Mrs Stocker*
>
> *I am much obliged to you for your letter giving details of Will's wound, and am indeed sorry to see that it is so bad. I have shown your letter to the other clerks and the principals all of whom express sympathy. We all hope that he might soon be about again, and even although artificiality will have to come to the rescue, we hope that with its aid he will not be much inconvenienced. There is a little consolation in the fact that, bad as it is, it might have been worse. I am writing to him by this post. If the new Bill goes through and they take all men up to 50, we shall be able to leave the office in charge of the*

caretaker and Mr Nevile, plus a lady clerk, so things look healthy just at present.
   With the kindest Christian regards
   Yours fraternally, Alf J Curtis (Secretary)

Friday 12th April 1918
Dearest,

Thanks for your letter. So my stamp meant 'I am longing to see you'. Where do I put the stamp for 'I am longing to see you, kiss you, hug you and spoon with you'? Let me know.

I had letters from Johnnie Blair and Curtis. When you come on Sunday you can read them. By the way, John has lost all his belongings but what he is sorry about is that he has lost our wedding photo and so if you have a spare one, I must send it to him or to his wife. When you come up remind me to ask you about chansons and pay book and also don't forget to ask me what Y.B. means.

15th April 1918
Dearest,

I'm already looking forward to seeing you again and I'm going to try and get the chair about 1.45 so as I can come and meet you and then I can have two x's (if nobody is looking), perhaps more. Comprenez? Now what about your present. I can guess you have something on your mind, but you hardly like telling me. What is it? Shall I give you a maximum and minimum as you suggest – no I won't, I'll state an elastic figure (and I'm not referring to something blue). £2.

I would rather you bought something other than jewellery. I suppose you would not like something for the home for yourself. Send me a list of anything you want. Don't be too shy to ask for anything you want.

By the way, you said yesterday you did not like wearing the various flimsy articles you have made. My Word! They must be thin. I'm wondering whether the people who saw you make them thought I put you up to it. Makes me feel funny. As they are so very flimsy it certainly looks like as if you have made them for my special benefit.

19th April 1918

Dearest,

 Thank you very much for your letter and also for the writing pad and photograph. So you would like an eiderdown quilt would you, righto! You ask me if I should like anything else. It's not my present, it's yours. I presume that for £2 it would be a first class article.

 The Daily Mail arranged a concert last night. It started at 7 o'clock, as I had been unfortunate on two previous occasions in getting in I got down there soon after five and being a chair patient was right in front in the special part reserved for such patients. My Word! It was a grand concert – I did enjoy myself.

 Yesterday, I had the tube taken from my foot and this morning I had a part of it burned away with a silver stick. One side of it stung, but the other side is still numbed. Sister Russell, the nice sister, said this morning that when I am better she will want me to help her with the dressings.

 What do you think – yesterday the Orderly Room sergeant came to see me about the letter I sent to the Paymaster at Chelsea. He had the letter in his hand I sent and after he had finished his explanations he said 'You write a nice hand and letter, I'd like to get you down in the office'. Fancy anybody telling me I write a nice hand. First time I have ever been told that. He may have been more or less correct about the letter. Hem! Well! I am not expecting any visitors today, but I am tomorrow and Sunday. I notice that some of the visitors roll in soon after one, so I do not see why you could not come in about 1.30.

24th April 1918

Dearest,

 Mother came to see me today. They have already made use of me and I have a light job sterilizing the surgical instruments, looking after the medicine cupboard, making dressings etc. I got on a pair of crutches today but I don't like them much they hurt my armpits and shoulders. I shall have to get another pair for hopping to and fro from my little job, which is mostly a sitting down job. Mother had a look at my papers today and Xray photo, none of the bones are broken. Tell Mother the words we could not decipher were 'tendons showing, some shattered'.

Have you got the quilt yet? What about letting me have it on my bed here till the honeymoon (Act 2). Well! How are the 'flimsies' going – not moth eaten, I hope. My Word, I am looking forward to the 2nd honeymoon, makes me feel quite spoony.

25th April 1918

Dearest,

I have got another pair of crutches which suit me much better so I shall soon be able to get a Sunday afternoon pass from 1-7 o'clock. The London pass I shall have to wait some time yet for and find an excuse in the meantime.

I understand from Mother that my Father and Uncle Bob are going to come up on Sunday, but I suppose you will come on your own, I think I should if I were you. I was wondering whether on Saturday – or some other Saturday, you could come up and book up a room for the night and stay until Sunday. I don't know how much it would cost, or how you would get on for food. If you could so arrange I could get a pass from 1-7 on Saturday and from 1-7 on Sunday. Why I suggest this is that (providing the people did not mind) we would have somewhere to go as I could not trudge about on crutches from 1-7. We could have tea at the place you have booked up on our own I presume, which would be lovely. Think about it and let me know what you think about it. By the way, if I were you, if you could, I should find a cheaper way to come than your present way. There must be dozens of ways of getting here. Get on a bus going somewhere in this direction and then go to the nearest station on this line, or bus all the way if you can, the boys here say it's possible and much cheaper. I should wangle something. Every time you come make an experiment and come a different way and find out which you like best and the most reasonable. I should not be surprised if you could come for a third of the amount you are at present paying. And if I'm going to be home for a long time you'll, or we will, save pounds.

If you go about it thoughtfully I do not see why occasionally you could not stay a weekend at a reasonable price including fare. It would be so great if we could arrange it.

29th April 1918
Dearest,

I hope you arrived home safely. By the way, before I forget, when you come up on Saturday I should like you to bring me a button cleaning kit:- button stick[184] and nail brush will suffice and a tin of Soldier's Friend. I expect we have a set or two at home. Perhaps only a button stick, if so will you please purchase one for me at Woolworth's, a nail brush and brass polish of some kind – Soldier's Friend preferably. You might also at Woolworth's (I say Woolworth's because they are very reasonable) get me a small boot brush.

Seeing that you are not having a quilt, what do you suggest? I am very much looking forward to next Sunday and am anxiously awaiting a letter from you stating that you have been fixed up. I suppose that she will take it for granted that you would expect me to be allowed inside. Are you bringing any flimsy gear? I suppose if you did, you could not adorn yourself while I was there. I've just been enquiring about late passes from 1–10 or 11 instead of 1–7.30, but I don't think it would look well for the first week. If, however, you are unfortunate don't forget to let me know early so that I can endeavour to arrange somewhere else. How great it will be to spend our weekends together and alone.

I must now bid you goodbye. Anything coming round the corner – no – Righto X!

Wednesday April 1918
Dearest,

I had some visitors yesterday, Ethel and Aunt Hannah. Maud, who you have heard me mention, was coming too, but thought it was rather too cold for her baby. Ethel is coming again on Saturday. Jolly

---

[184] A small piece of brass with a slit up the middle. It was put behind buttons when they were being cleaned to prevent any polish getting onto the fabric. Soldier's Friend was a brand of metal-cleaning paste.

good of her, isn't it? They all seem to take a great interest in me. I'm looking forward to a letter this morning from you. Elsie's friend, the Australian, is leaving today for his own hospital in Dartford.[185] After you had gone he said, referring to Elsie, 'she's a nice girl and tell her I said so'. Well! I don't know as I have any more to say only that I'm looking forward to Sunday and ~ ~ ~.

2nd May 1918
Dearest,

I am so looking forward to the weekend. Mind you don't catch cold through wearing too flimsy a wear.

I had a letter from Shrosbree yesterday and he says that at present the Division are having a posh time for a while.[186] I was thinking this morning that my being here is <u>almost</u> as good as one long leave, now that you intend to come every Saturday and Sunday. How great this is after three years separation!

Mother came on Tuesday and I was out, I did not expect her. However, luckily I came in fairly early. I spoke to her about Edie and Irene and she agrees about our being on our own. When you come on Sunday bring a few shillings extra, I shall want some. How about your present? What are you going to have? A Singer sewing machine (I don't think). By the way I've got something to say about that if you remind me.

PS. . . . Does Elsie still correspond with the Australian?

3rd May
Dearest,

Just woke up 6.30. I received your letter last night just as I had returned from an errand for one of the boys. I also had been out all the afternoon and was tired so I intended to go to Dearden today. However, on second thoughts I strolled off. I saw Miss Dearden and explained matters. She said she thought we wanted a bed sitting room and the room she had was only a small room. She was very nice about it and said if that would suit us she would be pleased to

---

[185] No. 3 Australian Auxiliary Hospital.
[186] At Amiens, well behind the front line.

have you. She is a school teacher at Plough Road, Clapham and is not unlike Miss Windybanks at Mrs Barbers. She wanted to know if you would stop Sunday night as if you did it would not cost you so much as you catch the workmen's which is only 8d (I think she said), she goes by that train. So if you get a single fare down and stay Sunday I think it would be best. When you have slept there once you will be able to arrange exactly how you are going to manage. So everything seems alright and I think you'll find Miss Dearden a very nice person. I stood (or sat) talking to her for a long time.

Ward 15, etc
Thursday 9th May
Dearest,

By the way when you come on Saturday will you please bring along my Sports Watch. I am glad to hear of your intention next Saturday 'if it's not freezing'. Comprenez? As far as a late pass goes, I have my doubts about it, but if I did get one it would be for Sunday. I should not make any cake for next Sunday, they must be very expensive considering the price of eggs and as for butter, if you can only get what they allow you for a week, ¼lb, I'll go without, but see you bring all you want for yourself. Don't bring any oranges etc for I'd sooner go without than pay 3½d. Last week you were talking to me about your fare. What's the matter with a workmen's from Hammersmith to Holborn 2d and a 1d from there to Newgate St 4d a day. Let me know what you have to say, a saving of 2/- a week. We have a joint income of:

£2 your wages
16/- your allowances
10/- Western's allowance
12/- my army pay
£3-18-0.

Say £4 and only you to keep out of it and I reckon we ought to do much better than we are. Including Orpington expenses we should save without any difficulty £2 a week if not £2-5-0. I've been thinking about these things lately and when the war is over it will be such a lot to us. To be perfectly frank I do not think you make the effort I do, if you do try and organise your expenditure you haven't made much of success.

PS. . . . Doctor has just looked at my wound and does not seem so satisfied: it's now to be dressed twice a day.

16th May 1918
Dearest,

I have just made application for a pass from 10am Sunday to 10pm Monday and if I don't succeed I expect I shall take it and chance the consequences. Naughty boy! In that event I shall see you on Saturday as usual and go with you home on Sunday, sleeping somewhere Sunday night and returning Monday evening.

22nd May 1918
Dearest,

Sorry first of all I have not written before. I got in all right and was not marked absent, although by error I suppose, my pass was only made out for one day and no night. I am today looking for a new abode for the weekend. Green had his mother, father and wife stay for 3 nights for 5/- (3 people for 3 nights). I was thinking once every 3 weeks or perhaps a fortnight I shall go home which will be cheaper. I had a nice letter from John Blair yesterday, he says he was just about to write you when my letter arrived. Well, goodbye for now I expect I shall write again tonight.

23rd May 1918
Dearest,

Have just been searching in a little street about 20 seconds from the Hospital: has about 12 houses and I tried them all, being recommended by one house to another: the last house about the best of the lot, old lady and daughter, seemed taken to me (not the daughter exactly) and after refusing, said that they could fix you up Saturday fortnight as the next two Sundays they are off to London. I should think that they would be reasonable too. I accepted and told them I would be round a few days beforehand.

I think that will do although I wish we could have gone on Saturday, I don't like being 'rushed' as we have been by Miss Dearden. When you come on Saturday, I will show you the street. When you come on Saturday, <u>remind me</u> if I forget to arrange something definite as regards our finances. Sunday week I may put in for a weekend pass: it will be cheaper than your coming down. By the way would you please remind me to give you your books on Saturday.

PS. . . . A lot of the boys in the ward are being discharged to their units today and a big crowd of Canadians go to Canada on Tuesday and I shall soon be the oldest in the ward. Our new sister today while dressing my foot said 'Stocker, this will get you your ticket'

PPS. . . . My pal, Green, is leaving tomorrow and the room he had, 1 bed (double) and use of sitting room he is tonight booking for me, price 1/6 a night. What a difference! I'll let you know as soon as possible if he is successful.

30th May 1918
My Dearest,

I have received your letter and have acted straightaway. If I have construed Miss Dearden's letter aright, it's mad if she expects 27/6 a week. At any rate I'm sending her the enclosed letter or rather a facsimile. I have also been to see the people in that little road and arranged for you to stay there from next Monday and henceforth for weekends. I'm more pleased than ever with it – it's quite a nice house and so now you have to be fixed up for Saturday and Sunday and so I'll see what I can do at Ransom's or somewhere else perhaps for two days.

I went to Western & Sons on Thursday and singularly enough Maddison turned up in goggles after I had been there a few minutes, he hasn't been there for two years, it looked like a worked affair!

PS. . . . After I had been to Western's I found difficulty in getting on the crowded buses at Catford and so I went by the only train which arrived at 9.2 at the station. After scheming how I should wangle it being so late, I got on a taxi at the station and took my hat off so as to look like an officer. The fellow at the gate, MP, saluted; I nodded and got out at the top of the hill at the foot of the wards.

10th June 1918
My dearest,

I have just been looking at some adverts and note a lot of property going cheap if only I had more to invest. I have also written to an advert, which I enclose. I note the profits are high £450 pa (if true). It's not in a very nice district, East. However it will be interesting to find out how much they ask for it. I have simply written for full particulars, giving your address and 'W Stocker'. And you will probably have a letter of some kind in a few days. If the individual should come round to see you (I don't suppose he will but you must be ready for any eventualities), you must of course keep it dark and smuggle him upstairs, shut the door and keep away 'nosy' people. You know what I mean.

I am now going to write RWB.

> *Dear Mr Black*
>
> *I understand that the Bishop of London has recently given his residence at Fulham for a hospital, and although I am quite happy where I am at present, if a transfer could be arranged so near home and Twynholm, it would be much better for me. I do not know the method of procedure for such transfers, but I presume the intended hospital would have to be approached to see if there is a vacancy and if so whether they will accept me, once matters were arranged that end I could push it through here. I should be much obliged if you will do what you can for me.*

PS. . . . The fact that I am an up patient and likely to be some time in hospital might be worth mentioning.

13th June 1918
Dearest,

Thanks for your letter received this morning. I quite see what you mean about the advert. I merely wrote by way of curiosity, it will be interesting to see what they ask. Did you receive my letter of yesterday? I think if we can secure the money it will be a good thing. Freehold property is always worth its money and it will not touch, only in solicitors fees, our capital. If I can get this one started, I shall try others too. By the way the term 'no agents' means that the owner is getting an agent to advertise. Consequently the agent who has the business in hand does not want a crowd of letters from agents asking for the house to be placed on their books, as if somebody else transacts the business he has no commission himself. Comprenez?

Sorry I caused you any unnecessary trouble by not stamping the envelope. But I lost, or rather mislaid, the ½d stamps I had, (I've found them since) and did not feel inclined to put 2d on, as I had to RWB, and some of the boys were saying that if the letters 'W.S.L.' (Wounded Soldiers Letter) was put on, it would go free. So I thought I would try and see. As I am not going to pay 1½d when I can pay nothing. However, apparently, it cannot be done.

I am pleased to see you take such an interest in the Economy Stunt and have seen about the buses. I have been scheming to see if you could come down some other way. Is this possible:- On Saturdays you could get up early and get up to Cannon Street about, or before 8, and get a workmen's to Orpington (<u>if</u> they are issued from London and at that time) and use the London to Orpington half later in the day. Is that possible? 8d. But if I get a transfer to Fulham it will not be necessary. I am very much looking forward to this weekend. Unless I hear to the contrary I'll go to Farnborough to meet you. Should you not be able to come by bus and arrive by train you can proceed to Farnborough where you will find me. Well! I must now resume my hard work viz reading Rider Haggard's 'Pearl Girl' lying on my back on the bed, most fatiguing!

With love a hug and a kiss (encore beaucoup)

PS. . . . Re your writing and mine. Whose leg are you pulling?

My Dearest,

On Saturday I am going with a chum, a Welsh Guard, to Westminster Abbey where a Welsh service will be held.[187] I hope you do not mind, dear; he is all on his own and I know would like me to go with him. So from there I shall go home to Waldemar where I hope to find you, I suppose about 5 o'clock and I am going to see the night sister and see if I can work Saturday night and Sunday night. It's now 10.10 and no light so I cannot see what I'm writing hardly, so excuse scribble. By the way did Mrs Mardle accept the additional 1/-? And will you by letter tell her I'm on a weekend this week and so we shall not turn up. And if you think fit forward 2/- for the room. Tell her of course you will be up Saturday week as usual.

25th June 1918

Dearest,

First of all let me tell you, I fell in it for Sunday. Saturday night all was well. I was rumbled Monday morning, my bed was not unstuffed when the boys got up and Sister looked to see if I was unwell and of course I was missing. If my slow confederate had, on getting up, rearranged the bed at the right time all would have been well from what the boys tell me. I was paraded down to the orderly room, I put up a good case. I went home to see a brother on leave. I had put in for a pass and was refused and as I had made up my mind to go I took it. I also told him that it was my first crime since I joined up at the outbreak of war. However, he said he was obliged to punish me with forfeiture of one day's pay and 3 days stoppage of

---

[187] "Two Prime Ministers, Mr Lloyd George and M W M Hughes (Australia), Lt-general Sir Francis Lloyd and a number of Welsh MP's acted as sidesmen and took up the offertory at Westminster Abbey on Saturday, at the special Coronation Day Service in aid of the Welsh Prisoners of War Fund. It was the first time a Welsh service had been conducted in the Abbey, the Hymns being sung and the lessons read in the poetic Welsh tongue. Queen Alexandra attended. The stirring Welsh National Anthem 'Land of my Fathers' was brilliantly rendered by Mr Ben Davies. The Bishop of St David's (Dr Owens) who preached in Welsh, said they thanked God that Wales had not been slow at the call of the King to do its duty and share the sacrifice made by the British and its Allies."
Western Daily Press, Bristol, Monday 24th June 1918.

pass. I've had a good run for my money so I ought to be satisfied but my slow confederate let me down, silly pie!

Thursday 4th July 1918
Dearest,

I'm glad you have asked me about treacle which I've bought, the last tin, and I hail with delight signs from you of economy and thrift: <u>the first I've ever seen</u>. Our whole future depends on discreet moves during the next few years. Although you obviously don't realise as much as I do this fact, I'm beginning to feel there's hope yet. Have you heard from the Paymaster yet?

If in your travels you can buy <u>ridiculously</u> cheap anything in the way of lino for our new abode, get it: that's if you want it and it's <u>CHEAP</u> and good, there's no hurry, heaps of time, but if you see a genuine bargain you might as well have it. Don't buy anything unless it's almost given away.

I suppose on Saturday you can't take a train say to Bromley and bus from Bromley saving 6d probably. Perhaps you could get a tube to Elephant and Castle and then get on a bus or tube to Clapham Junction and then by train you might save 3d. Several stunts you could try, I'm sure. I'd stake my life I'd get down from London reasonably quick for less than it would be by the present extortionate train fares.

Tuesday 16th July
My dear Daisy,

Thanks for pipe etc, I was just about to buy a cheap cherry wood when it arrived. I had a singular dream last night, I dreamt I had a son – some dream! When you see Mother this week let her know I'm coming up on Saturday and is Harry likely to be coming. Here! Ask my father if a (good as new) pair of Army boots large 6 for 12/- is any good to him. Not bad looking either, been worn a week.

31st July 1918
Dearest,

Thank you very much for such a useful letter. I am very pleased to hear about season ticket. So after all, my remarks on Sunday were not futile. I like the way we spent last weekend. So you had a few gnat bites too. I was well marked. However, they helped to recall happy days of the past.

I sold the rest of my tobacco and I found afterwards a client who would have given more. I've also bought some lovely boots. Two pairs. One for my father. So if you go round to Leslie House tell him I've got a new pair of boots, size 6, lovely boots, worth £2.2.0 and I'm bringing them along on Saturday and don't forget they are 12/-. Tell him price. Last him 50 years (more or less). Also send me £1 in 10/- notes as I might see some more good things.

Ward 15
10th August 1918
Dearest,

All's well for Saturday night. I have just been thinking about your business tonight. I hope you will settle everything satisfactorily. When we have got the houses in good running order, it will behove us to take especial care of our money as we shall be, for a time, stumped. Won't we?

I must really thank you for the help you are giving me and although at times my remarks seem harsh you may rest assured I notice and <u>don't forget</u> the willingness which you display in going out of your way to please my erratic nature. I hope you are better after a night's sleep. Just watch yourself, study yourself and look after yourself a little more. The 'ornament' to which you referred last night will be fashioned to a large extent by how you from now and henceforth do this. And don't be quite so lugubrious. If you just compare yourself even to the average person you have a lot to be thankful for – a jolly lot. So show it on your face – like the officer I showed you yesterday, a tonic to look at. That's that. Next time I see you let me realise you know what I mean.

By the way if in your travels you hear of or see a good bargain in the way of bicycles let me know at once and we will see about getting it. <u>Because</u> (a reason notice) it will come in handy occasionally to enable you to visit Bromley for rents possibly. Now if you want one look about 'seeking'. Comprenez? And I will too.

I'm thinking of trying to write an article for a London magazine, do you think I could manage it? It would pay well if it came off, would it not.

Wednesday 14th August 1918
Dearest,

It is just about 9 and I am in bed after a strenuous day of basking and reading in the sunshine. This is a really fine life the 'good time' I often used to refer to in France: the glorious dawn after a dismal night portending a brighter day. I had my foot examined today by the ward doctor and after he had finished he only said 'all right'. So whether I'm now going to have electric treatment I do not know.[188]

I received your letter and am pleased – very. The case of Waldemar shows the benefit of prompt action. As for Bromley, I think the report too severe and although I'm not disappointed I'm not in agreement with the report: 'The poorest people live there' was wrong and the remark about the district is obviously wrong also. However, as you say, Waldemar ameliorates everything. I note you say you were never keen on the property. I wish you had said so before. In future if you are not keen on any move I take, say so, it may save a bloomer. I think a lot of your opinion, that's why I always seek your criticisms. But, usually it's only under great pressure I get it. But I again thank you for your invaluable help – I mean this – I would not say so merely for flattery. <u>And just thank your father for me for his kind assistance.</u>

Wednesday 21st August 1918
My dearest,

Thanks very much for your letter – glad to hear things are progressing as regards 10 Waldemar Avenue. I was rather surprised at your aunt's ideas. I should have thought she would have jumped at the idea. If she had a room of her own or more if she wished to pay for it, I can't see how she would be dependent on us any more

---

[188] Electrotherapy, using galvanic current, was intended to increase blood supply to the injured area, thereby improving the condition of skin and muscle tone.

than she would be if living in your mother's rooms. However, it's quite immaterial to me what she does – absolutely. So press nothing – only I considered it a bounden duty to ask her seeing she would be otherwise on her own. I only hope you approached her diplomatically as it is not exactly nice to be refused. Of course, I suppose, she knows her own business best and I presume she understood what you meant. I trust you did not upset her. It seems to me funny though, especially as I understood from you she once mentioned living with us and on another occasion I understood that your aunt hinted at our living with her at her house in Inglethorpe Street. And several times before the war you distinctly told me your aunt looked forward to living with us. What you tell me now seems contradictory.

As for furniture I'm sure I'm done there. If we can, without squandering, get fixed up, I should say move right away. We shall have 3 rooms to furnish and staircase I suppose.

Reception room

1 carpet	3.0.0
overmantel	2.0.0 (your aunt possibly)
chairs etc	10.0.0
table	1 or 2 (? aunt for less)
pictures	5.0.0

Kitchen

table & chairs	4.0.0
oilcloth	2.0.0

Bedroom

bedstead	(you already have I believe)
drawers	2.0.0
dressing table	3.0.0
washstand	1.10.0

A casual and very rough estimate of £40.10.0. What have you to say? If you intend moving you had better just look about anywhere and everywhere 'seeking' and be careful. I hope this week to have quite a list of things you've seen and look for good pair of pictures too. Now if you would move, look about and get us fixed up.

PS. . . . I heard from Mr Dennis and I am speaking at the Institute on Sunday.[189]

Thursday 22nd August 1918
Dearest,

I had my foot examined more or less, and I understand from the clerk that I am marked 'Command Depot' which I suppose is Blackpool. So I expect on Tuesday or Wednesday I shall draw my khaki and go first of all on 7 days leave. I suppose the officer thinks that as I am in the R.A.M.C. it will be better to get to my own people. I should think that when I get there I shall be 'classed' and given a job suitable to my disablement. It's certain I shall not go back to France as I am unless it's a base job. If when I get to Blackpool I am given a light, clerical job or something, or if I am sent to some hospital on the staff, I shall be well satisfied, especially if it's near London. What do you say? Of course I can't stay on here everlastingly. At Command Depots boards are given and I <u>might</u> even get my ticket. However we will wait and see. My idea is that I shall have a home job somewhere, both disablement and service are in my favour.[190]

10 Reads Road, Blackpool
27th October 1918
Dearest,

I am getting on fairly well here. Only a few visitors are here and the town is normal unlike when Alex and I came a few years ago. I

---

[189] 'W. Stocker seems to be making good progress, and although still lame, is as happy as can be. In the afternoon of Sunday August 25th, he gave an address to the Twynholm's Youth Institute, which was both helpful and enjoyable.' **Joyful Tidings, September 1918.**

[190] No letters were found from the next two months. If Will was home on sick leave he got more than the seven days he was expecting. Until his discharge, when he 'drew his khaki', he would have been wearing the military hospital in-patient uniform known as 'blues'.

have met a good many of the old boys here including Horrocks[191] who was married recently at a registry office; he asked to be remembered to you. I had an examination the morning after my arrival and am marked B3 III White – white is home. I may remain here for a good while and I may not. I went to a fine show at the tower on Saturday for 5d, children only acted. The charge of 5d to soldiers including entrance to menagerie, aquarium and dancing.

30th October 1918
Dearest,

Thanks for your letter; am so glad Waldemar is fixed up. I expect you will be able to tell me in your next letter all the arrangements. I enclose a letter for you to copy and send to the Fulham Military Hospital as I understand that if a vacancy can be arranged by a soldier's people it is fairly easy to get a transfer, if the CO makes application for you. I should get some very nice note paper or if there is any Leslie House paper left write on that and call home for the reply. It would be good if it could be arranged.

> *To CO, Fulham Military Hospital, London SW6*
> Sir,
>
> *My husband, Pte Stocker 536373, of the RAMC, has recently been discharged from hospital and is stationed at Blackpool in a very low category BIII White, Home Service, and is awaiting a job in a home hospital, preferably clerical as his disability, ankle wound, causes lameness. I am writing to enquire whether you have a vacancy in the Fulham Hospital and if so if you would facilitate a transfer for him to your hospital*
>
> *I trust you will excuse the liberty I am taking by writing you but I understand this is the most effective procedure.*

---

[191] Presumably the same Horrocks who told Will in November 1914 that he looked like Asquith.

1st November 1918
Dearest,

I have just turned in, but I must write you first before I sleep. You ask me how I spend the day. I used to go on parade but was always turned off as I could not march and now I miss all parades and have nothing to do. I do not go sightseeing as I might be pulled up and so I spend most of the day reading. After tea I meet Horrocks at a Soldiers Club and play for hours at chess. We are about equal and have some keen games. It's a good life in a way but too useless to be over enjoyable. I am looking forward to the day when we can live together and work together in earnest. You say you are pining for me and I can assure you I long to be back again with you in our own home. This is an easy life but I don't want only ease. I want a life of usefulness in your company. However, the War will soon finish now.

I suppose you have sent off to Fulham Hospital? I understand that that procedure is out of order, but it might come off – that's the main point. How did the idea strike you? One of the boys said he knew of a case where it came off.

Dearest, I shall be very glad if you will endeavour to get in plenty of practice on the piano before I come home – really as much as you possibly can. If you like you can continue lessons with Madame Worby (practical only). Don't let anything stand in your way. You know, just to make me happy and you like doing that, don't you? And then I'll kiss you when I come home.

By the way, I received my kit thanks – no towels though, I left two at home. It's rather awkward – besides at kit inspection I shall fall in it. The pants you can keep – I mean for me. It's now getting late and so I'll say goodnight. X.

RAMCT, 10 Reads Road
Saturday 2nd November 1918
Dearest,

Have just returned from a hot sea water bath and feel A1. I got your letter, or rather short note, and had the same idea about St Marks Harrow but we must of course wait and see what happens at Fulham Hospital. I feel rather fed up tonight and so I am going to try and write you a line or two. I have just been in The Tower just to kill time by myself, apart from the menagerie and aquarium there is only dancing on, and seeing other fellows with girls it made me want you – jealousy I suppose – you know what I mean. I always get fed up when I am unemployed, and one can't read all day long. Tomorrow, Sunday, I am going to two or three services and, I hope, to the address of Miss Pickering's: it's just a little way off, a 1d tram ride I think. I hope it is somebody interesting – can't stick dull people. When interests in life ceases one might as well pack up.

I wish you were here – there's something missing in my life when I am away from you – I feel like Adam before Eve appeared, although she brought him trouble! There is only one time I don't miss your company and that is when you 'get my rag out', but it doesn't last long, a sign of true love, eh – I mean the inseparable part. What a difference a girl or woman can make in a man's life – can make it felicity or just the opposite. I think you'll make mine the former, don't you? I believe I'd be an awkward man for any woman to get on with – well! I'll say sometimes – but to counterbalance it I know I have great affection if appealed to the right way. You must not think I'm unhappy up here – I always try to be happy wherever I am but I feel moody tonight somehow, lonely – I suppose really it's lovesickness, eh? Say, "No". You always make out I'm not in love with you, don't you – all women do, don't they? It's a foolish whim of theirs. I suppose it's a natural propensity by which they hope to get more evidence of it and more attention – not a bad idea if it comes off.

I think married people get bored by each other because both after a while cease trying to be captivating, cease wooing, cease endeavouring to be as attractive in dress and manners. You know how angelic both strive to make themselves when trying to get off. If the spirit of affection the best behaviour and of attractiveness continued in married life married couples could never tire of each other's company. But as a rule they display themselves at their worst and there is such a difference in everybody at their best from their worst, isn't there – at their best would honesty be always 'one glad sweet song' not one constant discord. Very few make each other's lives a glad sweet song, one in ten thousand – but I know of two who are going to be the one exception in ten thousand. But to be frank, one or two little points of harmony must be watched – it only takes one little slip off a note to make a discord.

Expression in music is everything – well, not everything – but a jolly lot – and in love expression of all kinds is a jolly lot too – not unnatural expression known as swank – but natural expression fully displayed. I must now cease, I feel a happy man because I've written this letter, I've given vent to my feelings, which is what moodiness is after all.

5th November 1918
Dearest,

I expect you will be glad to hear I am moving from Blackpool to a place called Spalding in Essex. I do not know of a Spalding in Essex, I know of one in Lincoln and I hope it is not there as that is too far away. I understand it is in Essex so it will be fine, won't it – more weekenders eh? It is to a German Prisoners Hospital and I am looking forward to it. Good news for you isn't it?

I went to Mrs Reynolds on Sunday and had a nice time. Six of us broke bread: the old boy, his married daughter, a widow of 33 or thereabouts, another young lady and 3 RAMC, nice people exceptionally so. Write more later, in a hurry, pal waiting.

6th November 1918
German Prisoners Of War Camp, Spalding, Lincoln.[192]
Dear Daisy,

Not in Essex: a dull awful show, no good at all. I am in a prison not a hospital, rough and rotten. Arrived at the office early and have received from you two short letters and parcel of towels – thank you very much. So you have the 'flu' have you? As I told you in my previous letter all our wards here are full of flu and pneumonia cases and nearly all the staff are down with it including the doctor – so it may be my turn next. You must look after yourself you know – I wish I could come home and nurse you – how would you like that – nice! I do not know if you are still bad, if you are you should get the

---

[192] The letter is stamped 'Prisoner of War Repatriation Camp, Spalding'.

doctor's permission to send me a telegram or rather get somebody to get a form and you fill it in and get him to sign it. 'Your wife is ill and your presence is requested – Dr so and so'. Anything that would bring me up – that's if you would like me to come – I can easily be spared from here for a few days. I wonder you have not done it before. Why didn't you? If your doctor is a sport he will sign a telegram – just explain. See what you can do. I should not think it any good sending a telegram without doctor's signature – it looks too much like bluff. Even if you are up the doctor might sign such a telegram if he is a sport. I then can help to recuperate you – eh? Any rate just do what you think best if it's not too late. I do not think I can get up for the moving.

Friday 8th Nov 1918
My Dearest,

    I am just writing you a line in the office of the prison camp: it is six o'clock and I push off at eight. When I go out at 8.30 or thereabouts it is dark as sin, all the shops shut at six and only the barren fens are left to see or rather walk across: our sleeping accommodation is poor and dismal. I hate the show, but thank the Lord it's only a temporary job – or at least so they tell us. The wards are full of flu and pneumonia cases and everyday somebody snuffs it. When coming from the station there I had one other occupant in my compartment of the lorry – a dead Bosch.

    When you write me please write expressively. I mean to say, if you are happy show me it in your letter. I need a love letter. You are usually so cold in your letters and I might add in your manner – very. When I came home on leave you met me at the door as if I had seen you a minute before. As a rule you are the recipient of my caresses, they are not reciprocal. Last Sunday when I went to the breaking of bread I was most cordially welcomed by Mrs Fyles, as if I had known her for years. When one is absent a hearty reception does one good – Ernest is dull because Ada is dull. Let's hope our future will not resemble theirs: may ours be <u>warm</u>, <u>responsive</u>, <u>expressive</u> and carressive friendship and reciprocal too. It certainly will have to improve before it is. I often have thought what I have just written about your inexpressive love and tonight being somewhat fed up I'm in the mood of saying what I think.

Sunday 10th November 1918
Dearest,

I am just writing you a note in the office, while I am unemployed. I have not received a letter from you for about ten days, I expect the post has gone astray, so I feel sort of abandoned here. The three other RAMC who came here are a very funny crew and find enjoyment in the village public house and consequently I'm on my own. However, the war is almost over and today I'm waiting to hear the village peace bells ring out – probably by the time you receive this letter the war will be over. Fancy Christmas at home for the first since 1913 – how lovely – all fixed up in our own home – eh? I want to come home very much – I've had enough of being slung about at the mercy of the British Army, what do you say? Might as well not have kinsfolk if one is everlastingly absented from them. Well! I must now say goodbye I have just been handed a job.

My previous letter please modify; I was in a forsaken sort of mood. You know how I pour myself out sometimes and you understand me by now. When I come home for good and the hardships of War cease, I shall not be so fond of the loud pedal and explain myself in a more loving way – you know what I mean.

12th November 1918

So Peace has arrived at last. I felt so happy yesterday I did not know what to do with myself – how I wanted you to give you a real peace hug and kiss. Soon we shall be together again for always in our own home – how great! No more khaki and separation when I get home next time – can you really realize how delightful it will be. And all of us three boys safe and only one 'crocked', haven't we a lot to be thankful for. The village here went mad last night, fully lit up – fireworks and bands, singing and dancing. It's the happiest day of my life. Soon I shall be in civvies – soon both together in our home.

I enclose a little casket from a German prisoner all hand made.[193] I hope you will treasure it as it is a work of art done with improvised tools. Do you like it? It will do for your wedding ring or engagement ring – which? I get on extremely well with the prisoners and we are very friendly. One gave me a book and another a good copying ink pencil for 'friendship' another wants me to look him up after the war because 'I am his friend'.[194]

Tuesday 12th November 1918
My dearest,

It has just struck 11 o'clock and I am on night duty watching over a serious pneumonia and flu ward. I have a German orderly by my side and except for occasional coughing and groaning all is quiet. I rather like night duty, it is so restful and soothing and as I have nothing to do just now I thought I would try and write you a nice long letter. I received your postcard and letter today and I also got the towels, there is still a shirt I believe to come which I am responsible for.

How are you feeling by now dearest, much better I hope, are you? Please take the greatest care of yourself, I do wish I could be with you when you are unwell I'm sure I could be useful. If there is anything you want please get it, anything in the way of warmer underclothing or nourishment please get it. Look after yourself well. I would so much like to be with you just now, and then I should see that you lacked nothing.

If we are going to Ringmer Avenue on Saturday send me straightaway <u>by wire</u> £1 in case I haven't enough and I manage a

---

[193] Unfortunately this box was lost during a house move in the 1950s.
[194] While still a patient in Orpington, Will had been told to stop fraternising with the German patients as they were the enemy – he fetched them books from the library and bought tobacco and sweets from his own allowance. Will was not a great respecter of rank and told the sergeant that if he did not leave him (Will) alone and treat the prisoners better, then he would report the sergeant to the Commanding Officer for breaching the Geneva Convention. The situation ended with Will reporting the sergeant and having to make a statement in front of the hospital adjutant. The sergeant was transferred.

pass. If you do move I'll try hard for a pass. Of course, if the doctor will sign the wire I spoke, we can kill two birds with one stone. I should think the doctor would sign a telegram – he can't lose and it would do us a good turn.

I am looking forward to seeing you so much. I do not know exactly why, but I very very much want to see you, perhaps it's because PEACE has brought us still nearer together. I notice in your postcard you say you are too shy to demonstrate your affection for me publicly (or in other words in front of anybody), you have not been too shy to show obvious displeasure before people, why not obvious affection? I think it is very foolish to camouflage love, I do not mean ostentatious show but deep and real affection. I love to see it and much more, I love to receive it – a stroke of the hair, a pressed hand, a loving smile and all these other things go such a long long way or even a sly kiss. I'm open to improvement in that respect I know but I think it's one of the few in which I beat you really.

> *You <u>know</u> that I love you, and you love me*
> *And we both love each other you see*
> *I've got a mortgage on some happy days*
> *Now that I'm wise to your loving ways*
> *Our ideas just seem to harmonize*
> *My heart with love is nearly twice its size dear*
> *<u>We don't care what other folk say (should not care)</u>*
> *Don't care what they think*
> *So long as I've got You – hug me close dear*
> *And you've got Me*

Do you remember that song?

19th November 1918

Dearest,

I arrived back this morning at 4 o'clock after a fair journey and a 3 hours wait at Peterborough and so I only had 2½ hours sleep and feel somewhat tired now, but I'm going to turn in early tonight you may guess. Well! I leave for Blackpool tomorrow morning, Wednesday, and I am glad of it. I may get a job in London from there, hope so, I shall try hard. This has not been a bad place though, I worked a nice leave so I haven't much to grumble at. I sold all the tobacco and cigs to civilians interned and enclose ~~£2.0.0~~ 35/- which leaves me 5/- to carry on with. I charged a fraction less I think although you can judge I did well.

We had a fine time on leave didn't we? 'In our own home next time eh? Well! Look after yourself dearest, finish off that onion porridge and write frequently.

10 Palatine Road, Blackpool, Lancs
21st November 1918
Dearest,

I hope you are feeling much better by now – you certainly did not look in the pink of condition last weekend. I suggest you now get plenty of porridge in you and fats, if butter and so on is rationed get cocoanut fat and eat it in chunks. I'm certain in my own mind that the 'flu' is getting such a hold of European nations for one great reason – inadequate consumption of fat – owing to the War. So if you can't get one kind get another, I only know of one fat cocoanut or cocoa fat, whichever it is, that is not rationed and although you may not like it <u>go for it</u> and <u>get it down</u>. All fattening foods go in for, not half-heartedly but <u>bang smash</u> right in for them like you know I would have you. Porridge, barley, these despised cereals. <u>And</u> until further notice get yourself cod liver oil and take it regularly absolutely every day <u>3</u> times – let me know when you have got it. As much as you like, a bottle a day or 2 or 3 if you like but have it as much as you can and don't play the fool with the stuff, no shelving, get it down – DOWN. Got me? Righto – do it! And when I see you I shall tell you frankly if you look better – if you haven't made a big – an obvious improvement, Beware!

PART II

Part I didn't seem much like a love scene but it's a practical one the result of love. Did you see in the paper this morning the gratuities to soldiers – my service home and abroad will bring me just over £20 – good, isn't it – another house.

Well, how is 'Our Little Home' getting on, have you moved yet yourself? I think our next investment should be a nice kitchen table a big one, that little chap looks lost and have you done anything about the lamp & stand? Let me know, dear, I am so interested. Do the lamps give ample light? Got the coal yet? Any of the clocks go? Got that quilt from home? And you might get that oil stove from Mother, which she promised to give us – it may come in useful for boiling.

PS . . . What about 12 Months ago tomorrow eh?[195]

'Don't you be late' – DP
'All right about one' – WS
'No before one, 12.45 at latest' – DP

Saturday
Dearest,

Have spent this evening reading and playing chess and feeling lovesick. I thought I would try and write a line or two. I am sorry to hear your aunt is so queer; from what I can see, number 65 is a hospital – I suppose you couldn't by chance do with a first class orderly?

I am reporting sick tomorrow with my foot – yes – I'm taking it with me – and I'm going to see if I can do myself a bit of good in some way. At present I'm on light fatigue which yesterday meant cleaning the windows of the RAMC headquarters, some 'light fatigue'! Tomorrow I'm after a chit to excuse me all parades for good. I heard today that all men who joined up in 1914 are to have Xmas leave and so if I do not see you before, I shall at Christmas – about 5 weeks time – that seems long now, doesn't it, dear. And yet we patiently waited when I was in France – the more we have the more we want.

You will let me know when you move yourself to 45 Ringmer Avenue. Are the lamps quite good? And what about a strip of oilcloth from passage to kitchen. I suppose a good staining all over and polishing wouldn't do? It might look nice if it's really well polished – what do you say? And by the way when you do move

---

[195] It is their first wedding anniversary.

round do not allow the piano to rust and practise some pieces for when I come home – no excuse about piano out of tune now, you know – oh well – what were the voluminous excuses you used to make. Practice some songs and let me know what you are going to especially practise. And when I come home for good I want you to help me – don't forget. I want us both to be first class players and if we can't manage it helping each other studying we shall have to both spend some more money and be taught – I think we shall be able to do it by studying together and by books from libraries – at any rate I am <u>determined</u> (and you know what I mean by that) that we shall both make big advances – immense strides – in our playing. Opportunities and money which <u>you</u> have thrown away we both of us must make good and so in the meantime if you want to really gladden my heart methodize your time so as to get in each day a definite and good amount of practise. Let me know in your next letter if you are willing to do this. Now I'll turn over, you are not pleased with this side.

I wish I could come home this week I miss your presence more each time I leave you. Won't it be a fine time when I shall come home for good – and it's soon coming too – only a matter of weeks. 'No more to roam'. Won't it be LOVELY!

Dearest,

Thank you for your letter. And so you are taking Cod Liver Oil regularly, I'm glad to hear that and do not forget to tell me how you are progressing. I want to fatten you up for Christmas, it doesn't sound very nice, but you know what I mean, and so do all you can to help yourself along. Exercise, fresh air, and practical food – don't forget you have a bicycle when you visit Ringmer – keep your eye on it and don't let the tyres go down and perish. You have not used it ¼ enough yet – make it strengthen your constitution and save <u>us</u> money, that is what I bought it for. Do you go to Ringmer on it?

You ask me about Xmas leave – I have no doubt about getting it and I believe in a week I shall come up for voting for a few hours I believe facilities will be made for warrant etc.[196]

---

[196] The General Election of 14th December 1918.

Regarding lamps – you say that one wick won't turn up. Before you speculate on a new wick try doctoring it. Does one lamp give a sufficient light and I shall be glad to hear you have made a good job of the improvised lamp stand. Keep expenses low dear on unnecessary things.

The stove I spoke about I trust you have got – it should do admirably for the amount of breakfast you will want cooked. When I come home, instead of a gas ring, I expect I shall buy a primus oil stove which is much quicker than a gas ring and I am used to them too – had experience with them in France. Have you taken the cushions round yet? And would it be possible to use the bottom of the cupboard in the kitchen for our books pro tem? Because we shall use the kitchen as a study too – that is why I want a big table and so when you can get one, but watch finance. I shall be glad when you go to Ringmer, I shall feel then you are doing justice to our home – a burning bubbling interest . I know you haven't been in a fit state to set about the job in earnest, but if you watch yourself and try to strengthen yourself against all these breakdowns you are constantly having, fresh air, exercise, appropriate food, you'll soon be as strong as a lioness.

Now for something brighter, the above subjects I always let carry me away and I know you'll forgive me for anything I have said which seems unkind. I think when I come home I shall buy some 'civvies' before they get too dear. I shall buy a suit and hat I think. They reckon in the billet a good suit from £5 to £8 at least. I shall be very surprised if I can't get one for £2.10.0 and a good one at that. I know where I shall try. I didn't dispute the fact in the billet but I should want a suit and hat and overcoat and shoes too for £8 and not cheap stuff either.

You know you suggested buying some wool for a jacket and making it and save 30/- you said I think. I should have thought you could have got a good one ready made for 10/- and use the ardent toil on something else. How much is the wool going to cost? Don't forget to tell me. I paid 10/6 for that lovely woollen cardigan I bought last year. And if I remember rightly you already have a thick white jersey I think I noticed last time I was up. And you will have to buy something you need not take off in business. I wish I could be with you when you bought it and I should feel satisfied that you were getting full value. Not four guineas[197] worth of style and 5/- worth of hat sort of thing.

* * * * *

The letters stop abruptly at the end of November 1918. There may have been others which were discarded or lost, but Will was almost certainly home for Christmas for the first time in five years. Joyful Tidings reports that on 4th December 1918 he was appointed as a church officer for Twynholm Church for the following year. William Stocker was officially discharged from the army on 29th April 1919.

* * * * *

---

[197] A guinea was worth one pound and one shilling.

Afterword

The 5th London Field Ambulance, as a unit, remained in France until May 1919, in gradually decreasing numbers. Most of their time was spent dealing with the repatriation of prisoners of war from both sides and with the flu epidemic. The last entry of the War Diary is on 2nd May 1919 at 1800 hours as the last of the unit finally left for home: 'Embarked on SS *Prince George.*'

'As ADMS of the 47th London Division from August 1915 to June 1917, I necessarily saw much of the 5th London Field Ambulance . . . The loyalty, devotion to duty and the camaraderie displayed by all ranks helped materially to contribute to the honour of the Division . . . I can write nothing but good of the 5th. They did all that was asked of them and at all times they did it well'
Colonel J. D. Ferguson CMG, DSO
in History of the 5th London Field Ambulance TF.

* * *

'On Monday April 28th at the Twynholm Church Forward Movement, a very interesting evening was spent in listening to the experience of three more of our returned soldiers. Messrs Charles Perry, William Sidnell and William Stocker told their stories of life in the army, with its strange mixture of tragedy and comedy in such a manner that at one moment caused their audience to be convulsed with laughter and the next to be near to tears. The prevailing feeling, doubtless of all, as of the writer of these Notes, was of relief that the war which made those experiences necessary, was ended, coupled with a firm resolve to use all one's influence as a citizen in the years of peace to make a repetition of this world calamity impossible.'
Joyful Tidings, May 1919.

It is unknown if Will went back to work at Western & Son or if he did, for how long. He studied at night school and in his spare time and eventually became a primary school teacher in 1924. Initially he taught children up to the age of eleven. As he neared retirement age, he became a supply teacher working all over London, teaching children up to the then school leaving age of fourteen. When he went to one job interview, one of the interviewers asked him what sort of study he had done during the war. Will replied that the trenches had not been exactly conducive to study. He got the job. Later he organised evening classes for the pupils in chess, music, school plays, and swimming. He also organised athletics and football despite his injury causing him to walk with a limping rolling gait for the rest of his life. Harry, who was also a teacher, said of Will: 'He was a born teacher, better than many in his school.' He was active in school and church drama productions and some of his playwriting efforts survive.

He and Daisy were still active at Twynholm Church as late as 1928 according to various papers held in the Twynholm archives and a Twynholm Old Boys cricket and football club dinner menu in the family papers. However, their involvement tailed off after they moved to Putney. They had two daughters and two sons; the younger son was given the middle name Blair after Will's great friend John (Johnnie) Blair. Their younger daughter's middle name is Grace, after John's wife.

John Blair returned home safely in 1919, with the rank of sergeant, and went back to his previous job as a railway clerk but could not settle to work in an office. With his wife Grace, and their baby daughter, Joan, he emigrated to Canada in June 1920 to join his brother Joseph, farming in Alberta. Their daughter was eventually joined by four brothers. After twenty years in the harsh world of homesteading, John and Grace moved to Calgary, where John became an accountant. He died in 1978 aged eighty-seven. Unfortunately, Will and John had lost contact after John and Grace emigrated; Will regretted that for the rest of his life. In later years, he made several attempts to trace John but was unsuccessful.[198]

Will rarely took part in any reunions, parades, or memorial services as he did not want to be reminded of what he had experienced. He never again went abroad, preferring to take his young family on camping trips around Britain, driving them to their destination in an Austin 7 Tourer. During these holidays, he could always get a fire going, even when it was raining. The children all remembered that his fires looked odd but were effective. He started by digging a deep trench and making walls around the fire with the earth and grass. He said that he had learned and used this method in the trenches where his fire was usually the first one 'up and cooking'.

After he retired from teaching, Will and Daisy moved to Hayling Island, Hampshire, where Will took up fishing and keeping flat-coated retrievers. Around 1960, Daisy went on holiday to Europe with their daughter Iris and her family. Before she went, she wrote in a small notebook the names of some of the places where Will had served and a few comments in case they passed through them. The entry for the village of Houchin includes *'Ernie Austing, jam tart'*; we will probably never know what happened there but it was clearly memorable! John Blair's son Jim recalls that his father had talked about jam tarts but did not recall any details.

Harry's son, Julian, remembers that his father was always a little reticent about his life during the First World War. It transpired that Harry, with his deeply held religious and pacifist beliefs, had braved the storm of public opinion and been a Conscientious Objector. He had tried to join the RAMC in 1915 after finishing a course of study but recruiting had been closed. Despite being recommended for non-combatant service by a Exemption Tribunal, the army continually tried to conscript him into combatant units. He was held for a short time in an open prison, doing voluntary work in the community during the day, returning to the prison each night. He

---

[198] With the advent of the Internet and the availability of online records, finding, and making contact with, John's family proved to be relatively straightforward with the assistance of a genealogical and local history group in Alberta, Canada. – Ed.

eventually joined up in a strictly non-combat role in November 1917. Harry was awarded his BA degree in Religious Studies in December 1919. Ten years after the death of his fiancée Annie, he found love again and in 1925 he married Dorothy Lamb of Fulham.

The third brother, Alex (Alec), also survived the war. The Minute Book of the church Forward Movement notes on 4th April 1919 that he had just returned from the East. He eventually became an architect. His early work took him all over the country before he settled in North London, where he was chief of a power station in Essex. He is remembered as the real gentleman of the family. In 1923 he married Lillian Sears and had a son, Peter.

In a letter to the editor, Peter wrote: '*My father never used to talk about his war experiences which I doubt were as jolly as some of the old pictures would suggest. However, when they returned, safely thank goodness, I think my father (and your grandfather) did relate some of their experiences to the family. My aunt Irene, who was considerably younger than the others, told me that she found some of what they had to say so upsetting that she became very pacifist inclined.*'

Peter wrote of his uncle Will: '*I occasionally heard of some of uncle's exploits in later years, such as making bricks in the kitchen sink and baking them in the oven. I have fond recollections of him as being something of a character.*'

Of Daisy's three sisters, only Edie married, late in life. Ivy was thought to have been engaged to someone who was killed late in the war but it was never spoken about. She and Elsie shared a house through their long retirements; for many years living opposite Will and Daisy on Hayling Island.

Daisy died in 1974 and Will lived alone for the next fourteen years before moving to a nursing home after a bad fall. While putting out the milk bottles one night, he had slipped over on a patch of ice and broken his hip. He said afterwards that he wasn't too worried as he had his heavy winter coat on and he knew that the milkman would find him in the morning. He just snuggled up with his Sheltie dog for company and watched the stars. However, despite the best of care, he never fully recovered his independence. A few weeks before he died he said: 'They can take away my pain now, but they can't take away my memories of the war.' To the end of his life, he was always very reluctant to talk to any historians who contacted him. William Stocker died in 1989 aged ninety-six.

From his funeral address:

> *An early volunteer for the RAMC, he knew at first hand what the words 'Somme' and 'Ypres' really meant in terms of human suffering as he worked among the wounded and dying as a stretcher bearer. He was wounded on active service, but returned to duty caring not only for those who were Allied soldiers but also for those who were then considered to be the enemy. He was held in high esteem by them all and it is a mark of his intensely held humanitarian principles that differences in race, even in warfare, did not make him sacrifice those beliefs.*

* * * * *

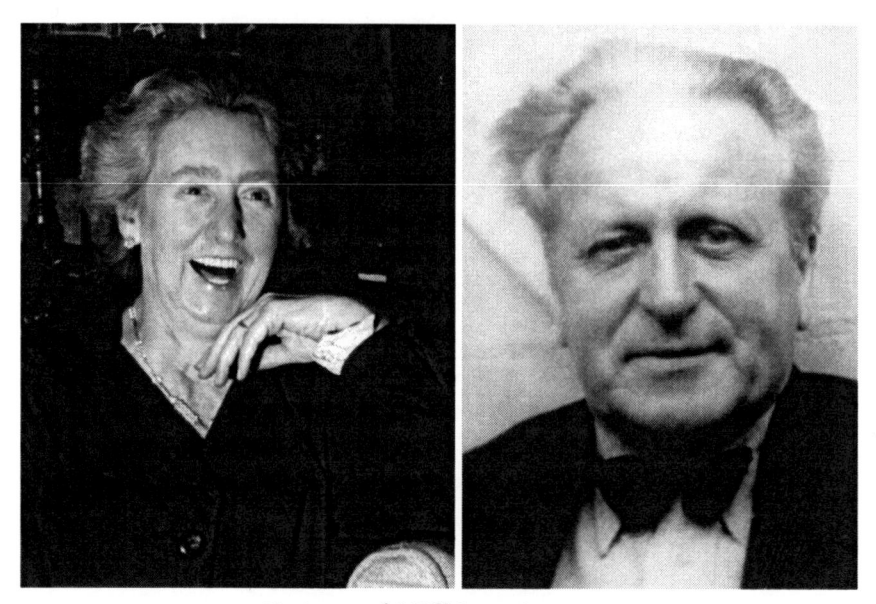

Daisy and Will in retirement

Daisy and Will on their fiftieth wedding anniversary 1967

Appendices

Appendix One

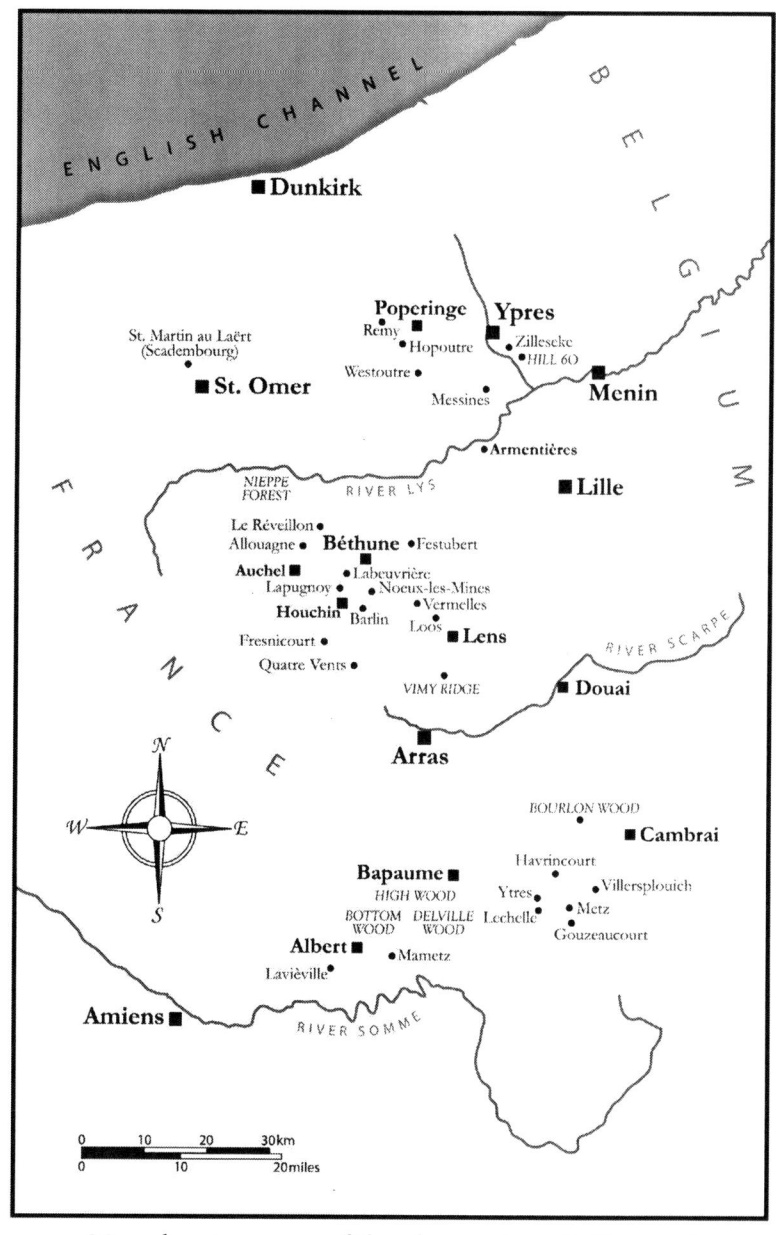

Map showing some of the places where Will served

Appendix Two

<u>GOING HOME</u>

This is an account of what happened the day Will got his 'Blighty One'. The main part of it was found in two different notepads, some of it written in shorthand. Other details were found on some odd sheets of paper and in an unfinished letter to his daughter, Connie.

If you were asked what was the best day of your life, I wonder what you would say. I have no doubt which day I exalt to this category – it was 21st March 1918. I was in France at the time on the Cambrai Front with the RAMC in the 47th Territorial Division. We had been in France 3 years and a rumour went around that we volunteers would go home after 3 years abroad. But that rumour was scotched by another that went round that General Gough, in charge of the 47th Division, had heard it and sent back the message: "You can tell the 47th Division that when I can take them all home in a rowing boat they will go back home." The generals well behind the lines playing chess with men's lives cared little for the men. Another rumour followed it that the Germans would launch their biggest attack yet to end the War in the Spring. If such an attack happened we knew our Division would be in it. Then 6 weeks before 21st March, all letters were banned from going to England.[199] We could receive letters from home but no replies were allowed. Something big was on. This was the first time that letters home were banned. All leave was suspended. We got fidgety – something big was afoot. Every night for many months we had heard the traffic going up the line. For many nights we heard the guns rumbling up to the Front.

On the 20th March 1918 the 47th Division moved up the line and the 5th London Field Ambulance was ordered to take up positions at Havrincourt, a village existing in name only – just a massive pile of

---

[199] However, there are letters from this period.

rubble, a place already flattened by gunfire. Things were fairly quiet, apart from the random shells coming over. We arrived in little groups at dusk and were told to find dugouts in a given area. Most of us chose a deep old German dugout which was down many rough steps. We sat on our haunches and dozed and woke all through the night. At dawn we made some tea and had bread and jam to eat and then all hell broke loose, apparently it was heard in London. The Germans had pushed forward and broken through on both sides of us and we were in a salient. Then, when we were expecting to have orders to RETREAT, we stretcher-bearers were ordered to go forward 100 yards to Havrincourt Wood where there were lots of wounded to be picked up. The wood was being heavily shelled and it seemed madness to go in but orders are orders and have to be obeyed and we picked up our stretchers.

We were all very scared of course, it seemed sheer madness, certain suicide to go forward. Vic Saunders, Charlie Double and 'Yanto' Evans[200] were on my squad and I was in front. Poor old Yanto was very white. I said to him: "Come on, Yanto, we've done it before and so I suppose we can do it again". Hardly were the words out of my mouth when suddenly a salvo of shells burst on the top of us. Men and stretcher went up in the air. You don't just drop down, you are blown off your feet into the air and you don't know where or when you are going to fall. Charlie Double lay dead, Vic Saunders was struggling to his feet. The lads in the dugout came rushing out. Young Roberts,[201] a jolly good chap, came running over to me as I tried to get up. He said, "Are you alright, Bill?" I said, "I think so, but I can't seem to get up". He said, "You've been wounded in the foot, half your foot has gone, put your arm around my shoulder I'll take you down into the dugout", which was only a few paces. I hopped along on my good foot and went down on my knees. I said to him to go in front in case I tripped. When I got down, they lifted me on to a stretcher and set to work on me. They cut off my boot and cut off my trouser leg to my knee. Len Clark, captain of our football team, got off my puttees. He was on Fulham's Football Club to play for Fulham

---

[200] Probably Owen Watkin Evans.
[201] Vernon Burgoyne Roberts was injured later the same day but was able to return to duty the following day.

after the war. I was looking up at them and Len said: "You've got a cert Blighty one here – turn your head away. Don't look at it, come on have a fag." It was the usual procedure to a wounded man. I took the fag and started smoking it. Every now and then I glanced at the boys attending to me, "Now don't look at it." I never at any time saw my wound, I was not allowed to. They bound up my foot securely. Then someone said: "A motor ambulance has arrived with Sergeant MacKenzie and a driver. Get the wounded out as quickly as possible". I went up on my knees and sat at the back. "Get away as quick as you can" said Sergeant MacKenzie. It was his last words, he was killed.[202]

The ambulance travelled slowly down the broken road. I sat at the back watching the shells bursting around. After 7 or 8 miles we stopped at Duisans at a railway siding. On the track was a very long train with Red Crosses painted on a circle of white. Lots of motor ambulances had arrived there, loading stretcher cases on to the train. Shells were coming over and looking up to the sky I saw a German observation balloon high up probably directing the fire. I said to a sergeant: "What do I do?" He said: "Get aboard the train anywhere, be quick it's about to go off." I hopped off on my good foot and clambered up into the train. I sat in the corner seat watching the shells bursting around. I was up near the engine. Then I thought: "That German gunfire is trying to knock out the engine. I'm climbing out and getting down somewhere near the end of the train." I clambered out and hopped along the railway track and got in near the end of the train. I sat down on a seat. Then I said to myself, this is as bad as the front. Shall I clamber out again and try and find a seat in the middle of the train? And then I thought if I tried to find a safer spot I might be left behind. That would be disastrous so I stayed where I was. Then the engine driver blew his whistle and we began to move. Hooray! I thought. I'm safe at last. We travelled about 6 miles and another salvo of shells exploded each side of the train. Then the train really did get a move on and there were no more shells.

---

[202] I have been unable to identify a Sgt Mackenzie, in the RAMC or the Army Service Corps who was killed on this date. Will may mean transport Sgt Frank Cosens, who was attached to 5th LFA and who died of wounds on 22nd March 1918. – Ed.

Then I remembered a letter I had been given in the dugout just before I was wounded, it was from Daisy. I smiled as I read it. *'It's very bad of you not to write more often. People are saying* (it wasn't difficult to guess who the people were) *why is it that since you were married you get so few letters?'* Of course, it was easily explained: all outgoing mail for 6 weeks had been prohibited. I just smiled. Nothing was going to upset me now. AT LONG LAST I WAS ON THE WAY HOME.

The train rumbled on now very fast. I suppose because it was full of wounded and dying men there were many nurses on board. At last one came to me. "How are you feeling?" I said, "Very well, thank you." "I'll take your temperature. That's quite normal," she said. "How does your leg feel. I presume it hurts a bit." I said, "It doesn't hurt much, but it aches a lot, I can't lift it, only by putting the good foot under it and moving it slightly." Then she changed some of the top bandages. When the nurse had finished she slowly lifted my foot on to the seat opposite. The train rumbled on mile after mile through the fields. Every now and then we passed a level crossing where there was a group of women holding up little union jacks and calling out 'Brave Anglais soldiers'. Evidently this train passed the same time every day from the British Front.

A tin of M & V rations

Eventually dinner time arrived and the nurses said we must all help each other. The orderlies brought in cases of M & V rations in tins. "Anybody good at opening tins?" "Yes," I called out, "I am." When I first came out to France I had sent home a message: *'Send me as soon as possible the best tin opener you can buy'*. Behind the lines I was always a cook and the tin opener on the jack knife was a poor thing and the boys got some nasty gashes in consequence. So from the earliest days I had a first class tin opener in my left hand top pocket. They passed over all the tins to me to open. Dinner over, the nurses said: "All wooden cases and empty tins and half finished out of the window."

We went on and on and at last when it was quite dark we halted. The name of the station was Le Tréport. Orderlies came running onto the platform and I was put on a stretcher and carried out to one of the waiting ambulances. After a short ride I was taken to a building and carried inside. There were nurses in the hall so I knew it was a hospital. A nurse came along and said: "I have one vacant bed towards the end of my ward," so I was carried down and lifted on to a bed. The ward was dark except for one or two tiny lights. "Now, can you undress yourself?" "Yes" I said. "Well, I'll go back to my room and watch you through the window, any trouble just wave your hand." I got off my uniform and put on the pyjamas. The nurse came down and put a cushion under my foot and a sort of cradle on the bed to warn others that my foot was wounded. Then she took my temperature and said that it was satisfactory. She said: "I shall come down every now and then, don't worry. I won't wake up a doctor. The doctors have had a heavy day. How do you feel in yourself?" I said: "Very well but a bit tired you know." "Now don't worry I shall keep my eye on you during the night. Now is there anything you want, drink or bedpan or bottle?" I said "Nothing thank you." She made me comfortable and said good night. I watched her walk down the ward with the little torch in her hand, looked at the clock with a little light over it and just turned my head and in seconds I was fast asleep.

It seemed I was only asleep for a few minutes when I felt somebody tugging at my shoulders trying to wake me up. I momentarily thought I was dozing in a dugout and it was my turn to go out. I opened my eyes and said, "What's up?" I saw the smiling face of my nurse. "Well, how is Private Stocker this morning?" "What, is it morning already? I must have slept well" "You certainly did" said my nurse. "I came to look at you 5 times, you didn't stir an inch all night..."

> *(Unfortunately, a page is missing here: there are torn edges in the pad. From the size of the pad and number of sheets used, there are about 200 words missing. – Ed.)*

... has grabbed it. I replied, "That's alright, that's going to get me home!" Then the doctor went to a patient opposite me and came back to me. Then he said "How long have you been out here?" I said "3 years." Then he said with a smile, "Would you like to go back to Blighty?" I replied, "Would I not!" "Mark him down for Blighty, nurse." Then he said to the soldier next to me who had been watching me as they dressed my foot and had a wounded arm: "And would you like to go back to Blighty too?" "The gentleman who sends me home will have good luck for the rest of his life." The doctor and nurse burst out laughing and said: "Mark him down for Blighty too." The doctor went off and the nurse said to an orderly: "Now put on our special record for the new arrivals." The orderly went over to the old horned gramophone, wound it up and put on the special record. I wondered what it would be – perhaps *God Save the King* or *Land of Hope and Glory* which would not have interested me a bit, but it was not. It was a woman's voice and I often think of it now, I've forgotten the verse but the chorus never. Here it is:-

> *You are as welcome as the flowers in May,*
> *We have waited for you day by day*
> *We love you in the same old way,*
> *You are as welcome as the flowers in May*[203]

The nurse said, "Did you like it?" I said, "Wonderful." Then I asked nurse if she had an envelope and sheet of paper and pencil. She brought them to me. I remember what I wrote was something like:

---

[203] 'You're As Welcome as the Flowers in May', Daniel J. Sullivan, 1902.

'You will be surprised to know I am in hospital wounded in the lower part of my leg and foot. Don't worry – I'm very happy – so you ought to be. I'm coming home for good next week. Finished with France.'

Now perhaps you can understand when I say the 21st March 1918 was the best day of my life.

Appendix Three

The following is a transcript of a tape recording made a few weeks before Will died. Will's grandson, Ashley (A) was visiting him. When Will suddenly started to talk about his army memories, Ashley hurriedly switched on a small office tape recorder in his briefcase. The tape starts abruptly with a few unintelligible words. Will rambles a little at times and there are a few places where the words cannot be made out, indicated by (. . .), a long pause is indicated by . . . . Sadly, the recording was made before anyone was aware of the existence of the letters. There are so many questions which might have been asked and answered that afternoon.

Will: "(. . .) a chap called Ernie Austing, he was our left-back at football. . . . and the shell came over and exploded and knocked us over and I turned to Ernie and said: 'My goodness, that was near' and he was still laying there and the fellows came running out of the dugout. I said to the officer, 'Is Ernie badly hit?' He said, 'No hope whatever' and in about five minutes he was dead . . . of course our worst part was the Somme because it rained all the time we were up there, six weeks of it."

A: "The lines of the trenches are still there, you can see just how close the Germans and the Allies were, it's incredible."

Will: "Yes, they used to chuck from the front row, front trenches, hand grenades and if they didn't explode, the Germans used to pick them up quickly and sling them back. . . . the hand grenades, about as big as that cup. Oh yes, I know them, I know the Somme. Thierry Wood, High Wood, Flatiron Copse. High Wood I remember very well. We used to go out at night to get in the wounded, and when you got out there, you were the distance from here I suppose almost to Havant[204] and the star shells going up all the time and shells

---

[204] About four miles.

coming over all the time and you just lost your way. You'd pick up a chap and carry him; you used to have six to the stretcher because it was raining so hard and we didn't stop in the trenches but right out on the top.[205]

I remember one night we picked up a Scotty and we went on and on and on and then we had a rest. At last we began to argue. They said, 'Well, we go that way.' And I said, 'I'm not going to go that way, you're going to go back again. I think our FA post is over there, what are we going to do?'[206]

The Scotty that was on the stretcher was fast asleep. And then a fellow came along in the trenches. We said, 'Here, have you passed the First Aid post?'

'Yes,' he said.

'Where is it?' I said.

'Somewhere over there,' he said.

So we all turned round and made our way back to this Aid post and then the Scotty woke up. As we put him down he said, 'Are you the chaps who picked me up last night?'

'Yes.'

'Have you been carrying me all night?'

'Yes.'

He said, 'In my kilt there's a little pocket with fifty francs in there. Share it between the lot of you.'

---

[205] 'The "carry" from the Cough Drop to Bazentin-le-Grand took a squad of six men four to six hours to accomplish owing to the mud and shells holes ... increasingly difficult on account of direct enemy observation. The wounded had therefore to be carried out at night. The intense darkness of the Somme nights, and the circumventing of shell holes and batteries in the quest for the Cough Drop, were, and still are, a nightmare to the RAMC of the 47th Division.' **History of the 47th Division – A. H. Maude.**

[206] Will's grandson, Ashley, remembers Will telling him that they had heard voices and stopped to get their bearings. Then they realised that the voices were German and that they had strayed close to the German lines. They had to retreat as quickly and quietly as they could, still carrying the casualty on a stretcher.

'We mustn't take money, Jock.' So we just left him there in this dugout and then an ambulance came along on the broken road and he was parked on there and went home to England.

Oh, I remember the Somme. I don't suppose there's a day that I don't think of the Somme and all the boys that were there and the way some of them were lost. There was one, a very good officer, all our officers were toppers. . . .[207] Captain Clark. . . . When we used to come back we were in such a state. There was one sandbag tied up to there and another sandbag up there and a sandbag down tied round there and another one there, overcoats were no good. We put a big blanket round our shoulders with a big safety pin and then over that the groundsheet with another couple of safety pins in the little brass holes, tin hat and that's how we went. I remember when we came back one night, he said: 'It's a bit rough out there, I'll come out with you tonight, boys, and see what it's really like out there.' So that night again we went out and we got up to what they called the Cough Drop Dugout and then a shell came over and Clark was killed.[208] That was the end of Captain Clark.

Oh, the Somme, the men that were lost on the Somme. It wasn't the first battlefield we'd been on but nothing like the Somme anywhere else. Over on the Somme at night the dead were all over the place, the Germans and British and all. A fellow said, 'It looks as if the British army's wiped out.' Thousands. 'Cos the machine gun had come into use instead of the rifle. They used to wait for the chaps to come over and turned their handle and. . . . I often think of it.

We were six weeks on the Somme. I shall never forget when we came out of the Somme. Sergeant Major who was in one of the dugouts right at the back, when we got down there he said: 'Well, boys, make your way back to Lavièville, you're going out.' Another troop was coming up. 'As you go through the dugouts tell the boys to make their way back to Lavièville.' And although we'd marched up there we came back in twos and threes and fours.[209] There was a very

---

[207] A well-liked person.
[208] Captain Sydney Clark was killed by a sniper on 2nd October 1916.
[209] 'Seriously depleted, with beards and in rags' – Daisy's notebook.

tall chap there, very nice chap but he was not a stretcher-bearer, he was too tall for anybody, about 6 ft. 2 in. He went along the hut and he said: 'Look, take your trousers off and all the trousers you want in that tent and your tunics chuck them down there, get another tunic in there, puttees in there, boots in there, over there is the pump.' And the fellows gradually undressed and they chucked the stuff down and they got up to the pump and started washing themselves down to the waist and he said: 'Your kitbags are in there with all your shaving kit.'

We hadn't washed or shaved for about six weeks. The fellows began to shave themselves and look clean and then a clerk said: 'Look in the tent, there's all the fags that you want, there's hundreds of packets. Help yourself.'

And it was marvellous to see all these chaps come back in such a filthy state and then change over and have a wash and shave and get a smoke and talk. I remember one chap saying, 'You know, Bill, it doesn't matter how long we live, we shall never forget those things.' He said: 'How do you feel now?' I said: 'I feel alright.'

The Somme was the worst, well, it wouldn't stop raining! My word. Shocking. And then of course, when we got behind the lines and slept in the huts, one after the other couldn't go to sleep and had to be drugged and about twenty fellows had to go back, their nerves had gone. Of course, there was such a blooming row going on all the time. It seemed like the shells going over and our shells going back, nobody could hear properly. And they had to go down to the whatsername and have their ears syringed and they syringed them out with hydrogen peroxide. You put your head on one side and they put this stuff in a bubble and it went in and a great big piece of wax came out big as a cherry stone and then the other ear. But the noise was so terrific it just messed up a fellow's ears.

And then of course we had mustard gas and tear gas on the Somme and pineapples, they used to call it. They'd say: 'I can smell pineapples' so the gas mask – in a box. 'Gas masks on!' and we used to put them on. Ooh, they were blooming awkward what with powder and shell holes and two little goggles in the dark. You know the fellows only put these gas masks on at the very last because it hampered them so.

I was actually wounded at a place called Havrincourt. I don't know whether you thought of that? But High Wood, the trees were about a yard high, that's all, just stumps. You would come along in the dark and crawl into all the little stumps and they'd say that's High Wood and we turned right and came across a lot of stumps about that high which had been trees and Perce said: 'That must be Devils Wood.'

What a shocking waste of life. Dammit, we hadn't been on the Somme five minutes. They never talked about chaps getting killed, it was always 'going west'. They said: 'Cornish's squad's gone west.'

'Cornish? Cornish? Cornish?' said the chaps. 'Who the dickens is Cornish?'[210]

'Well,' they said, 'he only came up last week.' And I was out there three years, so you know, luck of the draw. 'Cornish's squad, he's gone west. He only came out last week.'

But I don't think there'll ever be any more wars quite like that. You see in the Second World War they'd got the Siegfried Line. Did you see that? Tremendous rampart, like the Chinese wall, stretching right across France. In the Second World War they got up to the Siegfried line, but the Germans went right down to the end into Switzerland and came round that end that time. Then of course there were more aeroplane bombings. But I wasn't in the Second World War, only the First.

But one thing always, Bruce said the same thing when he came out[211] – he was in the army towards the second part of the Second World War, he was in Egypt: that was a piece of cake, you never saw any enemy – the wonderful camaraderie between the chaps. It didn't matter who he was and a fine old mixture. You'd have a chap

---

[210] Will probably means Maurice Cornwell, who was killed alongside Sidney Foxon on 18th January 1918. He had only joined the 5th London Field Ambulance two weeks earlier.

[211] Will's younger son, a Royal Signals despatch rider in World War Two.

who was a costermonger, then on my stretcher squad I had three sculptors: Reid Dick, Campbell, and Oakley.[212]

So when you were in the army you didn't know whether you got a costermonger's barrow boy or a bank clerk. We had two chaps training for parsons, we got a proper mixture but they all fell in. It didn't matter as long as you pulled your whack and played the game you were all good friends. But I don't think there ever again will be wars like the old wars. I doubt whether there ever will again because I mean what with these atomic bombs nobody's going to win. The Germans went into the war knowing they'd got a preponderance of guns and men and they were going to win and would have done if the Americans hadn't joined in. When America came in, you got all the American wealth. One thing about the atomic bomb, it'll make old-fashioned wars obsolete.

Just before the war broke out, just weeks, I was on holiday in Germany on a walking tour and we went to such places as Koblenz and Cologne. Köln I think they call it. And of course, mark you, the Germans had colossal losses too. I remember a chap saying to me, this was while we were on the Somme, 'Did you see that last batch of prisoners who came in, a dozen or so? They're not soldiers, they're baby-faced boys.' So chaps of sixteen were called up, you know.

. . . . 440 yards. That was my favourite distance. I used to like it because when I ran for West London in the London Sports, I used to say to the quarter milers, 'It's a quarter mile sprint.' I mean, when I first saw the quarter mile I went trotting off like it was a mile. But when I got to France and we went down and the gun went off, I shot off like it was a hundred yards sprint. I got miles in front. Course if you've got good bellows (. . .) and by the time I got to the whatsername, I was well away. My brother Harry didn't like the quarter mile. He could run alright for 80 yards, 100 yards, but when it came to a quarter he wasn't broad-shouldered enough and hadn't got the bellows and he was absolutely done up. I used to like the

---

[212] Sir William Reid Dick, 1879–1961. His works include 'Lion' above the Menin Gate in Ypres and the Kitchener memorial chapel in St Paul's Cathedral in London.
John Campbell, artist and illustrator 1885–1935.
Alfred James Oakley, 1878–1959. He sculpted the memorial for the 1st/5th and 2nd/5th London Field Ambulances in the parish church of St Alfege, Greenwich.

quarter. I loved the 100 and the 200 and the mile. I won the mile. I didn't like the half mile much. I always used to lead the mile in France.

I remember one chap who came up to us, Tom Hickling, a very nice chap. He says, 'I believe you're a bit of runner, so am I. You can have all the other distances but you're not having the mile, the mile's my distance.' And I said to his pal,[213] 'Is old Tom any good?' He says, 'Well, I saw him run when they had a lot of regiments down at Stamford Bridge and he came in first and very comfortably.'

So the day came and I was running in the various races and in the evening it was the mile. I started off steadily and I led all the way until the last 50 yards I heard footsteps behind and he came up and the two of us came in running together, absolutely abreast. But in the last 10 yards I altered my step and I got in front and won the mile too. But I think it was the toughest race I'd ever been in and the last race. I used to love running. I was quite good at swimming, I got two of the three championships at school but I never reckoned myself as good at swimming as I was at running. It was a strength being rather short. It's very good for you though, that sort of thing when you're young.

Oh well, it's nice to see you."

* * *

---

[213] Frank Herbert Orchard.

Appendix Four

'A Meditation from the Front'
by **Alexander Stocker**

Some time ago I participated in a scene which is unfortunately only of too common occurrence in this once peaceful village. I assisted in removing from its improvised hearse the body of a British Soldier, killed in action. The cart drew up at the door of what was once a charming village church, but whose splendid steeple is now pierced with huge shell holes, and whose altar, from which the priest a foretime blessed his rural flock, is now but a picture of confusion and ruin. We removed the remains reverently, and with slow measured steps, which echoed with hollow resonance throughout the sacred building, carried them to the end of the church, and there deposited them until the grave-diggers could come and complete the melancholy duty. I gazed for a moment at the tragedy of blighted youth, the first of its kind I had yet seen. The cold, stone-flagged church, with its dirt-strewn floor and empty window casements, through which streamed the moonlight, but made colder the resting place of him whose whole course was now run. I did not know who he was, or whence he came; all I knew was that the fury of war had claimed him for a victim, and swiftly and remorsefully his soul had been borne away, but footprints had been left on the sands of time. A small white cross on a grass mound, with nothing but a name and number, to distinguish it from its host of fellows – a few heart-broken friends at home, and they seem all the footprints he could leave. With sad feelings I turned away, and stole silently out of the church.

It was a sombre enough picture, but impressive. Was this the final result of all his hopes and aspirations, and the culmination of all his struggles and efforts? Was it for this that he was given life – to die alone, forgotten, save but a few, in a strange land, just when he was beginning to live! I am not alone in such questioning; the whole world is asking this today. The mourning thousands, hugging their shattered dreams ask us with complainings and grief, 'Is this all you can do? Is this the only message which your boasted civilization and Christianity can give to us?' May the trump of victory soon sound. Our terms we dare not dictate to Thee, but God, in Thine own time, may the olive branch once more be extended, so that out of the blood-like sunset of a tempestuous and raging day their own harbinger may usher in a better dawn, with all passion spent and impurity gone in the healing of Thy Eternal Light.

Abridged from *Joyful Tidings*, **January 1917**

APPENDIX FIVE

The lyrics to most of the songs mentioned by Will can be found online. Several of them can be listened to on Youtube or downloaded from various music websites.

'A Little Bit of Heaven', 1914 J. Keirn Brennan & E. R. Ball

'A Little Love, a Little Kiss' (Un peu d'amour), 1913 Lau Silesu, English lyrics by Adrian Ross

'Absent', 1913 Catherine Y. Glen & John W. Metcalf

'Dear Love Remember Me', 1903 Charles Marshall & Harold Harford

'I Hear You Calling Me', 1908 Charles Marshall & Harold Harford

'I'll Sing Thee Songs of Araby,' before 1889 Frederic Clay & W. G. Wills

'In the Twi-Twi-Twilight', c. 1910 Charles Wilmot & Herman E. Darewski

'Keep the Home Fires Burning', 1914 Ivor Novello

'Nirvana', 1900 Frederic Edward Weatherly & Stephen Adams

'Now I Have to Call Him Father', c. 1908 Charles Collins & Fred Godfrey

'Oh Dry Those Tears', 1901 Arthur Pryor & Teresa del Riego

'Put Me Amongst the Girls', 1907 C. W. Murphy & G. Arthurs

'Robin Adair', c. 1750 Lady Caroline Keppel

'Somewhere a Voice Is Calling', 1911 E. Newton & Arthur F. Tate

'Spring Song', 1904 Charles Ives

'Take Me Back to Dear Old Blighty', 1916 Mills, Godfrey & Scott

'The Holy City', 1892 Frederic Weatherly & Stephen Adams

'The Rosary', 1898 Robert Cameron Rogers & Ethelbert Woodbridge Nevin

'The Sweetest Story Ever Told', 1892 Robert M. Stults

'Until', 1910 Teschemacher & Sanderson

'You're as Welcome as the Flowers in May', 1902 Daniel J. Sullivan

'You're the Flower of My Heart, Sweet Adeline', 1903 Armstrong Gerard

SOURCES AND BIBLIOGRAPHY

6th London Field Ambulance (47th London Division) History, notes and autobiographical accounts re activities during the First World War, Wellcome Library, London, RAMC/801/20/5

ANON., *5th London Field Ambulance, 47th (London) Division T.F. 1914-1919*, London, Lake & Bell, n.d. c. 1935

BREWER, Rev. Dr., *Dr Brewer's Guide to Scripture Histories*, London, 1874

CAINE, Hall, *The Eternal City*, William Heinemann, London, 1901

COLEMAN, Frank, *A Brief Record of the 6th London Field Ambulance, 47th Division, During the War*, John Bale & Danielsson Ltd, 1924

GILBERT, Martin, *First World War Atlas*, Weidenfeld and Nicolson, 1970

GORDON, Samuel D., *Quiet Talks on Power*, F. H. Revell Co., Chicago / New York, 1903

GOUGH, Sir Hubert, *The Fifth Army*, 1931, 2nd edition Chivers, 1968

HAGGARD, H. Rider, *The Pearl Maiden, a tale of the fall of Jerusalem*, Longmans, London, 1903

HEADON HILL, *Caged! The Romance of a Lunatic Asylum*, London Ward Locke, 1900

HERINGHAM, Major General Sir Wilmot, *A Physician in France*, Edward Arnold, London 1919

HURST, Sidney C., *The Silent Cities, an illustrated guide to the War Cemeteries and Memorials to the 'Missing' in France and Flanders: 1914-1918,* The Naval and Military Press, first published by Methuen, 1929

Joyful Tidings, the monthly newsletter of the Fulham Cross Christian Mission 1891-1972

LIDDELL HART, B. H., *History of the First World War,* Pan Books, London, 1970

MACPHERSON, Major-General Sir W. G., *History of the Great War Based on Official Documents – Medical Services,* HMSO, 3 volumes 1921, 1922, 1923

MAUDE, A. H. (ed.), *The History of the 47th London Division 1914-1919. By some who served with it in the Great War,* Amalgamated Press, London 1922

MUNRO, Donald (ed.), *Diaries of a Stretcher-Bearer 1916-1918 L/Cpl Edward Munro MM, 5th Field Ambulance AIF,* Boolarong Press, Australia, 2010

NATIONAL ARCHIVES, *British Army Medal Index Cards 1914-1920*

ORCHARD, Frank, *The Private Papers of F H Orchard, RAMC,* Imperial War Museum Docs 6671

PARTRIDGE, Eric, *A Dictionary of Slang and Unconventional English,* Routledge & Kegan Paul, 8th Edition, 1984

POWER, Frederick D., *Bible Doctrine for Young Disciples,* Revell, 1899

ROYAL FIELD LEECH, *The Tale of a Casualty Clearing Station,* W Blackwood & Sons 1917

SERVICE, Robert W., *Rhymes of a Red-Cross Man*, T. Fisher Unwin Ltd, London 1916

SMILES, Samuel, *Duty: with illustrations of courage, patience & endurance*, John Murray, London 1880

STRATTON-PORTER, Geneva, *The Harvester*, Hodder & Stoughton, London 1911

The Fulham Chronicle Newspaper 1914–1918

WALLACE, Lew, *Ben Hur, a tale of the Christ*, Walter Scott Ltd, London 1887

War Diary of the 1st/4th (London) Field Ambulance, The National Archives, Documents WO 95/2725/1

War Diary of the 1st/5th (London) Field Ambulance, The National Archives, Documents WO 95/2725

War Diary of the 1st/6th (London) Field Ambulance, The National Archives, Documents WO 95/2725/2

War Diary of ADMS, 47th Division, The National Archives, Documents WO 95/2713

WARDLEWORTH, Dennis, *William Reid Dick, Sculptor*, Ashgate Publishing 2013

WILLIAMSON, Anne, *Henry Williamson and the First World War*, History Press, 2004

USEFUL WEBSITES

Ancestry
www.ancestry.co.uk

British Newspaper Archive
www.britishnewspaperarchive.co.uk

Commonwealth War Graves Commission
www.cwgc.org

Find My Past
www.findmypast.co.uk

Imperial War Museum
www.iwm.org.uk

National Archives
www.thenationalarchives.gov.uk

The Great War Forum
1914-1918.invisionzone.com
1914-1918.net/fieldambulances.htm

The Long Long Trail
www.longlongtrail.co.uk

The RAMC in the Great War
www.ramc-ww1.com

Wellcome Library
wellcomelibrary.org

Wikipedia
en.wikipedia.org

INDEX

A

Advanced Dressing Stations (ADS) xvii, 57, 67, 80, 87, 103, 116, 123-4, 132, 134, 163, 166
aircraft 50
Allouagne 46 n. 39, 80 n. 70
Archer, Arthur J. 14
Auchel 93, 97, 99 n. 92, 108
Austing, Ernest A. P. 108, 164 n. 148, 245, 259

B

Baswitz, Albert 37, 45 n. 34
baths xvii, 61, 86, 131, 139, 157
Battle of Loos 80 n. 70, 87 n. 77
Bell, Victor 30 n. 26, 44
Béthune 45, 55, 56 n. 50, 57, 58 n. 53, 65, 80
billets 4, 7-8, 11, 18, 25-7, 32, 43, 47, 57, 72, 74, 83-4, 94, 103, 116, 118, 120, 142, 153, 160, 164, 241
Bird, George S. 132 n. 128, 134
bivouac 82-3, 86, 118
Black, Annie 23, 61, 140 n. 132
Black, Robert W. xv, 11, 15, 85, 157, 186, 222-3
Blackpool xvii, 229-30, 233, 237-8
Blair, John N. ix, 5-6, 8, 10, 13-14, 19, 22, 26, 28-33, 38, 40, 99, 117-18, 125, 132-3, 139, 146, 151, 156, 167, 190-1, 200, 202, 207-8, 214, 220, 244-5
bombardment 55, 59, 84, 100
Bottom Wood 123 n. 114
Bull, Ernest A. 207

C

Calcutt, Lionel H. 14, 28, 53, 127
Cambrai 188 n. 170, 194, 202, 252
camping 245
Carrington, Cecil 14, 32
casualties xvii, 53, 57, 61, 88-9, 117, 123 n. 114, 126-8, 163-4, 187-8, 210-11
censor 45
Chateau le Réveillon 60 n. 54
Chelsea boys 7, 20
Christianity 6, 267
Church of Christ xv, 33 n. 28, 113 n. 104, 186
Clark, Leonard G. 253
Clark, Sydney 125-7, 261
Close, Lawrence 80
cooking 8, 125
Cornwell, Maurice W. 198 n. 178
Cough Drop dugout 124
Coward, Albert 45, 72, 181
Curtis, Alfred J. 31, 44, 61, 70-2, 93, 97, 174, 182, 214

D

Double, Charles 210 n. 185

E

engagement 6, 24, 32, 205, 236
Evans, Owen W. 253

F

faith xv, xxi, 16 n. 9, 56, 59-60, 67-8, 83, 85, 95, 100, 124, 132, 142, 148-9, 164, 189-90, 198, 210, 224, 257, 267
field ambulances v, xvi-xvii, xx, 4, 9, 21, 38, 43, 67, 80, 88-90, 105, 108, 119-21, 123, 125-6, 128, 159, 163, 167, 186-7, 243, 252, 263-4
4th London 88, 123, 125, 163

5th London v, 4 n. 3, 14, 26, 38, 42-4, 57, 89, 99 n. 92, 108, 121, 125-6, 132 n. 127, 139, 163 n. 147, 164 n. 149, 243, 252, 263-4
6th London xvii, 21 n. 15, 43, 57, 80, 88, 90, 120 n. 111, 125, 128 n. 122, 163 n. 147, 165 n. 150
Flatiron Copse 123, 259
food 8, 96, 192, 199, 216
football xviii, 7-8, 20, 35, 37-8, 53, 72, 108, 113, 130, 133, 135, 244, 253, 259
47th Division xvii, 89, 120, 123, 125-8, 179, 187, 194, 210, 243, 252, 260
Foxon, Sidney C. 198 n. 178, 263 n. 211
Fulham ix, xiii, xv, 2, 4, 21 n. 15, 29 n. 25, 45 n. 34, 113 n. 104, 127, 186, 222-3, 246, 253
Fulham Chronicle 3-4, 113 n. 104, 126 n. 117, 186

G

Germany xviii, xxi, 1-3, 94, 177, 264
Gozney, Charles M. 210
green envelopes 54, 65, 77, 119, 195

H

Haig, Douglas 194
Hall, Walter 30 n. 26, 45 n. 35, 122
Hanley, Grace 200
Hare and Hounds 117 n. 108
Hatfield 4, 6, 9-10, 18, 22, 25-6, 28, 40, 174, 207
Hearn, Arthur 14, 26, 156
Holgate, Ada (Mrs Ada Stocker) xiii, 24, 49, 176, 178, 208
Holgate, Stephen 183, 186
honeymoon 167, 180, 186, 202, 204, 207, 216
Horrocks, George G. 9, 53, 230-1
horses 43, 88, 112
Howard, Esme 82, 126, 128, 139, 172
hymns 147, 224

I

Indian Cavalry 44

J

John Bull 101, 146, 153
Joyful Tidings xv-xvi, 21, 45-6, 77, 124, 172-3, 181, 203, 211, 229, 242, 244, 267

L

Labeuvrière 60, 74
Lamb, Dorothy 246
laundry xvii, 52-3, 139
Lavièville 261
leave 15-18, 20, 24-5, 27-9, 33, 35-40, 74, 76, 78, 84, 91-2, 94-5, 98-9, 101-3, 105, 107-15, 117, 119, 130, 136, 139-40, 142-3, 145-6, 148-52, 156, 159, 166-9, 172, 174, 177, 179-82, 184, 186, 188, 190-1, 194, 197-9, 202-5, 213, 218, 224, 229, 234, 236-40, 252, 266
Lloyd George, David 88, 96, 123 n. 114, 224 n. 189
London Irish Rifles 30

M

MacFarlane, Walter J. B. 133-4
Maddison, William 90, 95, 126, 182, 221
Maisey, Ada xiii, 10-11, 140, 152, 154, 166, 176, 183, 205, 207, 227-8, 239
Mander, William xv, 29, 157, 181
marching 55, 60, 120
marriage 32, 141, 147, 170, 174-5, 180, 186, 193
Melville, Gavin 183 n. 166
Millson, Sydney T. 168
money 7, 11, 20, 22, 27, 32, 38, 40, 52, 54, 63, 72, 78, 92, 102, 121, 137, 139, 156, 166, 172, 197, 223, 225-6, 240, 261

Munro, J. Donald S. ix, 105-6, 129, 173

N

Nicholls, Horace W. 142 n. 136

O

Oakley, Alfred J. 264 n. 213
officers xvii, 7, 15, 21-2, 29-30, 40, 43, 45, 55, 80, 83, 86, 90, 90 n. 86, 93, 98, 100, 103, 105, 110, 112-13, 116, 118, 121, 125, 127, 130, 132 n. 127, 141, 151, 156, 160, 163, 166, 173, 210, 221, 226, 229, 259, 261
Orchard, Frank H. 164 n. 149, 165 n. 150, 193 n. 174
Owens, Basil xiv, 72, 99, 101, 213
Owens, Ernest xiv, 27, 98-9, 112, 129, 137, 154, 181-2, 203, 213, 234

P

parcels xv, 46, 49, 75, 99, 117, 126, 130
pay 151, 219, 224
poetry 56, 153, 161, 211
post xx, 13, 16, 111, 121, 180, 196, 213, 235, 255
post office 2, 92, 189, 213
postcards xx, 29, 43-4, 46, 73-4, 124, 236-7

R

raids 96, 168, 200, 206
RAMC (Royal Army Medical Corps) v, xvi-xviii, xxi, 4, 6, 12, 14, 18, 26, 30, 33, 42, 44, 46 n. 38, 62, 89, 113, 121, 126 n. 117, 128 n. 121, 139, 169, 186-7, 210 n. 184, 230, 233, 235, 239, 245, 247, 252, 260 n. 207
rations 6, 255
Reid Dick, William 18, 264
Riggall, Charles S. 210 n. 185
Roberts, Vernon B. 253

Royal Engineers 35
Russia 117, 155, 202-3

S

St Albans 16, 18, 20-1, 24-6, 29, 37, 39, 41, 54, 70, 75, 78-9, 108, 168
Sandilands, John E. 35, 89
Saunders, Victor F. 210 n. 185
Sears, Lillian 246
Second World War 263
Shrosberry, Harold W. 218
Smith, Arthur M. 132, 134
Somme 119 n. 109, 128 n. 120, 128 n. 122, 163, 179, 184 n. 167, 189, 191-2, 247, 259-64
songs 6, 8 n. 6, 15, 18, 19 n. 13, 63, 68, 75, 82, 86, 93, 115, 117, 144, 146, 204, 240, 268
Spalding, Lincolnshire 233
spies 168
sports 64, 80-1, 119-21, 165-6, 219, 234, 264
Stocker, Ada (Mrs Ada Owens) xiii-xiv, 11, 16, 50, 76, 97-8, 154, 157, 198, 213, 234
Stocker, Alexander xiii-xiv, xx, 16, 21, 41, 50-1, 65, 72, 76, 97, 105, 120, 137, 142, 144, 157, 191, 197-8, 206, 229, 246, 266
Stocker, Ethel 180, 213, 217
Stocker, Harry xiv, 105 n. 98, 139, 142 n. 138, 173 n. 159, 186, 264
Stocker, Irene xiii-xiv, 4, 15, 39, 46, 50, 90, 181, 186, 218, 246
Stocker, James xiii-xiv, 56, 77, 81, 83, 93, 121, 140, 157, 173
Stocker, Peter xx, 246
Sturt, Arthur 109, 168

T

Taubes 85, 168
trenches 49-50, 53, 57-60, 81, 84-8, 94-5, 99-100, 103, 123 n. 114,

133 n. 129, 149, 159-60, 177, 190 n. 172, 244-5, 259-60

Twynholm church xv-xvi, 4, 45 n. 35, 46 n. 38, 107, 113, 126 n. 118, 129, 140, 159, 170, 172, 181, 183 n. 166, 186, 222, 242-4

W

Walker, John A. 132, 134

War Diary xvii-xviii, 43, 55, 57, 58 n. 53, 65 n. 57, 74 n. 63, 77 n. 66, 87 n. 77, 89, 99 n. 92, 119 n. 109, 125, 127 n. 120, 132 n. 127, 142 n. 136, 163 n. 147, 165 n. 150, 167 n. 152, 210 n. 184, 243

War Loan 142-3

Ware, Herbert B. 36, 40

washing 262

weather 28, 43-4, 49, 60, 80, 82, 86, 107, 113, 119-20, 123, 140, 152, 195, 197

wedding 106, 148, 154, 158, 173, 177, 180, 184, 191, 199, 201-2, 214, 236, 248

Western & Sons 32, 70, 91, 93-4, 98, 102, 131, 221

Whitehead, Charles E. 89, 132 n. 128

Wreford, Barton St John 'Charlie' 196, 207

Y

YMCA (Young Men's Christian Association) 26, 28, 37

YWCA (Young Women's Christian Association) 37-8

Z

Zeppelin airships 96